Account of the Martyrs in the Provinces of La Florida

Account *of the* Martyrs
in the Provinces *of* La Florida

LUIS JERÓNIMO DE ORÉ

EDITED AND TRANSLATED BY
RAQUEL CHANG-RODRÍGUEZ AND NANCY VOGELEY

University of New Mexico Press ∾ Albuquerque

Library of Congress Cataloging-in-Publication Data

Names: Oré, Luis Jerónimo de, 1554–1630, author. |
Chang-Rodríguez, Raquel, editor, translator. | Vogeley, Nancy J., editor, translator.
Title: Account of the martyrs in the provinces of la Florida / Luis Jerónimo de Oré ;
edited and translated by Raquel Chang-Rodríguez and Nancy Vogeley.
Other titles: Relación de los mártires que ha habido en las Provincias de la Florida.
English
Description: Albuquerque : University of New Mexico Press, 2017. |
Includes bibliographical references and index.
Identifiers: LCCN 2016021177 (print) | LCCN 2017000732 (ebook) |
ISBN 9780826357984 (cloth : alk. paper) | ISBN 9780826357991 (electronic)
Subjects: LCSH: Florida—History—Spanish colony, 1565–1763. | Franciscans—
Missions—Florida—History—16th century. | Indians of North America—First contact
with Europeans—Florida. | Missions—Florida—History—16th century.
Classification: LCC F314.072713 2017 (print) | LCC F314 (ebook) | DDC 975.9/01—dc23
LC record available at https://lccn.loc.gov/2016021177

This publication is made possible in part by a generous contribution
from the Reed Foundation.

Cover illustration: *Floridae Americae provinciae Recens & exactissima descriptio* by
Jacques Le Moyne de Morgues [1591]. In Theodore de Bry, *Grand voyages*. Part 2. Latin.
Frankfurt, 1603. Courtesy of the John Carter Brown Library at Brown University.
Designed by Lila Sanchez
Composed in Minion Pro

Contents

Illustrations

Maps

Figures

Acknowledgments

Collaborative scholarship is a rarity in a profession where most work in isolation. In this case it is the fruit of a friendship of long standing and mutual affection; it derives from a shared desire to bring to the attention of general and specialized readers in the English-speaking world the writings of the Franciscan Luis Jerónimo de Oré, particularly his neglected narrative of the early Spanish presence in territories now part of the United States, *Account of the Martyrs in the Provinces of La Florida* (c. 1619). The project is the result of a long journey. It began with an investigation of Oré's life and writings in archives in the United States, Peru, and Spain; publication of the Spanish text of the *Relación* followed by translation of that text into modern English; and finally thought given as to how Oré's report fits into an inter-American history as well as into a large European political and religious context.

The Spanish word for "acknowledgments"—*agradecimientos*—perhaps captures better than the English term the need for expressing gratitude to the many in the long list who have helped in the production of this book. First we are grateful for the support our home institutions have given us over many years—the City College and the Graduate Center of the City University of New York, and the University of San Francisco. At the former we are particularly grateful to Eric Weitz, dean of Humanities and Arts at the time this book was being developed; Carlos Riobó, chairperson, Department of Classical and Modern Languages and Literatures; and José del Valle, executive officer of the Hispanic and Luso-Brazilian PhD Program. Initial research on Oré was enthusiastically supported by the Reed Foundation, and we would like to acknowledge its officers: President Reed Rubin, Secretary Jane Gregory Rubin, and Director of Programs David Latham.

The Hesburgh Library of the University of Notre Dame, in whose José Durand Collection Oré's manuscript resides, has graciously given permission for release of its property; at that library Sara Weber facilitated our use of the manuscript. We appreciate the persons on whose previous studies we have built and whose kindnesses to quote from we now honor: Maynard Geiger, OFM; Atanasio López, OFM; Antonine Tibesar, OFM; Jerald T. Milanich; Noble David Cook; and Amy Turner Bushnell. We acknowledge our lenders—institutions and individuals: the John Carter Brown Library, the Hispanic Society of America, the British Museum, the University of South Florida Special Collections, and the Ministerio de Cultura and Museo Nacional de Antropología e Historia del Perú. At the John Carter Brown Library, Leslie Tobias-Olsen aided in providing images. At the Hispanic Society of America, John O'Neill has been a steadfast guide. At the British Museum, Iain Calderwood patiently answered our requests. At the University of South Florida, we are particularly grateful to Andy Huse from Special Collections and Richard Bernardy from its Digitization Center.

We are grateful to Rev. John O'Malley, SJ, for an early reading of the manuscript; his comments helped immeasurably in our discussion of the Roman Church and its saints and martyrdom. We admire his generosity in responding to an out-of-the-blue request for help. Any straying from his advice is on our shoulders. John O'Neill helped in checking the bibliography format. Andrea Fernández attended to several research tasks. Marcos Gildemaro Alarcón Olivos contributed to securing the image from Museo Nacional de Antropología e Historia del Perú.

Finally, we thank Val Mathes, a wonderful friend, for suggesting we contact the University of New Mexico Press—and at that press we found an enthusiastic response from Clark Whitehorn. We are grateful to the anonymous readers who provided guidance and new insights when reviewing the manuscript. We have also benefited from the caring support of Morgan Podraza and Sandra A. Spicher in shepherding the manuscript to print.

Introduction

AN ACCOUNT OF THE MARTYRS IN THE PROVINCES OF LA FLORIDA
(*Relación de los mártires que ha habido en las Provincias de la Florida*,
c. 1619), written by the Peruvian Franciscan Luis Jerónimo de Oré (1554–
1630), makes several new claims on our understanding of the US historical
record. At the time of its initial release, it circulated principally in Castilian
court circles and the Franciscan world, and, we must assume, its story of
what seems to be a successful pacification was influential. Today's readers of
the *Account* in this English translation, however, will perhaps instead focus
on the work's portrayal of the early Spanish history of La Florida—an area
that in the sixteenth and seventeenth centuries included not only the pan-
handle and the peninsula, but also territory north to Virginia and west into
present-day Kansas and beyond. In representing La Florida, Oré describes
the interaction between indigenous populations and Franciscan friars. He
offers documentation of people-to-people encounters, which has often been
lacking, as military and settler accounts have concentrated more on land
possession. Traditionally, New England and Plains Indian cultures have represented the US past, and Florida has been a footnote to Mexican histories.
Both English- and Spanish-language historians have tended to ignore the
area's early contact record; they have often failed to appreciate the significance of how European struggles played out in that vastness. Fought over by
Spain, France, and England, the area manifests the international politics

1

behind those countries' economic jealousies and claim disputes. In this study the region will be called "La Florida" to avoid confusion with the modern state.

The encounter between Europeans and American indigenous peoples Oré describes in *Account* differs from other contact narratives we are familiar with for several reasons: Oré—born and raised in Peru at a time late in the sixteenth and early seventeenth centuries when Spanish governance had taken root and acculturated many in the indigenous population—was accustomed to dealing with Andean peoples. In composing the *Account*, he was called upon to view and write about dispersed and often-hostile Floridanos in their first exposure to Christianity. The Spaniard José de Acosta (1540–1600), who was the Jesuit provincial in Peru and participated with Oré in the Third Provincial Council of Lima (1581–1583), wrote several treatises for authorities in Europe on the nature and beliefs of Peru's Indians and the natural world they inhabited; in contrast, Oré seems to have been more interested in the friars and their dealings with La Florida's peoples. There, in La Florida, he is thrown back to an original moment of contact as lone Franciscans entered the American wild. Oré, a criollo, records the hardships each experienced, their successes and failures in winning conversions, and the outposts' gathering into an organizational structure. If geographical detail enters Oré's narrative at all, it appears as land minimally cultivated by the Indians and rich vacant stretches ready for occupation. His report on measurements of marshes and inland waterways seem to be directed toward military strategists interested in repelling foreign encroachments into Spanish territory. From this Franciscan's point of view, Indians are no longer strange, to be handled by either philosophic musings or the curiosities of travel literature, but instead by the management practicalities imposed by Philip II and the Church for the natives' pacification.

With Oré's work, readers today must consider the context in which he was writing as they face terse lists of friars' martyrdom and summaries of inspection visits. They must situate these dry reports into a missionary literature, usually written by Europeans, which present scholarship has thought aimed only at justifying conquest and classifying the human species. It is helpful to consider, in Oré's work, not only its content in terms of the picture it paints but also its function as a bureaucratic exchange whose readers, in the late sixteenth and early seventeenth centuries, no longer needed impassioned theological argument or spiritual coaxing but did need an explanation of how new and costly missionary experiences fit into imperial and

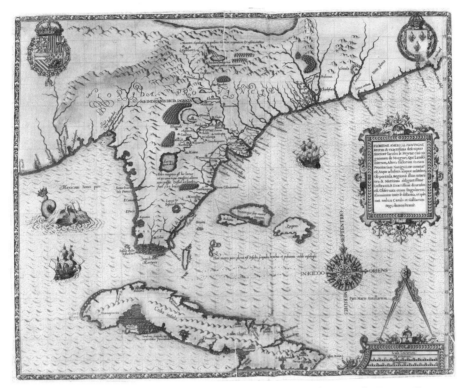

MAP 1 *Floridae Americae provinciae Recens & exactissima descriptio* by Jacques Le Moyne de Morgues [1591]. In Theodore de Bry, *Grand voyages*. Part 2. Latin. Frankfurt, 1603. Courtesy of the John Carter Brown Library at Brown University.

post-Reformation Church thinking. Letter writing and reportage between Europe and the Americas, increasing as the empire and the Roman Church were extending their reach, in fact created the operational mental framework for institutional survival and development. "La Florida" highlights the degree to which "America" was a European construct, a place where men's minds as well as their bodies created newness.

First, Oré belongs to a generation of criollos, persons born in the Americas who were of Spanish descent. Educated according to European standards, this generation was slowly beginning to enter Spain's governing elite as viceroyalties were established. Criollos viewed the world around them through two main lenses. They inherited European legal and theological classifications of strangeness. However, familiar with native peoples and aware of the difficulties of incorporating them into Spanish governance and Catholic behavioral modes, they understood other complexities. Oré, bicultural and multilingual, missionized in what then was the viceroyalty of Peru—which included all of Spanish South America—as well as in Cuba and La Florida. But he also traveled to Europe (Spain and Italy), where he was made aware of changing attitudes toward the New World. Thus, his *Account* is a valuable measuring stick, plotting Oré's awareness of how American experience was increasingly challenging and problematizing European rules and theories.

Secondly, he was a Franciscan, a member of a mendicant order in the sense that he worked independently of episcopal jurisdiction and was obedient to the order's rule. Particularly after the Council of Trent (1545–1563) had set out new guidelines in an effort to reform the Church, bureaucracy was building and new alignments were taking place.[1] The mendicant orders, the secular clergy with their episcopal structures, and civilian appointees of the Spanish kings worked rather differently together in the Americas than in Europe; friars and brothers had come early to work in the field alongside Spanish soldiers, preparing the way for priests and urban developers. Consequently, Oré's *Account of the Martyrs in the Provinces of La Florida* must be seen in the context of Counter-Reformation change— pursuant to Church demands but also in line with the Crown's regulations. His report can be read as an update for readers in Madrid, Seville, and Salamanca (Franciscan headquarters for the empire) and also for officials at the Holy See who needed information regarding success or failure in the missionary field as they weighed continuing support. The careful list of missionaries—where they were from in Spain, their individual talents, and their stories of conversion and martyrdom—suggests a report to higher-ups. Indeed, the whole question of martyrdom is central to Oré's narrative and will be examined later.

Accordingly, awareness of the *Account*'s readers makes us look at the information Oré chooses to supply and to question what is missing. There is little or no content in which the author muses over the essential nature of La Florida's Indians, their spirituality, the best options for conversion and

---

1 O'Malley states that bishops in Europe often lived at a distance from their bishoprics, collecting their benefices without regard for their pastoral duties (2013, 16). He argues that the council, wanting reforms, intended to strengthen bishopric structures. However, Bireley indicates that "[d]espite the emphasis on bishops at Trent they saw their authority diminished with respect to the papacy and to the secular power" (1999, 60).

indoctrination, or concern for the natives' salvation; it is as if Oré's generation understood these questions to have already been answered.[2] Franciscans had a history in Europe of itinerant preaching, going to areas beyond population clusters where established churches already existed, so their order was thought to be especially suited for pastoral work in the Americas. Trent had renewed emphasis on deepening Catholic faith among illiterates, reaching out to dissident Protestants and unchurched peoples on the peripheries of Europe (Goths, Irish, Slavs, sects in the eastern Mediterranean).[3] As a consequence, Franciscans in La Florida first of all thought to learn the natives' languages as preliminary to preaching and teaching. The religious brought about conversions and peace between warring tribes, yet one reads that such peace was often the result of fortuitous circumstance; "miracles" are told as if they were the consequence of God's justice in punishing or rewarding Indians and his benevolence in furthering the missionaries' work. Oré describes the actions of La Florida's natives without saying whether the actors were good or bad—or even sinful; instances of their cruelty are attributed to the devil's influence. He repeats one missionary's account of his horrible captivity without concluding the Indians possessed an evil nature. However, he comments that some ethnic groups are especially fierce. Trying to understand them, he says that the Floridanos do not have the vice of drunkenness of the Andeans, with whom he is familiar, and appreciates that they are intelligent and easily taught. He seemingly sympathizes with an Indian husband's logic as to why he wants several wives to cook for him and his children since his first wife, to whom he had been married by the priest, had left—and then records the priest's specious solution to the theological problem posed.

Thirdly, Oré's account of Spanish penetration into wilderness areas where indigenous peoples often were at war with one another shows that the Jesuits, the first delegation to the area, and the Franciscans were encountering hatreds already at a high pitch. Spanish conquistadors had previously entered some of those areas and terrorized the population, so the natives were primed for retribution. As a consequence the friars were either killed or nearly killed. Oré registers a tone of matter-of-fact tolerance of violence in his description of how the Spanish soldiers seized Indians and diplomatic coolness in telling how the captives often suffered and died as a result. Unlike the religious who accompanied soldiers earlier into Mexico and Peru where

---

2 Codignola (1995), for example, makes this point.
3 Michelson (2013) ties this itinerant preaching after the Council of Trent to diocesan reform in Italy.

natives had been accustomed to indigenous rule and priests traveled more safely, Oré's religious encountered scattered tribes—or groups he calls "language families"—living in separate territories. Adding to problems, Franciscan advances in La Florida beyond Spanish fortifications were running into English and French encroachments; each power had different motives for wanting to press inland, but all wanted to assure control of a coast where rich shipping passed. Thus Oré's *Account* can be seen as not only a report for superiors in his order but also as advice to the Spanish king as well as to civil authorities that the peaceable means religious manpower afforded was preferable to military force in planning for La Florida's future. In order to address these issues and related concerns, the introduction will cover the following principal topics: (1) Oré's life, career, and other writings; (2) the *Account* and its historical context; (3) the author's Franciscan identity; (4) La Florida as a contested site for Spanish, French, and English dominance; and (5) criteria for an annotated translation.

The Life, Career, and Other Writings of Luis Jerónimo de Oré

Oré was born into a deeply religious and well-to-do Spanish family in Guamanga (today Ayacucho) in southern Peru. His father, Antonio de Oré, was an encomendero charged with maintaining and instructing in Christianity the Indians on his land in return for their labor. Period testimony shows Antonio de Oré to have been cultured and pious, well versed in Latin—a language he taught his sons and daughters—and also fluent in Quechua, acquired in daily contact with the area's native population. Luis Jerónimo's childhood was spent in an atmosphere imbued with religious fervor. He learned Gregorian chant and to play the organ; remembering the importance of music in his own education, he later recommended it as a tool in evangelizing the native population. The boy also grew up in contact with several languages: he spoke Spanish with his family, he learned Latin from his father and from listening to religious services, and he acquired Quechua and Aymara in exchanges with household help and other native speakers. These linguistic skills marked Oré's career, setting him apart from other ecclesiastics. Years later during the Third Council of Lima, summoned by Archbishop Toribio de Mogrovejo in 1581, Oré was invited to participate in preparing a trilingual catechism (Spanish, Quechua, Aymara), *Doctrina cristiana y catecismo para instrucción de los indios* (Christian Doctrine and Catechism for the Instruction of the Indians) (1584), the first book printed in Lima by Antonio Ricardo. How much Oré contributed to this publication is not clear; according to Franciscan sources he worked on it with other *lenguaraces*, or experts in Amerindian languages. In any case the effort brought Oré together with the aforementioned Acosta, and Oré is credited with heavily influencing Acosta in understanding the need for a catechism intelligible to natives. Acosta is said to have acquired some knowledge of Quechua himself in his travels in Peru, yet it seems likely that he relied on others, particularly criollo priests, translators, and native informants, for the real work.[4]

The First (1551), Second (1567), and Third (1582)[5] Lima Council decisions to bring Catholic teaching to the populace by means of catechetical literature in translation was the result of new emphases at the Council of Trent. Recognizing that in Reformation Europe, Protestants were forsaking Latin in preference for vernacular languages and making use of the new print medium to produce their own teaching tools, Trent began to pay more attention to the Church's teaching mission. In fact the first two Lima Councils had tried to legislate change but with limited success. It is worth remembering that in the Americas, while evangelizing in native languages seems logical today, some in the colonial Church did not approve of the practice. As reflected in the Royal Decree of 3 July 1597, indigenous languages were often considered deficient for transmission of doctrinal complexities (García Ahumada 1990, 927). It has been speculated that the Third Lima Council also brought Oré together with Guaman Poma de Ayala, an indigenous writer and artist whose illustrated *Primer nueva corónica y buen gobierno* (First New Chronicle and Good Government) (1615) is a landmark work. It is not certain that Guaman Poma attended the council or knew Oré personally (Adorno 2000 [1986], xlviii). However, there is indication that the native chronicler was familiar with some of the Franciscan's writings as they circulated in manuscript form. Guaman Poma criticized Oré for omitting from his *Símbolo católico indiano*[6] (Catholic Indian Creed) (1598) details of the ancient Andean stages of development, and not telling about the lives of the Inca sovereigns (1980 [1615] 3:998).

---

4 Burgaleta (1999, 123) here draws on María Luisa Rivera de Tuesta in *José de Acosta, un humanista reformista* (1970, 119).
5 Bishop Mogrovejo summoned the council in 1581. Meetings began in 1582, when ecclesiastical authorities had arrived in Lima.
6 *Symbolo catholico indiano*; to present the title we use the modernized spelling.

Oré's religious vocation manifested itself early. He began his studies around the age of fourteen in 1568 at the Franciscan monastery in Cuzco and then continued on in the Franciscan convent in Lima and at the University of San Marcos. He was ordained a priest in Lima on 31 March 1582 (Richter 1986, 4) by Archbishop Toribio de Mogrovejo.[7] Luis Enrique Tord has noted two events that likely had an impact on the youth's sensibilities—the nativist movement of Taqui Onqoy (dance sickness) that erupted in 1565 in the areas of Parinacochas, Lucanas, and Soras (all near Oré's home in Guamanga), and the brutal decapitation of Tupac Amaru I in the central square of Cuzco in 1572 (Tord 1992, 22–24). In the first, the followers of Taqui Onqoy wanted to return to worship of the ancestral *huacas* (revered objects or shrines) and rid Inca territory of Spaniards. The uprising was violently crushed; Jesuits and other religious orders in Peru were committed to governing policies that pursued and extirpated idolatry. When the rebellion started Oré was eleven, and when it was eradicated in 1570, sixteen. A second instance of severe Spanish justice, which Oré surely witnessed when he was eighteen years old, also probably affected the youth. The viceroy Francisco de Toledo (1569–1581) ordered the execution of Tupac Amaru I, the last Inca leader, who had held out against Spanish rule from the Andean stronghold of Vilcabamba. These events, in which two worlds clashed, likely caused the young man from a wealthy family, whose ordination into the Franciscan Order showed his European leanings as well as his concern for Peru's natives, to reflect on his personal responsibility to bridge the gap between the two.

Shortly after his ordination, Oré was assigned to Franciscan posts in the Colca Valley (c. 1586) and Jauja (c. 1595). He then went on to serve in Indian parishes, first in Potosí and later in Cuzco. During his stay in the mining town of Potosí, his skills impressed the Hieronymite friar Diego de Ocaña, who toured in the region between 1599 and 1606. Ocaña wrote commenting on Oré's linguistic ability and Marian devotion:

> And the miracle was that the very reverend father Friar Luis de Oré, preacher of the order of Saint Francis, preached every Sunday to all the Indians in their language one of the miracles of those that are in the book of Our Lady of Guadalupe. When the octave ended, the image of

---

7 Bishop Toribio de Mogrovejo was canonized by Pope Benedictus XIII on 10 December 1726. Following Richter, Oré's ordination as auxiliary deacon was 23 September 1581; as deacon, 3 March 1582 (1986, 4). Oré was ordained together with Ludovico Bertonio, a Jesuit famous for his studies of the Aymara language.

Our Lady was placed with great reverence on the high altar, above the sacrarium where it is now; and the whole town is so devoted to this image that when in need, they go to her and pray to her to request a remedy for their problem. And they give alms, which the stewards collect and which remain in perpetuity in this town.[8]

Oré continued to perfect his knowledge of Quechua and Aymara, producing three manuscripts that circulated in several areas of the viceroyalty (Cook 1992b, 42–44): *Símbolo católico indiano*, *Sermones del año* (Sermons of the Year), and *Arte y vocabulario en romance y en las lenguas generales deste reyno, quechua y aimara* (Grammar and vocabulary in Romance [Spanish] and in the general languages of this kingdom, Quechua and Aymara). *Símbolo* contains explanations of the Apostles', Nicene, and Athanasian Creeds. His contemporaries praised Oré's command of indigenous languages and his missionary zeal; for example, the Franciscan chronicler Diego de Córdoba Salinas wrote that he was "an angel of the ministry" (un ángel del ministerio) who "as a major planet was far above his brothers in the wonderful gift he had to learn and speak many and various Indian languages from several nations and provinces, where he preached with an insatiable thirst for their conversion and spiritual benefit" (1957 [1651], 346).[9] Because of their importance to the task of evangelization, Church notables and colonial administrators—including Father Friar Hernando de Trejo, bishop of Tucumán, and García Hurtado de Mendoza, viceroy of Peru (1589–1596)—recommended that Oré's manuscripts be published.

A KEY BOOK, *SÍMBOLO CATÓLICO INDIANO*

Símbolo católico indiano appeared in Lima in 1598.[10] In this treatise we find the principal ideas that structured the Franciscan's thinking throughout his career. He relates Indian origin to the biblical story of man's fall from God's

---

8 "Y el milagro le predicó a todos los indios en su lengua el muy reverendo padre fray Luis de Orée, predicador del orden de San Francisco, el cual, todos los domingos que predicaba a los indios, les contaba algún milagro de los que estaban en el libro de Nuestra Señora de Guadalupe. Y con esto se dio fin al octavario y se colocó en el altar mayor la imagen, sobre el sagrario, adonde agora está, con mucha veneración; con quien toda la villa tiene tanta devoción, que en tiniendo alguna necesidad, luego acuden a ella a pedir remedio della. Y ofrecen sus limosnas, las cuales recogen los mayordomos y con esto quedan perpetuas en esta villa (Ocaña 2013 [c. 1608], 497–98).
9 "Como planeta mayor predominaba a sus hermanos en el don maravilloso que tuvo de hablar muchas y varias lenguas de indios de diversas naciones y provincias en que les predicaba con una sed insaciable de su conversion y provecho espiritual" (1957 [1651], 346.
10 The printing press was established in Lima in 1584.

grace and as a result concludes Americans' participation in a common humanity: "Our first beginning was that of Adam and Eve. Then when God punished the world and all men perished except four—Noah and his three children—we have spread and multiplied."[11] Oré distinguishes between polytheistic and monotheistic practices and translates a prayer attributed to Inca Capac Yupanqui, associated with the cult of Pachacamac or supreme creator (Oré 1992 [1598], 157–58 [f. 40 r/v]), citing it as evidence of native monotheism. He identifies the devil as responsible for the outrages he sees in native practices (Oré 1992 [1598] 161–62 [f. 42r/v]).[12] And he condemns the Spanish for their exploitation of the native population and criticizes their failure to provide good shepherds for instruction in Catholic doctrine. If Christianity is to flourish, he argues, every Indian village must have a school, a teacher, and singers; the natives, he insists, are fully able to understand and assimilate Christian doctrine along with other Western cultural tools:

> Let there be a school, a teacher, and singers, paid sufficiently, so that the children be taught to pray according to Catholic doctrine, to read, write, sing and play a musical instrument. Let them leave the school skilled in doctrine and capable of teaching it to the entire village. The school is like the soul of a village [essential] for it to be better indoctrinated and governed. Where there is no school there will be a lack of things like doctrine, music, adornment of and service to the churches, altar, and choir.[13]

In *Símbolo* Oré encourages devotion to the Marian cult, recitation of the rosary, and punishment for those who do not learn the basic tenets of the faith. He shows his conviction that the Franciscan mission will elevate Indians, and equates preaching the Gospel in the New World with the work of the apostles

---

11 "Nuestro primer principio fue de Adán y de Eva, y después, cuando Dios castigó al mundo y perecieron todos los hombres, de solo estos cuatro, de Noé y de sus tres hijos nos hemos propagado y multiplicado" (Oré 1992 [1598], 294 [108v]). In quoting from *Símbolo*, we use the modern pagination and put the folio number in brackets; punctuation and spelling have been modernized. Translations are ours. See Lamana (2014) for additional discussion of Oré's notions of Indian origins as they parallel theories of José de Acosta and Guaman Poma de Ayala, and also Chang-Rodríguez (2016).

12 Oré relates that he has collected other prayers but will not publish them until he gets permission from the bishops (1992 [1598], 158 [40v]).

13 "Que haya escuela y maestro de ella, y cantores diputados y pagados con salario suficiente, donde sean enseñados los muchachos a rezar la doctrina, y a leer y escribir, cantar y tañer, y de la escuela salgan hábiles en la doctrina, para enseñarla a todo el pueblo. Finalmente, la escuela es como ánima de todo un pueblo para ser mejor doctrinado y regido, y donde no la hubiere faltará todo lo dicho, de doctrina, música, ornato y servicio de las iglesias, altar y coro." (Oré 1992 [1598], 189 [56r]).

in carrying the teachings of Jesus to the Gentiles (Oré 1992 [1598], 153 [38r]). Ministers must "preach the true doctrine, live a saintly life, and behave with the piety of a father with his Indians." This ideal minister, then, "will be able with a clear conscience, if required by his vows of obedience to discharge the requirements of this doctrine, to receive it and love it as if it were his wife."[14] Oré offsets this example of a good minister with criticism of those who are more interested in profit than in preaching. This emphasis on clerical morality had been a principal concern of the Third Council of Lima; its delegates had received orders from the Council of Trent for reform of the Church's representatives but they already had seen sufficient greed and corruption around them to realize how those representatives of the Church hurt Indians.[15]

In *Símbolo* Oré reveals an ambivalent attitude toward the viceroy. He praises Toledo for having instituted the *reducciones*, Indian communities set up under ecclesiastical authority to facilitate conversion, acculturation, and tax collection.[16] He says that this resettlement measure helped in catechizing the Andean population (Oré 1992 [1598], 161 [42r]), and later in *An Account of the Martyrs in the Provinces of La Florida* suggests that it be applied there. However, this praise of the viceroy is tempered by his comment on the beheading of Tupac Amaru I, saying that it caused "incredible pain and sorrow" (increíble dolor y sentimiento) to Indians, Spaniards, and clergymen (Oré 1992 [1598], 161 [42r]).

TRIPS TO SPAIN AND ITALY

Admiring Oré's missionary work and realizing his intellectual qualities, but also wishing to see Oré's manuscripts published, Antonio de la Raya, bishop of Cuzco (1594–1606), had him sent to Europe. When he left, Oré had three manuscripts with him—the collection of sermons called the *Sermonario*, a work titled the *Manual for Administering the Sacraments*, and the *Arte y vocabulario* or grammar and vocabulary. He also hoped to have published there a new edition of *Símbolo*. Additionally, it has been suggested but not documented that Oré went hoping to recruit men for missionary work in the Americas (Reyes Ramírez 1989, 1103).

14 "Será idóneo ministro de Cristo y podrá con segura conciencia, si la obediencia le encargare alguna doctrina, tomarla y amarla como esposa" (1992 [1598], 165 [44r]).
15 For a useful summary of the Council's ordinances and historical importance, see Tineo 1990.
16 For further coverage, see Coello de la Rosa 2014. See also Mumford 2012.

His efforts in Europe soon bore fruit. Cook relates (1992b, 45) that on 22 March 1605 the Royal Council of the Indies authorized the publication of the *Manual*. Oré represented Bishop de la Raya before that council on two occasions: the delimitation of the jurisdictions of the dioceses of Cuzco and Charcas, and support for the creation of the University of San Antonio Abad in Cuzco.[17] Beginning to move in important administrative and ecclesiastical circles, Oré went on from Spain to Rome by the end of 1605. Since the *Manual* had not yet been published in Spain, he submitted the manuscript to Pope Paul V for publication in Italy; two years later it was printed in Naples as *Rituale, seu Manuale Peruanum, et Forma Brevis asministrandi apud Indos sacrosancta baptismi poenityentiae, eucharistiae, matrimonij & extremae unctionis sacramenta.*[18] This work contains prayers in Quechua, Aymara, Puquina, Mochica, Guaraní, and several Brazilian languages. In Italy Oré became friends with a confidante of the Pope, the scholar and teacher Vestrio Barbiano, to whom he dedicated his *Treatise on Indulgences*, written in Latin and published in Alessandria (Italy) in 1606 (Cook 1992b, 46). During this time Oré was also a reader of theology at the University of Naples (Vargas Ugarte 1978).

Returning to Spain, Oré was given several commissions—to prepare missionaries for evangelizing in La Florida and to travel to Venezuela. However, this latter charge was interrupted as he was preparing to sail on 20 June 1613 on the ship *La Esperanza*,[19] when he was asked to gather material on the life of the Spanish friar Francisco Solano,[20] missionary to the Calchaquíes of Tucumán (in present-day northern Argentina). The importance of that task, interviewing witnesses and writing up a summary of the life of this Franciscan in preparation for an appeal for his sainthood (published in Madrid in 1614), will be remarked on later.

17 It was founded in 1692, after documents were signed in Rome and Madrid.
18 According to the copy in the Biblioteca Nacional del Perú (Fondo Antiguo), the sections in Quechua and Aymara were translated by Dominican, Franciscan, Augustinian, Mercedarian, and Jesuit priests. Alonso de Barzana, a Jesuit, was in charge of the segment in Puquina, and there were additions after he died in 1597; the section in Mochica was translated by secular and regular priests and approved by the Archbishop of Lima. Father Luis de Bolaños took charge of the section in Guaraní and it was approved by the Río de la Plata ecclesiastical authorities. The section on "Brazilian languages" was attended to by monks of San Benito and Jesuit priests from Portugal (Oré 1607, 384–85).
19 According to the passenger list in AGI, Contratación, 5538, Lib. 2, ff. 125v–26v.
20 Francisco Sánchez-Solano Jiménez (1549–1610), beatified in 1675, and canonized in 1726.

ORÉ AND EL INCA GARCILASO IN CÓRDOBA

Early in 1612, traveling from Madrid to Cádiz, a port where missionaries gathered on leaving for America, Oré stopped in Córdoba and met his fellow Peruvian, El Inca Garcilaso de la Vega (1539–1616). This meeting between the two, whose views on an America increasingly being explored and developed by Spain, was significant for both. Garcilaso was an accomplished chronicler, by then having published his major books, *La Florida del Inca* (1605) and *Royal Commentaries* (part 1, 1609). Oré particularly wanted to discuss with his compatriot *La Florida del Inca*, a chronicle he was familiar with and that he thought would be helpful for his missionaries to read before leaving for work there. Garcilaso, son of a Spanish conqueror and an Inca princess, had left Peru to live in Spain so as to pursue in his father's world an intellectual life devoted to Renaissance culture and thoughtful examination of his double heritage. In Córdoba he had met a veteran of the Hernando de Soto expedition (1539–1542), Gonzalo Silvestre, who had told him stories of that frontier. Thus Garcilaso, like Oré, had a unique perspective on Spain's expansion in the Americas, where a second phase of the empire's push required that the native population, instead of just being subdued, be converted and acculturated.

Garcilaso described Oré's visit in the second part of *Royal Commentaries* (also known as *General History of Peru*, 1617), characterizing him as a "great theologian" (*gran teólogo*). He gave Oré three copies of *La Florida del Inca* and four of *Royal Commentaries* and wished him success in his missionary work: "May Divine Majesty help you in the task of bringing those idolaters out of the abyss of their darkness" (*HG*, book 7, chapter 30, 182).[21] It is also recorded that the men reminisced about the past, particularly events relating to Peru's early history when Gonzalo Pizarro touched off a civil war, rebelling first against the New Laws of 1542 and later against the Crown. Garcilaso had heard different versions of what had happened to the heads of Pizarro and the rebels Francisco de Carvajal and Francisco Hernández Girón and later wrote:

> Speaking to me of these heads, Oré told me that in the convent of San Francisco, in the City of Kings [Lima], five heads were to be found— of Gonzalo Pizarro, Francisco de Carvajal and Francisco Hernández

---

21 "[. . . que] la Divina Majestad se sirva de ayudarles en esta demanda, para que aquellos idólatras salgan del abismo de sus tinieblas." Quotations from *Royal Commentaries* are from Ángel Rosenblat's edition (Parts 1 [1943] 2 vols., and 2 [1944] 3 vols.). The following abbreviations are used: *CR* (*Comentarios reales*) and *HG* (*Historia general*).

Girón, as well as two others that were unidentified. They were kept there unburied. He wanted to know which was Carvajal's because of his fame in the empire, and I told him to look for the sign underneath on the iron cage where the heads were kept. But he replied that the heads were not in cages but loose, each one by itself, without any sign that would enable recognition.[22] (*HG*, book 7, chapter 30, 182)

The two men's discussion of the fate of the heads of the dead Spanish conquistadors can be seen as more than macabre curiosity; rather it points to their memory of early factional politics in Spain's takeover of Inca territory.

THE BISHOP OF THE SANTÍSIMA CONCEPCIÓN (CHILE)

Oré's visits to La Florida will be discussed later. However, his administrative career took another turn when on 17 August 1620, King Philip III appointed him bishop of the Santísima Concepción, at that time the southernmost bishopric of the Church in present-day Chile.[23] En route Oré stopped off in Lima where, in 1621, he was consecrated bishop by a fellow Franciscan Fernando de Ocampo, bishop of Santa Cruz de la Sierra in present-day Bolivia (1621–1632) (Richter 1986, 8). At first this bishopric in Chile was based in La Imperial[24] and later, in 1603, in Concepción as a result of the Arauco wars (Richter 1986, 8). The latter was a vast inland area where different ethnic groups warred against Spanish domination—among them the Mapuche whom Alonso de Ercilla immortalized in his epic poem *La Araucana* (part 1, 1569). Other threats existed along the coast where pirates and spies from European rivals of Spain threatened Spanish settlements.

Oré traveled extensively throughout his vast diocese and in Chiloé, a remote archipelago, urged that more missionaries be sent there. He initiated a system of *fiscales* (overseers) whereby specially selected individuals helped

---

22 "Y, hablando destas cabeças, [Oré] me dixo que en el Convento de San Francisco, de la Ciudad de los Reyes, estavan depositadas cinco cabeças: la de Gonçalo Pizarro, la de Francisco de Carvajal y Francisco Hernández Girón, y otras dos que no supo decir cuyas eran. Y que aquella santa casa las tenía en depósito, no enterradas sino en guarda, y que el desseó muy mucho saber cuál dellas era la de Francisco de Carvajal, por la gran fama que en aquel Imperio dexó. Yo le dixe que por el letrero que tenía en la jaula de hierro pudiera saber cuál dellas era. Dixo que no estaban en jaulas de hierro, sino sueltas, cada una de por sí, sin señal alguna para ser conocidas."
23 Pope Paul V confirmed the appointment in August of that year.
24 Founded in 1551 by conqueror Pedro de Valdivia and so called in honor of King Charles I of Spain who at that time was head of the Holy Roman Empire (Richter 1986, 8).

out in the celebration of mass and other ceremonies. In Concepción, the diocesan seat, he established a seminary to train priests. However, when that seminary did not produce the expected result, Oré was held responsible; the governor, Luis Fernández de Córdoba y Arce (1625–1629),[25] blamed him for ordaining unqualified individuals (Reyes Ramírez 1989, 1112–13). In exchanges with the governor in 1625–1626, Oré invoked his right to appoint chaplains and defended—as he had done before—the use of native languages for evangelization, as well as pleading for respectful treatment of all parishioners including indigenous neophytes (Cook 2008, 33–35). Although the king had asked for Oré's advice as to how to pacify the region, that advice to withdraw the army and allow missionaries to catechize the Mapuche was not followed (Cook 1992b, 57–58).[26] Instead war continued; the natives were imprisoned, branded, and sold as slaves in Lima and other parts of the viceroyalty.

Oré died on 31 January 1630 at the age of seventy-six. He drew up his will three days earlier. There he shows his concern for four indigenous protégés. He asks for shelter for a boy "seized in war" (coxido en la guerra) who had been Christianized for seven years and for his assignment to a chaplaincy "that we founded and do not consent that it be taken away from him by anyone by means of an encomienda or in any other way" (q[ue] dexamos fundada y no consienta se le quite por alguna persona por uía de encomienda ni en otra manera alguna); for Pedro Milla Quiñe, a native under his guardianship also captured in war; and for Anton and Juan, two others whom he assigned to serve his nephew, Father Pedro de Serpa. Oré charged his nephew with giving these protégés "the good treatment that I have given to all" (el buen tratamiento que yo les he hecho a todos) (Pello 2000, 169).

Overview of *An Account of the Martyrs in the Provinces of La Florida*

There is confusion about when the book first appeared (Geiger 1937, 285–86). Diego de Córdoba Salinas says in his *Crónica franciscana de las provincias del Perú* (1651): "In the account that Oré published in Latin in Naples in 1607, documenting the martyrs in La Florida, and the illustrious men who have flourished in their saintliness in the Indies, he placed our Villacarrillo

---

25 He was appointed by his uncle Diego Fernández de Córdova, Viceroy of Peru (1622–1629), Marquis of Guadalcázar, and Count of Posadas, and later confirmed by King Philip III.
26 Letter dated 4 March 1627 (Cook 1992b, 57–58; and Espinoza Soria 2012, 15).

among them."[27] Lino G. Canedo, whose reedition of Córdoba Salinas's *Crónica* was published in 1957, is unable to identify this 1607 work and suggests that it cannot be the same as the *Relación de los mártires* because it appeared several years after 1607 and has no reference to Villacarrillo (Córdoba Salinas 1957 [1651], 342n12). However, Córdoba Salinas offers another date, varying the title: "[in] the year 1604 [Oré] printed a *Relación de los mártires que padecieron en la Florida.*"[28] González de Barcia, likely following Córdoba Salinas, gives 1604 as the publication date and specifies the book appeared in quarto format (1723, 181). Nicolás Antonio, in his *Bibliotheca hispana nova*, also dates *Relación* to 1604 and notes its quarter-page size (1783–1788, vol. 2, 43). It appears that both followed Córdoba Salinas in that date. Although they add the publication's size, it is not clear if they had access to a printed copy. In his *Manual del librero hispanoamericano* (2d. ed.) Antonio Palau y Dulcet gives 1612 as the *Relación*'s publication date. José Toribio Medina in *Biblioteca hispano-chilena* believes that the *Relación* did not appear before 1612; and Medina even questions whether Oré visited La Florida (1897, 1:113–17).

However, internal evidence in the text of the only copy located in the United States, part of the collection of José Durand in the Hesburgh Libraries of the University of Notre Dame, does not support any of the three dates (1604, 1607, 1612). As indicated in chapter 11 of the *Relación*, Oré visited La Florida for the first time in 1614. In San Agustín (Saint Augustine), he organized a meeting of the province of Santa Elena (encompassing La Florida and the island of Cuba); he then returned to Cuba. From Havana he traveled to La Florida again on 6 November 1616, assigned to inspect the province of Santa Elena, and to celebrate the formation of its chapter. That meeting took place on 18 December 1616 in San Buenaventura de Guadalquini (in present-day Georgia) where the friars elected the authorities for the new province of Santa Elena, instituted in 1612. Taking into account, then, these and other factors (Oré's return to San Agustín in 1616 and then his trip to Havana early in 1617, his voyage to Spain in 1617 to attend the Salamanca meeting of the

---

27 "En la relación que imprimió [Oré] en lengua latina en Nápoles, año de 1607, de los mártires que ha habido en La Florida y de los varones ilustres que han florecido en santidad en las Indias, pone entre ellos a nuestro Villacarrillo" (1957 [1651], 342). "Villacarrillo" here appears to refer to the Franciscan Jerónimo de Villacarrillo, a Spaniard who served in Cuzco and died there in 1588 (Tineo 1990, 317; and Tibesar 1953, 48, 65–68, 76).
28 "[en] el año de 1604, [Oré] imprimió una *Relación de los mártires que padecieron en la Florida*" (1957 [1651], 343–44).

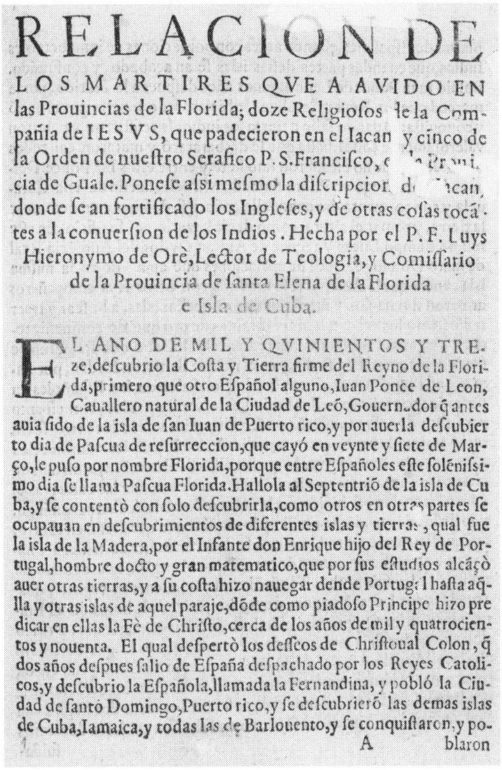

RELACION DE
LOS MARTIRES QVE A AVIDO EN
las Prouincias de la Florida; doze Religiosos de la Compañia de I E S V S, que padecieron en el Iacan y cinco de la Orden de nuestro Serafico P. S. Francisco, en la Prouincia de Guale. Ponese asi mesmo la discripcion de Iacan, donde se an fortificado los Ingleses, y de otras cosas tocãtes a la conuersion de los Indios. Hecha por el P. F. Luys Hieronymo de Orè, Lector de Teologia, y Comissario de la Prouincia de santa Elena de la Florida e Isla de Cuba.

EL AÑO DE MIL Y QVINIENTOS Y TREze, descubrio la Costa y Tierra firme del Reyno de la Florida, primero que otro Español alguno, Iuan Ponce de Leon, Cauallero natural de la Ciudad de Leõ, Gouernador q̃ antes auia sido de la isla de san Iuan de Puerto rico, y por auerla descubierto dia de Pascua de resurreccion, que cayó en veynte y siete de Março, le puso por nombre Florida, porque entre Españoles este solẽnissimo dia se llama Pascua Florida. Hallola al Septentriõ de la isla de Cuba, y se contentò con solo descubrirla, como otros en otras partes se ocupauan en descubrimientos de diferentes islas y tierras, qual fue la isla de la Madera, por el Infante don Enrique hijo del Rey de Portugal, hombre docto y gran matematico, que por sus estudios alcãçò auer otras tierras, y a su costa hizo nauegar dende Portugal hasta aq̃lla y otras islas de aquel paraje, dõde como piadoso Principe hizo predicar en ellas la Fè de Christo, cerca de los años de mil y quatrocientos y nouenta. El qual despertò los desseos de Christoual Colon, q̃ dos años despues salio de España despachado por los Reyes Catolicos, y descubrio la Española, llamada la Fernandina, y pobló la Ciudad de santo Domingo, Puerto rico, y se descubrierõ las demas islas de Cuba, Iamaica, y todas las de Barlouento, y se conquistaron, y po-
A blaron

FIGURE 1 First folio of Luis Jerónimo de Oré, *Account of the Martyrs in the Provinces of La Florida*. Reproduced from the original in the Department of Special Collections of the Hesburgh Libraries of the University of Notre Dame.

order in June 1618, and the necessary time to compose and publish the *Account*), it can be argued that 1619 is the most probable date for the work's publication. Oré likely wrote the *Account* in 1617 on his return to Cuba after having completed his second pastoral visit there. At that point he could enrich his report with details of Father Marrón's death in Havana in 1617 (at whose burial Oré officiated), the story of Father Ávila's captivity (which Marrón had preserved in Cuba), and the description of the chapter meeting in San Buenaventura de Guadalquini, as promotional evidence of the Franciscans' work in La Florida for presentation at the 1618 Salamanca meeting and probable circulation among sympathetic court circles. Since Notre Dame's edition—more details on its characteristics appear below—bears no title page giving information as to date or place of publication, one can only conjecture as to the 1619 publication date.

One reads in the author's selection an appreciation of the desire of the Spanish Crown and the religious orders to explore and establish a presence in La Florida. In 1562 French Huguenots led by Jean Ribault traveled along the coast of the modern states of Florida, South Carolina, and Georgia and founded the town of Charlesfort (on Parris Island). Although that colony was abandoned, two years later, René de Laudonnière returned and established Fort Caroline near the modern city of Jacksonville. Worried about this penetration into an area Spain was claiming, King Philip II sent Pedro Menéndez de Avilés (1519–1574) to expel the French and reassert control. This newly named adelantado[29] of La Florida and later governor of Cuba killed the French at the fort and founded San Agustín (1565) and Santa Elena (1566). He entrusted the Jesuits with missionizing, but in 1571 religious from that order were martyred by Powatan natives in the bay of Santa María del Jacán (or Ajacán, modern-day Chesapeake Bay). Thus the Jesuits decided to leave Florida, and Franciscans arrived shortly after (1573) to continue the task of evangelizing.

At the beginning the Franciscans limited their efforts to the area around San Agustín, but later they attempted to extend their radius. By 1600 Cuba, La Florida, and Venezuela were part of the Franciscan province of Santa Cruz, headquartered in Santo Domingo.[30] In 1609 La Florida and Cuba became a *custodia* under Father Friar Pedro Ruiz, and in 1612 the province of Santa Elena was established. It encompassed the above-mentioned territories, convents in Cuba, and a novitiate in Havana. Wanting to expand into La Florida, Franciscan superiors asked Oré to prepare catechists for preaching in that new frontier. When Oré first arrived, then, La Florida was a territory where rival European powers competed, but also where Spanish religious and civil authorities squabbled among themselves. He came, sent by the new commissioner general of the Indies, the Franciscan Juan de Vivanco (AGI, Santo Domingo 25, 1 folio).[31] Leaving Seville for Havana on 27 June 1614, accompanied by Father Friar Francisco de San Buenaventura and the servant Juan Tundidor, he

---

29 In medieval Castile the title designated the military and political governor of a frontier province. In the Americas, he held the military title of captain-general and was also the governor and chief magistrate of participants in the expedition; in a successful conquest, the adelantado also ruled over the native population (Burkholder 1996, 12).

30 For La Florida's early history under Church management, see Lopetegui and Zubillaga 1965, 449–88.

31 The resolution from the Royal Council of the Indies approving the request is dated 12 June 1614.

arrived in La Florida that same year.[32] Immediately he tried to establish contact with the diverse populations—particularly the Guale and Timucua—inspected the missions, and called a meeting of the order in San Agustín. He then went back to Havana, returning in 1616 to visit all the missions in the province of Santa Elena and to hold another chapter meeting.

At first glance, the *Relación* is an uneven compilation, giving the impression that Oré wished to bring together all the evidence he had, pertinent or not, from various sources of missionary activity in La Florida. However, the narrative proceeds according to the logic of a primer—presenting to faraway readers basic knowledge of the stages of the region's development and introducing the cast of characters essential to understanding the lead-up to the present state of affairs. Oré's sympathies and antipathies in selecting the information are evident: He appears to be critical of the tactics of Adelantado Pedro Menéndez de Avilés; he is scathingly critical of the English pirates who hide in safe havens throughout Chesapeake Bay and on Caribbean islands that he calls "thieves' nests" (ladroneras) from which they prey on Spanish shipping; and indirectly he is critical of the Spanish king who has failed to clean out these nests. In reproducing the long nautical report of the Jacán and San Pedro River (the Potomac), compiled by Juan Menéndez Marqués, so that the king can become acquainted with the terrain and expel the English, Oré's language—"so that the king will know the facts"—suggests that His Majesty has been slow to act on knowledge he has already.

Comprising eleven chapters of varying length and style, the first two sections of the document review the early major Spanish expeditions—La Florida's discovery by Juan Ponce de León; the incursions of Lucas Vázquez de Ayllón, Pánfilo de Narváez, and Hernando de Soto; and the arrival of Pedro Menéndez de Avilés. Oré mentions the evangelizing efforts of the Dominican Father Friar Luis Cáncer de Barbastro and the attempt by France to enter the region. Chapters 3 and 4 tell of the martyrdom of the Jesuits in the Bay of Santa María de Jacán, while the fifth and sixth describe revolts against the Spaniards in Santa Elena and Guale; these chapters also include the nautical report mentioned previously. Chapter 7 lists the twelve Franciscans who came to La Florida in 1595 and features Father Friar Francisco Pareja, who later became a leading expert in the Timucua language and

---

32 Passenger list for the ship *Nuestra Señora de los Remedios* (AGI, Contratación, 5538, Lib. 2, f. 128r/v).

HERHANDO DE SOTO:

FIGURE 2 Hernando de Soto (c. 1500–1542), *adelantado* of La Florida and governor of Cuba. *Retratos de los españoles ilustres*, 1791. Courtesy of the Hispanic Society of America, New York.

provincial of Santa Elena. However, the chapter's most striking section describes the massacre of four Franciscans in the Guale area and details how Father Friar Francisco de Ávila survived to tell the story of his captivity and rescue (chapter 8). Chapters 9 and 10 tell how the Guale conflict was resolved and provide information on early contacts between the Franciscans and the indigenous populations. Chapter 11 documents Oré's arrival in the area (1614), his visits to missions, and meeting in San Agustín. This chapter concludes by reporting on a second meeting of the province of Santa Elena in 1616 at Santa María de Guadalquini, when officers were elected.

In chapter 1 the narrator gives evidence of having read El Inca Garcilaso's *Royal Commentaries* and *La Florida del Inca*. This is apparent in the description of de Soto's role in Peru and in La Florida, and in the favorable view of him Garcilaso and Oré shared as a result of de Soto's request for fair treatment for Atahualpa and his offer to finance the conquest of La Florida with rewards from his Peruvian service. Information regarding de Soto's burial also seems to borrow from Garcilaso's *La Florida del Inca* (part I, book 5, chapter 7). In this chapter Oré details two expeditions—one in 1521, probably led by Pedro de Quejo and Francisco Gordillo in which Indians are abducted, and a second in 1524 under Lucas Vázquez de Ayllón when the Spaniards were invited to land, entertained lavishly, and then killed.[33] It is noteworthy that here Oré calls the natives "barbarians." The French episode is told minimally, instead focusing on Philip II's interest in La Florida and the personality of Pedro Menéndez de Avilés.

PEDRO MENÉNDEZ DE AVILÉS

The appearance of Menéndez de Avilés at this point would have raised several concerns in the minds of readers. As an adelantado who had signed a contract (*capitulación*) with the Spanish king to undertake exploration of La Florida, he was like an independent contractor—counting on the king's support but also putting up some of his own money for the enterprise. He had a reputation as a skilled navigator, a soldier known for tough campaigns, an employer who recruited family members but also members of the local nobility in the northern regions of Asturias for the open-ended expedition. All sought adventure but primarily reward in the form of noble titles and land grants for their "service" to God and country. As we have seen, Menéndez at first chose Jesuits as spiritual backup for his landing and penetration. As a result Jesuits were the first martyrs in 1571; their university studies little prepared them for evangelizing among natives whom they judged to be rough barbarians, so they abandoned the territory to the Franciscans.

Oré passes quickly over this Jesuit interlude, failing to record the names of the twelve martyrs as he does later for his Franciscan brothers. The Franciscan hierarchy, seemingly the readership that Oré was mainly targeting, might have judged Menéndez to have been ruthless and possibly also critical of the Jesuits who failed in their charge. Here it must be acknowledged that Menéndez was not just an ordinary sailor; there are records of letter exchanges

---

33 Oré gives 1524; however, in 1523 Vázquez de Ayllón was granted the royal charter (capitulación) to explore and establish a colony in the area of the southeast Atlantic coast known as Chícora; in 1526 he finally left Puerto Plata in Santo Domingo (present-day Dominican Republic) and founded the short-lived colony of San Miguel de Gualdape.

PEDRO MENENDEZ DE AVILES.
*Natural de Avilés en Asturias, Comendador
de la orden de Santiago, Conquistador de la Florida, nombrado Gral de la Armada contra Inglaterra.
Murió en Santander N. 1574 à los 55 de edad.*

FIGURE 3   Pedro Menéndez de
Avilés (1519–1574), *adelantado* of
La Florida and governor of Cuba.
Retratos de los españoles ilustres,
1791. Courtesy of the Hispanic
Society of America.

he had with such luminaries as King Philip II; the general of the Jesuit Order,
Francis Borgia; and with Pope Pius V.[34] Oré shows confusion over Menéndez's
name and omits mention of how massive the assault was that Menéndez led on
the French in 1565: five ships with five hundred soldiers, two hundred sailors,
and one hundred additional crew, including some wives (Quinn 1990, 269).
These numbers, however, suggest more than those required for military purposes; the large expedition, and particularly the presence of women, imply that
Menéndez intended to consolidate control in that area by founding a Spanish
settlement after he had driven out the French. Oré diplomatically omits mention of the fact that Menéndez later married the sister of a cacique so as to gain

---

34 These are reproduced in Lyon, *Spanish Borderlands Sourcebook* (1995, part 3, 141–219). Spanish and
US historiography has often focused on Menéndez. For Spain, see Solís de Merás (1990 [1565]) and his
letters edited by Mercado (2006). For the United States, see the several works by Lyon—particularly
essays in his *Spanish Borderlands Sourcebook*—and Cushner (2006).

support among the Indians (records dispute whether the marriage was consummated) (Reilly 1995, 383–409). Similarly he passes over bitterness in France over Menéndez's cold-blooded killing at the time of the attack on Ribault of unarmed French prisoners—fellow Catholics whom he had assured of his protection. David Quinn understands the Spanish conquistador's ruthlessness as contributing to the "long Hapsburg-Valois struggle" in Europe (1990, 274).

VIOLENCE AND MARTYRDOM

In describing the Spaniards killed on the beaches along the Bahama Channel in chapter 2, Oré says that only some were true martyrs since they died "as Catholics at the hands of infidels" (muriendo como católicos a manos de infieles) (3v). The question of martyrdom will be discussed in greater detail later, but here it is pertinent to recall distinctions between kinds of martyrdom that E. Randolph Daniel (1975) finds in a 1437 *Tractatus*.[35] There he identifies four types: "those who suffered death involuntarily . . . ; those who desired to avoid martyrdom but when faced with the choice of denying Christ or dying decided to die; those who could have fled but voluntarily died instead; and those who spontaneously offered themselves as victims because their *caritas*[36] made them desire to imitate Christ" (1975, 123). Oré's careful language here with regard to the Spanish soldiers and elsewhere in his descriptions of Franciscan deaths suggests his theological consciousness in his use of that term and sensitivity to the nuances his readership would have appreciated.

In chapters 3 and 4 Oré tells how a young Powatan native named Paquiquineo was, it seems, forcibly taken to Spain and educated by religious there under the patronage of the Spanish king. He later traveled to Mexico where he took ill and was baptized and renamed Luis in honor of the viceroy of New Spain (Mexico), don Luis de Velasco (1550–1564), who had supported various attempts to establish a Spanish foothold in the area of Pensacola.[37] This youth, returning to La Florida supposedly to help convert his brother

---

35 See his *The Franciscan Concept of Mission in the High Middle Age* (1975).
36 Latin for charity. According to St. Thomas Aquinas, the most important of the theological virtues, reflecting love of God above all things, and the central idea of loving our neighbors as ourselves sharing in the love of God for all beings. *New Advent: The Summa Theologica of St. Thomas Aquinas*, "Question 23. Charity, considered in itself," http://www.newadvent.org/summa/3023.htm, accessed 5 August 2015.
37 The most important expedition was commanded by Tristán de Luna y Arellano and left Veracruz in 1559. They established themselves in Ochuse Bay, probably today's Pensacola Bay. A hurricane destroyed the colony, the supplies, and most of the ships.

FIGURE 4 Jesuit Martyrdom in Santa María de Ajacán or Chesapeake Bay. Mathias Tanner (1630–1692). *Societas Jesu usque ad sanguinis et vitae profusionem militans in Europea, Africa, Asia, et America.* Pragae [Prague], Typis Universitatis Carolo-Ferdinandeae, in Collegio Societatis Jesu ad S. Clementem per Joannnem Nicolaum Hampel Factorem, 1675. Courtesy of the John Carter Brown Library at Brown University.

Indians, instead reverted to his old ways; his betrayal was responsible for the murder of the religious in the Jacán.[38] Another view of these events is told by Jaime Bartolomé Martínez, a soldier in La Florida who was sent on to Potosí. Martínez calls Menéndez's role in the Indian's transport to Spain gentlemanly, saying that the adelantado treated the Indians well and consulted with the youth's father before taking him away. Thus there was no abduction:

---

38 It has been proposed (without documentation) that the young Luis could be the native leader Opechancano (he who has a white soul), who in his old age attacked Jamestown in 1622, or perhaps the father of the native leader who led the attack (*Cronología histórica*, http://cronologiahistorica.com, accessed 5 April 2014).

When the Adelantado Pedro Menéndez (may God keep him) reached the Jacán, he discovered on the coast a large bay within the harbor and he sailed in. When the Indians saw the ships, they approached in canoes and came aboard. They entered the captain's stateroom where His Lordship (another Alexander) entertained them with food and clothing. Among the natives was a leader with his son who, for an Indian, was handsome and graceful in appearance. Pedro Menéndez begged the father to let him take the youth to see the king of Spain, his master, along with other young men he had. He gave his word and swore upon his faith to return him with many riches and vestments. So the Indian leader gave him his son and Menéndez took him to Castile, to the court of Philip II (may God keep him). The king and his court were very pleased with him and the other Indians from San Agustín and Santa Elena, and rewarded them with gallant, rich clothing. The youth became a Christian; they named him don Luis; and he remained in Castile six or seven years in the Jesuit house. Because he was very intelligent, like all the Indians from those provinces if they are brought up from very young with Christians, he received the holy sacraments of the faith and was confirmed. When he was more than twenty years old, he decided he wanted to return to his homeland so as to convert his parents, relatives and fellow Indians to the faith of Jesus Christ, and be baptized as he was (Vargas Ugarte 1940, 88–89).[39]

Anna Brickhouse (2015), in a book-length study of don Luis de Velasco's role in the murder of the Jesuits at Jacán, has gone back to several sources

---

[39] "Llegando el Adelantado Pedro Menéndez (que Dios tiene) al Jacán, descubrió en la costa una gran bahía dentro del Puerto y surgió en él. Viendo los indios los navíos, vinieron a bordo en canoas y entraron en la capitana adonde su Señoría, como tenía costumbre, que era en esto otro Alejandro, les regaló con comida y vestidos. Entre los indios vino un cacique que traía un hijo, para indio, de muy buen parecer y gracia, y rogóle el Pedro Menéndez que se le diese para llevalle a que le viese el Rey de España, su señor, con otros que llevaba. Que él le daba su palabra y fe de volvérselo con muchas riquezas y vestidos. Diosolo el cacique y su señoría lo llevó a Castilla a la corte del Rey don Felipe II (que Dios tiene). Y con él y otros indios de la tierra de San Agustín y Santa Elena que llevó el Adelantado aquel viaje se holgó mucho el Rey nuestro señor y la corte y su señoría los trajo muy galantes y ricamente vestidos. El indio se volvió cristiano y le pusieron por nombre don Luis, y estuvo en Castilla seis o siete años en una casa de la Compañía . . . y siendo de lindo ingenio, como lo son los indios de todas aquellas provincias si tratan desde pequeños con cristianos, vino a ser capaz que le administraron los santísimos sacramentos del altar y confirmación. Siendo ya de edad de más de veinte años, diole deseo de volver a su tierra por ventura con designio y voluntad por entonces, como él dijo, de que sus padres, parientes y naturales della se convirtiesen a [la] fe de Jesucristo, [se] bautizasen y se volviesen cristianos como él lo era" (Vargas Ugarte 1940, 88–89).

in an effort to understand his motive for turning against the European culture that educated and baptized him. She draws mainly on Jesuit records for knowledge of the event: contemporary letters, Pedro de Ribadeneyra's life of Francis Borgia (1592), the hearsay account in El Inca Garcilaso's *La Florida*, and the 1953 history of Virginia Jesuits by Lewis and Loomis. Her consideration of Oré's narrative is drawn from the latter; she does not compare his Franciscan version with those histories she studies, which are based primarily on Jesuit expectations for missionizing, slender eyewitness testimony, and military reporting. Oré emphasizes the Indian's education with Jesuits in Spain, whereas Brickhouse tells of his stay in Cuba and in Mexico—where, she indicates, Dominicans baptized him. Reading between the lines according to literary conventions of the period, she interprets don Luis's violent deed as residual loyalties to his ethnic group and his dawning realization of Spain's ambition rather than apostasy, a return to evil barbarian ways or wild vindictiveness. In her argument for native "unsettlement"—American pushback against European colonization—she sees in his murder of the Jesuits a calculated act to forestall further encroachment into Indian lands.[40]

In chapter 3, Oré inserts himself into the narrative by saying that "in my diligent search [into the names of the martyrs of Jacán] I have not found them anywhere. I have only found the name of Father Juan Bautista, their prelate and superior."[41] In a handwritten note in the left margin of folio 5v, someone wrote, drawing on Garcilaso's *La Florida* as a source: "These were the priests Juan Bautista de Segura, a native of Toledo, and Luis de Quirós, native of Jerez de la Frontera. Six were brothers named Juan Bautista Méndez, Gabriel de Solís, Antonio Zevallos, Cristóbal Redondo, Gabriel Gómez and Pedro de Linares . . . and he [Inca Garcilaso] does not account for more than eight."[42]

---

40 Because Brickhouse focuses on English entry into Virginia she has absorbed Spanish arrivals at what later became the US mainland into the English-language preference for the terminology of "settlement"; in this way she can develop her identification of the "narrative mode of unsettlement [as] a trenchant critique of Spanish colonial discourse" (2015, 10). As a result she elides distinctions between Protestant and Catholic reasons for sending expeditions to the New World. Nevertheless, her book is extensive in its coverage, careful in its several readings, and rich in making apparent how later authors returned to the story of don Luis, politicizing it for their various purposes.

41 "Que en la diligente pesquisa que [h]e [h]echo no los [h]e podido descubrir sino solo el del padre Juan Bautista, su prelado y superior" (5v).

42 "Llamábanse los dichos que están sacerdotes Juan Bautista de Segura, natural de Toledo, y Luis de Quirós, natural de Jerez de la Frontera. Los seis eran hermanos y se llamaban Juan Bautista Méndez, Gabriel de Solis, Antonio Zeballos, Cristóbal Redondo, Gabriel Gómez y Pedro de Linares . . . y [el Inca Garcilaso] no pone a más de ocho" (5v).

FIGURE 5 Natives of the Timucua ethnic group worshipping the sun. Attributed to Jacques Le Moyne de Morgues in Theodore de Bry, *Brevis narratio eorum quae in Florida Americae provincia Gallis acciderunt* (1591). Plate 35. Courtesy of the Special Collections Department, University of South Florida. Digitization provided by the USF Libraries Digitization Center.

CHRISTIAN INTERPRETATION OF INDIAN BELIEFS

In chapter 4 Oré goes on to attribute the young Luis's rejection of Christian teaching to the influence of the devil. The personification of evil in this way was standard in medieval thought, and Fernando Cervantes has studied how this European belief carried to colonial New Spain an easy explanation of the seeming appearance of the supernatural in the natural world (1994). However, this association was selectively used; it was invoked to alienate and demonize Indians whose idolatry and magical beliefs were called paganism and superstition and therefore demanding of eradication. Spaniards made it seem as though the devil was an invention of Indian belief, that the figure moved in the American mind in a way contrary to rational European thought. Yet belief

FIGURE 6 The Timucuas treating their sick. Attributed to Jacques Le Moyne de Morgues in Theodore de Bry, *Brevis narratio eorum quae in Florida Americae provincia Gallis acciderunt* (1591). Plate 20. Courtesy of the Special Collections Department, University of South Florida. Digitization provided by the USF Libraries Digitization Center.

in the devil was also conveniently used by Spaniards themselves to explain events. When Father Ávila recounts his captivity in Oré's chapter 8, the friar says the Indians were led to torture him by the devil; the devil, he claims, was also responsible for tempting him to break his vows by offering him a lovely Indian wife. Oré generally avoids discussion of what one might call native pre-Christian religious belief, though in this temptation scene he does say that the Indians insist that Ávila will have in the afterlife just what he has in this life; thus, if he wishes to be happy there he should enjoy a wife here.

CONVERSIONS AND REBELLION

Chapter 5 usefully provides background on why an initial peace between the Spaniards and the Indians of Guale and Escamacu was broken. This so-called Indian "rebellion" was precipitated by the military governor's adjudication of an Indian dispute. Outraged Indians violently turned on the soldiers and the friars but also on one another, ruining what had been the start of a promising arrangement for coexistence and the beginnings of successful Christianization. This incident has attracted the interest of historians, but Oré, in describing here the origins of the war, provides additional information on Spanish administrative politics and military tactics, reasons for the Indians' brutal reaction to the sentence—even documenting the complicating factor of the arrival in the area of a French galleon. Chapter 6 emphasizes progress in the Christianization of the native population. However, Oré tells how Indians who were not Christians (*hanopiras*) were being persecuted by their fellows who had become Christian. At first the converts had been the target of the heathens' anger, reviled as renegades and betrayers of Indian loyalties. The new Christians persisted, however, considering it an honor to embrace the Spaniards' faith, and turned the tables on the non-Christian natives to such an extent that the priests then were in the position of having to protect them. In this chapter Oré compares La Florida's Indians with the Andeans he knows, suggesting the beginnings of a classification system. He calls both populations "barbarous" but says, "Both are expert in the use of the bow and arrow. But in Peru they go about clothed, or at least less naked than the ones here. The Floridians have the advantage in that they are more warlike."[43] Indeed clothing as a measure of civilization is at the heart of Father Ávila's description of his torture; when he is stripped of his garments, this humiliation, he believes, reduces him to the level of the Indians. And when some garments of the martyred priests are found to have survived, Oré says the Christian Indians treat them as holy relics.

Chapters 7 and 8 narrate the Guale rebellion of 1597 in which four Franciscans (Pedro de Corpa, Miguel de Auñón, Blas Rodríguez, and Francisco de Veráscola) and a lay brother (Antonio de Badajoz) were martyred. They also tell how Father Friar Francisco de Ávila was kidnapped and then rescued. Ávila's account, in his own words, is one of the most affecting parts of Oré's report. The chapters also provide a description of how the governor Gonzalo Méndez de Canzo ruthlessly punished the Indians for the Franciscans' murders. This action touched off rebellion, and the Franciscan missions in present-day Georgia, except for San Pedro on Cumberland Island, were destroyed (Geiger 1940, 120). Oré gives as an explanation the fact that a friar told an

---

43 "Y los unos y otros son flecheros, pero allá andan vestidos, o menos desnudos que los de acá, y estos se aventajan en ser más guerreros" (10r).

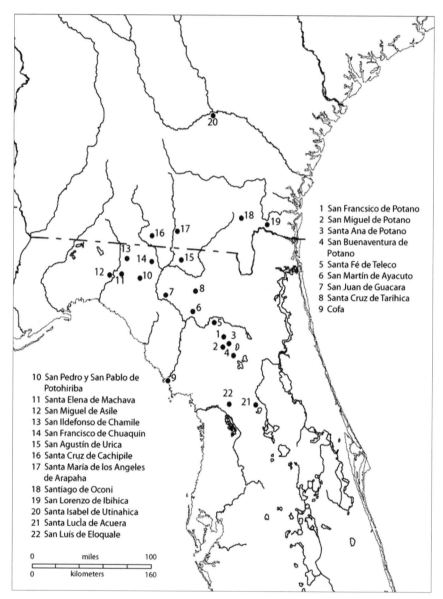

1 San Francsico de Potano
2 San Miguel de Potano
3 Santa Ana de Potano
4 San Buenaventura de
  Potano
5 Santa Fé de Teleco
6 San Martín de Ayacuto
7 San Juan de Guacara
8 Santa Cruz de Tarihica
9 Cofa

10 San Pedro y San Pablo de
   Potohiriba
11 Santa Elena de Machava
12 San Miguel de Asile
13 San Ildefonso de Chamile
14 San Francisco de Chuaquin
15 San Agustín de Urica
16 Santa Cruz de Cachipile
17 Santa María de los Angeles
   de Arapaha
18 Santiago de Oconi
19 San Lorenzo de Ibihica
20 Santa Isabel de Utinahica
21 Santa Lucla de Acuera
22 San Luís de Eloquale

| 0 | miles | 100 |
| 0 | kilometers | 160 |

MAP 2 Franciscan missions in La Florida, 1606–1630, prepared and revised by Jerald T. Milanich and published with his permission.

Indian cacique, whom he had married according to Christian sacrament, that he could not take a second wife since that was against doctrine.[44]

Christian teaching about matrimony begins chapter 9, telling how Guale was finally pacified. Starting in 1604, Franciscans returned and began to have successes in conversions. They were helped by "miracles"—superfluous spouses died, people were cured of illnesses, etc. Here Oré relies on the testimony of Father Friar Francisco Pareja, who emphasizes how, after fourteen years of Franciscan labor, the Indians learned to read and write with the help of materials he wrote and had printed. The new Christians were observant of the mass and respected the importance of confessions. Pareja says, "Among the Indians I have known I have not found any trace of idolatry, or witchcraft—but rather of superstitions such as when they say, 'With this you will be cured; or if this herb does not cure you will die; if the owl cries, it is a sign that some evil is going to befall.'"[45] It is only the old people, he goes on to say, who repeat these superstitions; the young people who are Christians make fun of them.

Chapter 10 continues the account of Franciscan successes with the testimony of Father Friar Martín Prieto. His teaching and personal example, after initial resistance, brought about conversions. These were accomplished particularly when a miraculous storm convinced an old man, who had been a captive of de Soto and hated the Spaniards, to relent; he became a Christian and brought hundreds of his followers to the faith. This is followed by another such story. But the most moving episode in this chapter is the account of a little boy who was dying; his words, verbatim, inspired others not to fear death but instead to hope for peace in a Christian heaven. Chapter 11, dating Oré's visits to La Florida to inspect missions and oversee the beginnings of Franciscan governing structures, is the most useful for concluding when the work was published.

44 J. Michael Francis and Kathleen M. Kole (2011) have recently uncovered archival evidence that further explains the rancor behind this hostile outbreak.
45 "Que entre ellos jamás [h]e hallado ni rastro de idolatría, ni de hechicería, sino de supersticiones diciendo; 'con esto sanarás; si no te curas con esta yerba, te morirás; si canta el búho; señal es que me [h]a de suceder alguna desgracia'" (25r).

FIGURE 7 Bridal party. Attributed to Jacques Le Moyne de Morgues in Theodore de Bry, *Brevis narratio eorum quae in Florida Americae provincia Gallis acciderunt* (1591). Plate 37. Courtesy of the Special Collections Department, University of South Florida. Digitization provided by the USF Libraries Digitization Center.

The Franciscan Identity of the Author

Franciscans were early arrivals in the Americas. Histories of both Mexico (Ricard 1966) and Peru (Tibesar 1953) tell of the entry of twelve Franciscans into each of those areas, whose numbers mythically recalled Christ's apostles in spreading the Gospel. The order was founded by St. Francis and approved by Pope Honorio III in 1223. The friars were noted for their poverty and humility, often begging for their keep. In sixteenth-century Europe they were known for their preaching as they traveled to areas where absent bishops had left churches devoid of pastoral care. In its Counter-Reformation years the Church particularly counted on this mendicant order, as well as others, in carrying out reforms the Council of Trent had decreed.

In the Americas, then, after the first phase of discoveries and conquest the Franciscans—along with Dominicans, Augustinians, Jesuits, Carmelites, and Mercedarians—worked as always under the direction of the Pope and their superiors, but now according to the dictates of the council. If scholastic dialogue with Moslem, Jewish, and Protestant scholars had served in the past to bring about conversions, churchmen at Trent now recognized that Catholicism's message had to appeal at another level to peoples whom they wanted to keep within the Church but also those they wanted to attract. Some of these were illiterate; others spoke strange languages and seemed immune to Christian approaches to their cultures. Since the council had been mostly a response to challenges in Europe and attendees were under duress to finish after long years of theological debate, they wrapped up their work so fast that they did not have time to address problems missionaries were having (O'Malley 2013, 21). American bishops were absent from Trent with the result that later councils in Mexico and Peru took European dictates for proselytizing as models. Trent decisions about preferring vernacular languages to catechize had a paramount impact in the Americas.

THE SECOND AND THIRD LIMA CHURCH COUNCILS

Thus the Second Lima Council (1567–1568) worked to present plans for missionaries to use for conversion and Indian instruction. Spanish, a modern language, was substituted for Latin and Indian tongues were deemed useful for communicating the Church's teachings. A passage from the Third Lima Council summarizes the spirit of the new regulations: "Each one should be instructed in a manner that enables understanding of doctrine, the Spaniard in romance and the Indian also in his own language."[46] Grammars, vocabularies, catechisms, prayers, sermons, guides to confessors—all now were newly required. The preparation of these catechetical instruments incidentally permitted the standardization of languages that lacked writing systems comparable to the Latin alphabet. Three publications resulting from these efforts were *Doctrina cristiana y catecismo para instrucción de los indios* (Christian Doctrine and Catechism for the Instruction of the Indians) (1584); *Confesionario para los curas de indios* (Confession Guide for Priests Ministering to Indians) (1585); and *Tercero catecismo y exposición de la doctrina cristiana por sermones* (Third Catechism and Presentation of Christian Doctrine through Sermons) (1585).

---

46 "Cada uno ha de ser de tal manera instruido que entienda la doctrina, el Hespañol [*sic*] en romance, y el indio también en su lengua." (Vargas Ugarte 1951–1954, t. 1: 325).

As previously mentioned, the Jesuit José de Acosta assembled the translating team in which Oré worked to prepare evangelizing materials in the native languages—one reason being that Acosta distrusted interpreters for transmitting Christianity's message.[47] Interpreters were thought to work on an ad hoc basis, sometimes with faulty knowledge and under stressful circumstances, whereas printed materials and friars trained in approved-of seminaries could be thought to regularize communication.[48] This early distinction between "translators" and "interpreters" reveals a centralizing preference that characterized other Church and civil governing policies but that also recognized the usefulness of American adaptations. This new linguistic policy must be seen as acknowledgment of other cultural modes of human understanding and equally adequate language systems, as a recognition of the need to accommodate the faith rather than perverting Christianity's message of love and charity by bludgeoned conversions. Following these trends in 1579 Viceroy Francisco de Toledo founded a chair for Indian languages at Lima's University of San Marcos.[49]

THE ORDINANCES OF 1573: THE RELIGIOUS AND THE MILITARY

In addition to oversight by the institutional Church, religious affairs in the Americas were also subject to the Crown. At the time discoveries were being made in that hemisphere, the Pope had delegated to the Catholic kings, Ferdinand and Isabella, responsibility for the conversion of indigenous peoples; Philip II, whose reign lasted from 1555 to 1600, took this charge seriously. In 1573 the king decreed new ordinances for discovering and populating new towns (Nuevas Ordenanzas de Población y Descubrimientos). Missionaries were designated as the principal agents of imperial expansion, thus relegating the conquistadors who overthrew great empires to the secondary role of defending their advances. To a great extent these ordinances were a response to complaints that the conquistadors had often been destructive; religious petitions for more men and supplies were being denied in favor of support

---

47 See Cobo Betancourt (2014) and Puente Luna (2014).

48 Quilis (1998, 67–75). In addition to writing *Historia natural y moral de las Indias* in Peru, Acosta also prepared there his *De procuranda Indorum salute*, which more fully addresses issues of pacification and colonization considered by the Third Council (see the 1984 edition). On the Council generally see Lisi 1990.

49 Porras Barrenechea (1952, ix); Martín (1968) is also useful in describing the Jesuit presence in Lima, and the order's founding of the Colegio Máximo de San Pablo in 1568. Its library, in 1750, reached 43,000 volumes.

for soldiers, and appeals for peaceful entry into new regions for "spiritual conquest" had been ignored in favor of a policy that supposed the need to acquire territory at any cost. Nonetheless, it is true that in remote areas such as La Florida and the Araucanian region of Chile, bordered by key maritime routes and where missionaries needed protection from often-hostile natives, presidios were understood to be necessary. Additionally, the 1573 ordinances stated that the religious, now servants of the Crown, had to be paid by the closest royal treasury, thus setting up competition between the two factions for the same monies.[50] In the case of La Florida stipends for soldiers and missionaries came from the Viceroyalty of New Spain.[51]

A second decree by the Spanish Crown in 1574, the Ordinance of Patronage (Ordenanza del Real Patronato de Indias), also contributed to changing the dynamics of authority in the Americas. Philip II entered even more fully into the business of religion by asserting his right to appoint bishops and name viceroys who would participate in Church affairs.[52] For example, Francisco de Toledo was sent to Peru as a civil administrator, yet he worked hand in hand with clergymen on projects to manage the territory's Indians. When delegates to the Third Lima Council came from as far north as Nicaragua and south from modern-day Bolivia, Argentina, and Chile, they also carried out the Crown's pacification work in their introduction of disciplinary literature, parish development, and resettlement schemes in the formation of reducciones.[53]

Relations between religious and civilian administrators were often explained by the metaphor of two knives or swords (*dos cuchillos*)—a medieval legal concept that joined spiritual to secular authority. That thinking was current at the time of the Councils but began to be questioned in later years as military and ecclesiastical factions competed for support from the embattled and indebted Spanish Crown. The bishop of Santiago de Chile, Gaspar de Villarroel, used the phrase in his 1656 work, *Gobierno eclesiástico pacífico, y unión de los dos cuchillos, pontificio y regio* (Pacific Ecclesiastical Government, and Union of the Two Swords, Papal and Royal), where he complained that the Crown was supporting an excessive number of friars with money

50 Bushnell describes these Ordinances of Pacification, particularly as they applied to missions in frontier areas dealing with dispersed mobile indigenous populations (as in the case of La Florida) (2004, 142–68).
51 About the *situado* or funds for payment, see Bushnell 1994.
52 Indeed Meier calls Philip II "a kind of vice-pope for America" (1992a, 63).
53 For a discussion of reducciones, see Mumford 2012.

that could be used to pay for more soldiers to defend the presidio. One reads the opposite viewpoint in a memorandum of 17 January 1617, signed by the friars of La Florida—Francisco Pareja, Pedro Ruiz, Lorenzo Martínez, Alonso Pesquera, Juan de la Cruz, Bartolomé Romero, and Francisco Alonso de Jesús. There they presented evidence of greedy colonial administrators, missionaries being slandered, abuses against the native population, the constant corrupting presence of soldiers among Indians, and prohibitions against catechism in certain areas (AGI, Santo Domingo 235, ff. 73–76, 17 de enero de 1617, 4 folios).

More evidence of this mutual animosity in the case of La Florida is contained in a letter dated 15 May 1616 that Commissioner Vivanco wrote requesting that a neutral person from Guatemala, Father Friar Francisco Hurtado, be sent there to verify what was happening, resolve problems and recommend reforms (AGI, Santo Domingo 25, Consejo, 15 de mayo de 1616, 1 folio). Oré's *Account* repeats these jealousies when, speaking in the third person, he says in his second visit to San Agustín that he "published an edict attacking the public vices that might be found among the soldiers in the presidio. With the agreement of the governor, he named an attorney and notary from among the soldiers. Without hurting anyone, he resolved everything that needed resolution and displayed the prudence and tact necessary for dealing with the soldiers so as to bring about the desired corrections [in a way that] should be hoped for."[54]

In what seems to have been a letter-writing campaign, Oré and other Franciscans wrote to the king on 14 January 1617 saying that "the most important thing is to appoint a person to this government who does not impede but rather helps with his favor and encouragement what the missionaries with immense labor and fatigue are achieving every day."[55] The signatories then recommended the appointment of Juan Menéndez Marqués as governor. In another letter (probably dated 1618, AGI, Santo Domingo 25, 1 folio, Resolución a 20 de febrero), Oré argued "for the need in La Florida of missionaries for new conversions of large numbers of people who request baptism in the

---

54 "Y publicó edi[c]to contra los vicios públicos que pudo [h]aber entre los soldados del presidio, nombrando fiscal y notario de los mismos soldados con permisión y beneplácito del gobernador. Y en todo se remedió lo que pedía remedio, sin agravio de nadie y con la prudencia y recato que entre soldados es necesario tener para que se consiga el fin de la enmienda que se debe desear" (30r).

55 " . . . porque lo más importante es proveer persona en este govierno que no impida, antes ayude con su fabor y aliento a lo que los religiosos con inmenso trabajo y cansançio van cada dia ganando" (AGI, Santo Domingo 235, ff. 71–72, 2 folios).

provinces of Apalache, Latama, Machagua, and Santa Elena. In these provinces, hoping for the arrival of priests, the Indians of Apalache have built churches. Captain Juan de Salinas, governor of said provinces, has written about this."[56]

In still another letter Oré requested more missionaries, and then noted his return to Spain so as to participate in the general chapter meeting in Salamanca of the Franciscan Order in 1618. On the journey he was accompanied by Lorenzo Martínez, custodian of the province of Santa Elena, who would return to La Florida via New Spain (AGI, Santo Domingo 235, ff. 77–78, 2 folios, Resolución de 23 de julio de 1618, 2 folios). At the Salamanca gathering the Franciscans agreed to promote the cult of the Immaculate Conception, a fact that probably explains the 1619 publication in Madrid of Oré's *Corona de la sacratísima Virgen María Madre de Dios nuestra señora . . . Dedicada a la misma Virgen sacrosanta, concebida sin pecado original, en su imagen y santuario de Copacabana* (Crown of the Most Holy Mother of God . . . Dedicated to the Same Holy Virgin, Conceived without Original Sin, in Her Image and Sanctuary of Copacabana). The title shows Oré's desire to insert an Andean devotion to the Copacabana Virgin into a larger European context.

EUROPE'S HISTORICAL ATTITUDES TOWARD CONVERSION

One now considers how these American letters might have been received on the other side of the Atlantic. Throughout the sixteenth century Spain was fighting wars in the Netherlands, in central Europe, in Italy, and in the eastern Mediterranean. Charles I's and Philip II's relations with the Pope, France, and England were often angry. Internally, although the Jews had been expelled from the Peninsula in 1492, the Inquisition that was established in Spain in 1478 was strengthening efforts to bring to trial crypto-Jews but also to bear down on Moriscos, descendants of Arabs who had been permitted to stay on in the south after Granada, their last Moslem stronghold, had fallen.[57]

---

56 "la necessidad que ay en ella de religiosos para las nuevas conversiones, de grande número de gente que piden el baptismo en las provincias de Apalache, Latama, Machagua y Santa Elena, en las quales, con esperança que an de entrar sacerdotes, los indios de Apalahe an edificado iglesias sobre lo qual escribe el capitán Juan de Salinas, governador de aquellas provincias."

57 The best account of the early years of the Inquisition, founded in southern France in the late Middle Ages to combat Cathar and Albigensian heresies, and introduced into Spain as Castile and Aragon were consolidating power, is still Lea's three-volume history (1955 [1888]).

Members of this economically important faction, who had been born in Spain and were converts to Catholicism or Christianized at birth, were rising up to threaten the new nation's prosperity and Catholic unity. The king at first had attempted a policy of pacification designed to suppress the use of the Moriscos' language, customs, and questionable religious practices. But when that policy of seeking to avoid violence failed, the population was expelled in 1609. El Inca Garcilaso, Oré's compatriot, fought in the Rebellion of the Alpujarras (1568–1571) against the Morisco population.

That initial decision to handle the Morisco threat peacefully was based on the population's education and resettlement. Yet the policy was not consistently peaceable because forcible baptisms did occur during those years (Perry 2005, 3). Indeed the question of forced conversions had long-standing roots in Catholic theology and had come to be an acceptable practice because, it was argued, it avoided bloodshed and eventually produced a unified, docile population. According to James Hitchcock, describing the Church's effort to resolve the question of how to subject conquered peoples with non-Christian beliefs to the true faith (an issue that historians have often subsumed into discussion over a just war),

> some Church leaders, notably Ambrose, condemned forced conversions. But . . . Augustine, after first rejecting the practice, reluctantly accepted it in the case of the warlike Donatists, who were an acute pastoral problem in his own diocese. His justification was Jesus' parable of the man who gave a banquet and whose final command to his servants, with regard to those they would meet in the streets, was "compel [them] to come in" (L[u]k[e] 14:23). Augustine pointed out that, even if the first generation of converts was coerced, their descendants might embrace the faith with sincerity (2012, 59).

Coerced faith or the use of violence is implicit in Oré's *Account*, in which he matter-of-factly notes how Spanish soldiers treated Indians—and perhaps reveals his own belief in the need for force. This attitude probably offends modern readers but, within the context of the period, was morally justifiable. When early in the narrative Indians who innocently board a Spanish ship are carried off, Oré does not moralize on the Spaniards' duplicity, which later causes the natives who initially were friendly to retaliate by killing Vázquez de Ayllón's expeditionaries; he simply records the two events. One may conjecture several reasons for Oré's coolness. His theological training may have suppressed his human reaction as he remembered argumentation learned in the seminary. His bureaucratic function to report just the bare facts, evident here and throughout the *Account*, may have constrained him and prevented him from making explicit cause and effect to distant authorities who might have favored the military's pragmatism. Indeed a relación, according to the *Diccionario de autoridades* (1726–1737), was considered to be a report that, like a deposition, functioned as a legal document. It was testimony that an individual, usually an eyewitness, made publicly in front of a judge. In that sense, it did not require the person's elaboration or argumentation, but instead was limited to a recitation of facts.

Early in the sixteenth century the Dominican Friar Bartolomé de las Casas (1484–1566), in criticizing Spain's tolerance of those means of conquest and "conversion," had angrily denounced the Spanish soldiers' harsh treatment of the natives and emotionally called them the real barbarians. However, by the latter part of that century the language of "pacification" or "spiritual conquest" was officially adopted (Bireley 1999, 157), displacing onto the friars the onus of the takeover. Hospitals, schools, seminaries and confraternities were founded with the purpose of peaceful assertion of Spanish controls. Rituals as part of the mass but also public celebrations such as processions and pilgrimages were encouraged so as to inspire piety and conformity. In the case of La Florida, evangelization and governance were accomplished through "persuasive" tactics that, although they often did demand force and discipline, also included appeasement through gift giving (particularly to chiefs), resettlement, and intermarriage (the case of Menéndez de Avilés) (Bushnell 2006a, 195–213). Verbs such as *rendir* (to cause to surrender), *sujetar* (to subject or bring under domination), and *someter* (to cause submission), with their various connotations of force and violence, were part of the period's language to describe the process of establishing authority.

Nevertheless, whether disguised or obvious, violence rooted in precedent, which had seen cooperation between civil and religious authorities, underlay pacification and conversion policies throughout Europe and the Americas in the sixteenth and seventeenth centuries. In 1232 Pope Gregory IX authorized the first appearance of the Inquisition with the purpose of suppressing heresy, particularly in northern Italy and southern France. That discipline countenanced secret denunciations, torture, and public executions of persons who threatened orthodoxy, that is, the established order. Throughout the fifteenth century several popes issued bulls allowing Spanish monarchs to establish an inquisition in their several kingdoms with the aim, under the guise of serving the popes and guiding faith, of forcing Jews and Moslems to accept Christianity or leave the Peninsula; in this way the monarchs could realize their goal of consolidating control over the diverse population. Ever since 1391, when Jews were massacred throughout Spain, hatreds had intensified; ghettos, vilification, and restrictions on their livelihood—all had deepened rifts where Christians ruled. However, when *conversos* (newly baptized Jews and Moslems) opportunely accepted baptism to protect their lives and property, old Christians felt threatened and jealousies grew worse, seemingly creating the need for an oversight body that would determine sincere faith. As a result in the late fifteenth century, the Catholic kings Ferdinand and Isabella (a title conferred on them by the Pope), whose marriage joined Aragon and Castile, expelled all Spain's Jews in 1492. Those few Jews who had stayed on at the upper levels of finance and medicine in the last years of the century, who had enjoyed the protection of powerful Christians, then converted or left. Serving other purposes as Spain extended to the Americas, the Inquisition went on to set up its tribunals in Mexico, Cartagena de Indias, and Lima to exercise control over populations there.[58] Thus, the idea of "forcible" conversions was rooted in the Spanish Catholic experience.

Yet conversion began taking on other forms in Catholic thinking in the sixteenth century. Protestantism with its emphasis on literacy, on the individual's ability to read and interpret the Bible without priestly interference, was giving impetus to printing; Catholics duly recognized the utility of printing their own books—not only to counter Protestantism and instruct new literates but also to begin dialogue with those they had previously damned. Franciscan emphasis on preaching and missionizing, as well as other orders' reaches into northern Europe, England and Ireland, the eastern Mediterranean, and Asia among equally cultured peoples who could not be ejected or beaten into submission, had caused the Church to turn to more accommodating methods of conversion. Books in the vernacular, but also political maneuvering to convince local princes to stay in the Church and decree the faith for their populations, as well as respectful negotiation with Eastern potentates, started to modify hard-line policies. Pope Gregory XIII, in his tenure from 1572 to 1585, began to promote the usefulness of catechisms for summarizing faith for neophytes but also *confesionarios* for use

---

58 This summary is based on Kamen (1997).

by priests so as to rout out deviation. This catechetical literature, along with the printing of hymnals, prayer books, etc., began to mean good business for printers in Spain as well as in other parts of Catholic Europe who exported to the New World.[59] In 1542 Pope Paul III, realizing the threat of Protestantism, established the Congregation for the Propagation of the Faith. In 1559 Pope Paul IV, assessing the dangers of uncontrolled reading, published the first Index of Prohibited Books. Already in 1554 the Spanish king Charles I (and Holy Roman Emperor as Charles V) had decreed two types of book censorship (pre- and post-publication) authorizing civil authorities to impose one set of controls while the Church-run Inquisition imposed another (Ramos Soriano 2011, 38). Thus the Roman Congregation firmed up boundaries of the faith through intellectual surveillance and economic restraints on publishers and booksellers, but also by means of more visible punishments. Inquisition book burnings and autos-da-fé accustomed the public to performances of violence. It is in this context, then, that one appreciates the work of Lima's Second and Third Provincial Councils, mentioned earlier. It represents the new and more compassionate, but also pragmatic, direction the Church was taking in consolidating and expanding its base.

DYING FOR THE FAITH

In seeking to understand further Spanish attitudes toward non-Christian peoples in that period, one also recalls how throughout the late Middle Ages a combative mentality arose in Europe as Christian princes sent warriors to reconquer Jerusalem. Spain had its own Crusade during the Reconquest years (711–1492) as Christians fought to expel Moslems from the Peninsula. Thus war was thought of as part of religious service. With the challenge of the Reformation in the fifteenth and sixteenth centuries, across the continent Catholic powers not only fought Protestants for territory or to gain prominence but also engaged in rivalries among themselves. Indeed the struggle between Spain and France was particularly heated, spilling into Italy. Within France, civil war between Catholics and Protestants raged throughout the sixteenth century; the Massacre of St. Bartholomew in 1572 was only one episode in that religious and political struggle.

---

59 González Sánchez (2014).

Consequently, violence suffered as the result of Christian faith, at the hands of pagans, barbarians, heretics, etc., was admirable at that moment; martyrdom for a religious cause was not strange. In fact, martyrdom was often a preliminary step to sainthood. In the late Middle Ages and on into the sixteenth and seventeenth centuries, *Ars moriendi* books describing the art of dying and the idea of a "good death" circulated in both Catholic and Protestant areas of Europe; the topic, in which suffering emulated Christ's sacrifice and was justified as the need for man to expiate his sinful nature (O'Connor 1942), further concentrated men's minds on pain and death. Suffering, whether in the form of fasting, flagellation, or a difficult pilgrimage, was a form of penance, often considered necessary in that historical context as proof of repentance. Denial of bodily desires, ideally in selfless service to others, affirmed one's spiritual purity. Endurance of pain and death suffered unjustly was meant to teach others. Living an exemplary life (perhaps without martyrdom but with sacrifice to Church ideals) was a means of attaining sainthood; being "a confessor," one who confessed the faith in his or her life like Elisabeth of Hungary (1207?–1231), was also a path to sainthood—indeed, Elisabeth of Hungary was canonized in the thirteenth century. In both instances, adherence to Church ideals were gifts the individual gave voluntarily, surrendering one's self in order to become part of a larger body, in a true spirit of *caritas*.

Peter Brown, in commenting on Christianity's spread in the pagan world, says that "the church was an artificial kin group. Its members were expected to project onto the new community a fair measure of the sense of solidarity, of the loyalties, and of the obligations that had previously been directed to the physical family" (1981, 31). La Florida's missionaries—leaving behind their biological families, joining a fraternity with other men in a foreign world, and representing in their deaths a willingness to leave their bodies behind in renunciation of self—made up a new kin group. To themselves and to the Indians they were walking models of new loyalties. Although native family structures might be understood to have been collective, Indians would have recognized in the friars' transplant from a foreign world to theirs, in their solitary existence, their celibacy, their humility, their peaceable nature, and then their voluntary deaths, a break with their own familiarities. Martyrdom, it can be argued, was a necessary tool in Christianity's campaign in America and Asia in the sixteenth and seventeenth centuries, as it dramatized how the old self had to be annihilated so that the individual could join a new community.

Martyrdom, violent and bloody, had its origins in the early Church. Candida Moss has recently studied this historical phenomenon in her *Myth of Persecution: How Early Christianity Invented a Story of Martyrdom* (2013); among other conclusions, she suggests how Rome's point of view, which saw the sect as threatening and gloried in abasing it, shifted as Christians themselves began to write and took on their victimization as a positive value. Christian martyrs thus started the legends according to which the underground Church rallied. Kate Cooper, in her review of Moss's book (*TLS* 10 Jan. 2014), calls attention to how in the fourth century Eusebius in his *Ecclesiastical History* features martyrdom: "With their heroism in the face of persistent attack, the martyrs play nearly as visible a role as do the apostles in carrying the Christian message to the world" (24).

MARTYRDOM REVISITED

However, Oré's narrative of martyrdom, surfacing in the climate after the Council of Trent, is strange. Even before the council, popes had begun to slow down and change the process for naming saints; Cook writes that no saint was canonized between 1523 and 1588 and quotes Peter Burke that in that century "the whole idea of a saint was under attack" (1998, ix). Therefore, Oré's story of faithful sacrifice asks questions about why he chose the language of "martyrdom" to tell the story of Jesuit and Franciscan missionaries. One of these questions is this: Who were Oré's readers? Probably not just pious lay people for whom hagiography was intended, but rather the upper reaches of Spanish civil administration and the Roman Ecclesia. Another important question is, Considering the Church's rethinking of qualifications for sainthood, what was the purpose of that interpretation of Christian life and service?

Indeed the Church's earlier emphasis on martyrdom as a precondition for sainthood can be seen to have been undergoing a change. Thomas James Dandelet, in discussing attitudes toward canonization in those years in his *Spanish Rome, 1500–1700*, tells how two requisites of sainthood—a holy life and the performance of miracles—were emerging in the new, tightened-up process. Martyrdom seemed to be receding in the Church's list of necessary attributes. In 1588, when the Spanish Franciscan Diego de Alcalá was canonized after many years when few Spaniards had been elevated to sainthood—and, indeed, few saints at all entered the calendar—international politics appear to have been behind the action. There was little documentation to support Alcalá's

FIGURE 8 Portrait of San Francisco Solano (1549–1610). Oil on canvas (c. 1810), by
Pedro Díaz. Courtesy of Ministerio de Cultura and Museo Nacional de Arqueología,
Antropología e Historia del Perú.

road to sainthood; but Pope Sixtus V, also a Franciscan, had repeatedly asked Philip II to invade England. Thus when the king finally obliged in that year, Dandelet argues that the canonization of this first Counter-Reformation saint was payback (2001, 172–75). Miracles, for which witnesses could be found and whose testimony could more easily be invoked, were beginning to supplant martyrdom. Martyrdom or death at the hands of enemies of the faith, which an increasingly Christianized Europe was making rare, was beginning to disappear from the canonization process. Rosa de Lima, the first saint born in the Americas, was canonized for her exemplary life in 1671.[60]

Oré's language of martyrdom, therefore, likely asked his readers to rethink the criteria for sainthood. One remembers that Oré had been assigned to gather evidence for beatifying, then canonizing, the Franciscan Francisco Solano, who left Spain to catechize in Peru. Oré's documentation was published in Madrid in 1614 but Solano was not made a saint until 1726. Based on interviews with witnesses, Oré emphasized Solano's preaching, which miraculously reached Indians who spoke different languages, and the fact that his body, when disinterred, was found to be uncorrupted. He had not died as a result of martyrdom, but his life and death displayed both exemplary service to the faith and miracles.

REPRESENTING SELF-SACRIFICE

One can read Oré's *Account*, then, as hinting at current theological issues if not also at a proposal for La Florida martyrs' nomination to sainthood.[61] The men are examples of sanctity and heroic virtue. They have chosen their life of service, knowing the risks of suffering and dying. Obedient to their vows and facing death at the hands of enemies of the faith, they accept it. Although there is some evidence in Oré's detail of how items of the friars' clothing were preserved as relics, of how memory of their burial place was forming, of how some conversions were beginning to be regarded as miracles, it is apparent that Oré is using criteria for sainthood as a kind of outline for his choice of information. However, because the *Account* ends by showing a stable world in which

---

60 Isabel Flores de Oliva (1586–1617).
61 Fr. Conrad Harkins has formally requested that the Catholic Church declare the Franciscan martyrs, the first step to sainthood. In March 2007, he hand-carried the official Acts of the Process, nearly five hundred pages, to the Congregation of the Causes of Saints in Rome. Fr. Harkins, OFM, is the vice-postulator of the cause. See Paul Thigpen, "The Georgia Martyrs: Heroic Witnesses to the Sanctity of Marriage," http://www.catholicculture.org/culture/library/view.cfm?recnum=7662, accessed 5 August 2015.

preaching has brought about conversions and peace among the chiefdoms, and mission stations are organized, there is a suggestion that the need for any more martyrdom, at least in this region, has passed. Nevertheless, the message is implicit that La Florida's conquest and development had to be based on initial destruction as well as in the exemplary lives of these religious.[62]

Oré's narrative of martyrdom asked clerics and lay readers to rethink the Church's idealism in teaching the values of self-sacrifice, bodily mortification, and voluntary obedience. It asks modern readers to understand how, in this literary instance, an American—a criollo born in the viceroyalty of Peru—was challenging European demands and expectations. The martyrs are not portrayed as spiritual heroes in the sense that they constantly prayed and performed superhuman deeds (or miracles), but rather as obedient servants of the Church who were trying minimally to survive and carry out missionizing tasks in the face of Indian belligerency and cruelty. Oré's lists of men, giving credit to their Spanish birthplaces, suggests that other young men could gain honor for themselves and their families by serving in the Americas. His careful naming of Franciscans in the field, as he met them in his supervisory role as provincial leader on an inspection tour, suggests a reportorial aim for his account. Oré's depiction of these episodes of self-sacrifice recalls Garcilaso's earlier contention in *La Florida del Inca*: so much Catholic blood had been spilled in the area that surely it would bear fruit when its inhabitants accepted God's word and came to obey the Holy Roman Church, and, of course, the Spanish king (1956 [1605] Book 6, Chap. 22, 448). The miracle would be achieved not by the sword but rather through the caritas of missionaries. Seen in this manner Oré's report on martyrdom is both pragmatic and idealistic as it anticipates an orderly future, made possible by the religious and their exemplary lives and deaths.

La Florida as a Contested Site

Unlike Spain, England and France provided a visual record of their early presence in La Florida. In addition to the written materials sent home by seamen, adventurers, and early settlers, maps, drawings, and prints done by travelers who accompanied them propagandized those countries' claims and

---

62 As background for understanding the canonization of saints and martyrdom, see also Molinari, Greene, and Gilby, all published in 1967.

perhaps have taken precedence over Spanish written accounts (which often were kept secret so as to protect routes and forays). The Frenchman Jacques Le Moyne de Morgues (c. 1533–1588) accompanied the 1564 expedition led by Ribault and Laudonnière to the area; his drawings of the Timucua were taken up and reproduced by Theodore de Bry (1560–1623) in his 1591 work published in Frankfurt—*Brevis narratio eorum quae in Florida Americae provincia Gallis acciderunt*. There were editions in German and French as well as Latin.

IMAGES OF LA FLORIDA

The English gentleman and watercolorist John White (d. 1597), who had personal associations with Queen Elizabeth and Sir Walter Raleigh, made at least five trips to the eastern coast of the present-day United States, beginning in 1577; surviving records suggest the 1585 trip was the one that allowed him to draw maps and sketch La Florida's native population. In 1584 Richard Hakluyt, arguing for the need to challenge Spain in the area, wrote the essay "Discourse of Western Planting" to try to convince the queen to continue her support for discoveries. The English colony of Roanoke Island, in modern North Carolina, was the result, the settlement that most histories of the United States feature.[63] Thomas Harriot's *A briefe and true report of the new found land of Virginia*, published in 1588, helped to establish the preeminence of that early English holding.[64] White's detailed portraits of the natives together with renderings of customs, done during that expedition, also had an impact on the English and Continental imagination. In 1590 Theodore de Bry published a new edition of Harriot's work with engravings after White's watercolors, and in 1591 another on discoveries in La Florida with accounts by Ribault and Laudonnière, accompanied by forty-three illustrations based on paintings by Le Moyne (this book was published in German, Latin, and French, circulating widely). Within a few years Italians reproduced some of de Bry's Indian images as decoration in maps, allegorical books, and coats of arms. White's single studies have only recently been located and reevaluated—principally in a 2007 exhibit mounted by the British Museum and its catalog, *A New World: England's First View of America* (Sloan 2007).

---

63 Remembered as the "Lost Colony." For recent discoveries in Roanoke, see Emery 2015.
64 On Harriot see Quinn 1990, 239–56.

 Hey haue comonlye coniurers or iuglers which vſe ſtrange geſtures , and often cõ-
trarie to nature in their enchantments : For they be verye familiar with deuils , of
whome they enquier what their enemys doe , or other ſuche thinges. They ſhaue
all their heads ſauinge their creſte which they weare as other doe , and faſten a ſmall
black birde aboue one of their ears as a badge of their office. They weare nothinge
but a skinne which hangeth downe from their gyrdle , and coueretch their priuityes. They weare a
bagg by their ſide as is expreſſed in the figure. The Inhabitants giue great credit vnto their ſpeeche,which oftentymes they finde
to bce true.

FIGURE 9   A conjurer or sorcerer. Engraving after a watercolor by John White. In
Thomas Harriot, *A briefe and true report of the new found land of Virginia*, Frankfurt
Ad Moenum, Typis Ioannis Wecheli, Sumptibus Vero Theodore de Bry, 1590. Plate 11.
Courtesy of the John Carter Brown Library at Brown University.

XVIII.

Theirdanſes vvhich
they vſe att their hyghe
feaſtes.

A T a Certayne tyme of the
yere they make a great,
and ſolemne feaſte whe-
runto their neighbours of
the townes adioninge re-
payre from all parts,euery
man attyred in the moſt ſtrange faſhion
they can deuiſe hauinge certayne marks on
the backs to declare of what place they bee.
The place where they meet is a broade
playne, about the which are planted in the
grownde certayne poſts carucd with heads
like to the faces of Nonnes couered with
theyr vayles. Then beeing ſett in order
they dance, ſinge, and vſe the ſtrangeſt geſtures that they can poſſiblye deuiſe. Three
of the fayreſt Virgins, of the companie are
in the mydſt, which imbraſſinge one another doe as yt weat turne about in their
dancinge. All this is donne after the ſunne
is ſett for auoydinge of heate. When they
are weerye of dancinge, they goe oute of
the circle, and come in vntill their dances
be ended,and they goe to make merrye
as is expreſſed in the 16.
figure.

FIGURE 10 Dancing during high feasts. Engraving after a watercolor by John White. In Thomas Harriot, *A briefe and true report of the new found land of Virginia*, Frankfurt Ad Moenum, Typis Ioannis Wecheli, Sumptibus Vero Theodore de Bry, 1590. Plate 18. Courtesy of the John Carter Brown Library at Brown University.

Yet France had the publicity advantage more broadly as a result of de Bry's use of French visual materials. A Protestant from Liège, de Bry was a refugee fleeing Catholicism who had gone to Frankfurt-am-Main to work; for personal reasons, it seems, he was sensitive to the fact that the East Coast of the United States was an important contact zone where Protestants contested with Catholics. Using his engraving skills he communicated the religious politics playing out in the area (with Indians in the background, intended as exotica). France's rights to La Florida derived from prior penetration by Breton fishermen of Nova Scotia, and its mapmakers contested Spanish claims (Galloway 2006, 75–90). Like England, France wanted to gain a foothold there so as to challenge Spain and put a hold on its further occupation; but it also saw it as a place to expel its Huguenots, who were disrupting Catholic rule. Too, France had dreams of following the American continent's waterways, leading inland, as passageways north to China and south to the gold and silver fields of Mexico. However, as Oré says, Spain quickly expelled the French, so that country's tenancy, at least as Spaniards read his report, was made to seem negligible.

STRUGGLES FOR POWER

France and, later, England generally gave little thought as to how their citizens might interact with La Florida's native population. The two powers were more interested in (1) encouraging traders to establish sites in a coastal chain linked to Caribbean waypoints and (2) using the area to place dissidents. They gave land grants to settlers without regard for any legal code that might authorize seizure from previous owners. Except for Jesuits who entered the Great Lakes region in the eighteenth century, France and England made no attempt to missionize; contact with Indian groups was initiated principally to gain allies in wars against one another.[65] Hakluyt's sixteenth-century essay on "planting," for example, meant planting English people on the eastern seaboard in order to counter a Spanish presence (Chaplin 2007, 55); in the minds of sponsors back home, or the settlers themselves, the natives existed only as food providers for people unaccustomed to working the land or

---

65 For background on early English and French attitudes toward America's Indians, and disinterest in converting them, see Codignola 1995. Pope Gregory XV established the Sacred Congregation de Propaganda Fide in 1622, proclaiming the obligation for conversion of infidels by spiritual means; but by then those countries could ignore it.

hunting to feed themselves. When Indians themselves had little food to eat, let alone share, the colonists died. White's drawings show the Indians as classically proportioned figures or in exotic poses. Le Moyne effectively cancels their existence by removing horror from depictions of their scalping practices (which written accounts describe) (Honour 1975, plates 64–65). Instead Joyce E. Chaplin in her essay in *A New World* notes that English illustrators focused on portraits, scenes, creatures, and maps (2007, 55) in renderings that incorporated the Indians into new scientific categories. As English, German, Danish, French, Austrian, and Italian collections of American artifacts were built in the seventeenth and eighteenth centuries, the religious significance of feather headdresses, idols, etc., disappeared in favor of labels emphasizing their appeal as curiosities (Feest 1995, 324–60).

SPAIN'S WORLD ORDER

On the other hand Spain—with its historical allegiance to Catholicism and that faith's interest in converting pagans—can be seen to have understood the need to include evangelizing in its imperial designs. Early on priests, but especially friars, saw natives through the lens of theology and later, according to various pronouncements by Rome, they saw them as part of a "Spanish world order"—the title of James Muldoon's book (1994) in which he studies the importance of the legal scholar Juan de Solórzano Pereira (1575–1654) for the formulation of Spanish policy and its contribution to an emerging sense of international law. Solórzano worked in the Audiencia[66] in Lima as a judge (*oidor*) from 1609 to 1627, returning to Spain from Peru to serve on the Council of Castile and on the Royal Council of the Indies. His *De Indiarum jure, sive de justa Indiarum Occidentalium inquisitone, acquisitione, et retentione tribus libris comprehensam* was published in Madrid in 1629–1639.[67]

Solórzano's thinking in this book about the relationship between the Papacy and secular rulers (Catholic and Protestant), as regards to their authority over America's territories and peoples, is important to understanding Oré's

---

66 The Audiencia de Lima was the highest royal court of appeals for the Viceroyalty of Peru.

67 Muldoon uses the original Latin edition (1629–1639) rather than the 1647 Spanish translation, *Política indiana*, because, as he says, the king ordered some evidence of Spanish cruelty in the original removed from the vernacular edition—which would have made it known to Spain's enemies. Additionally, the Latin version preserves medieval argumentation, allowing for insight into Solórzano's scholastic and humanistic training and their effect on his legal thinking (1994, 10–11).

Relación. Solórzano begins by taking into account the early theological writings of Bartolomé de las Casas and the legal formulations of Francisco de Vitoria (1485–1546). However, Solórzano faced more complicated problems, writing one hundred years later, when Protestant powers (particularly England) were questioning Rome's spiritual purity and legitimacy and breaking with that domination, when traditionally Catholic monarchies (particularly France) were either ignoring the Pope or invoking other papal bulls that they argued justified challenges to Spain's monopolies in the Americas. By then a new international vision was called for, so Solórzano had to contend not only for the pontiff's right to claim jurisdiction over American territories and peoples but also for Spain's special charge to establish that authority. Unlike the Ordenanza del Real Patronato de Indias relationship, referred to earlier, England and France had no such royal charge to Christianize the native population; new lands were considered to be under the direct rule of the Pope. However, by the end of the sixteenth century, as Luca Codignola argues, the Holy See was filled with men far away from the mission field—"secretaries and chamber clerks," only preoccupied with everyday business; they did not concern themselves with theology (1995).[68] Therefore, Solórzano had to reestablish some sense of Spain's understanding of international law and order—in opposition to the secular formulations of legalists like Hugo Grotius (1583–1645), which were emerging to justify Protestant rights.

It is not inconsequential, then, that Oré begins his *Account* with mention of the Portuguese Prince Henry the Navigator and that country's early Christianizing in Madeira and other Atlantic islands. So as to avoid war between Portugal and Spain, which was beginning its own expansion westward, the Spanish-born Pope Alexander VI had been led to proclaiming the bull of *Inter caetera* (1493), ratifying the Treaty of Tordesillas so as to divide any future discoveries in the Americas by the Portuguese and the Castilians along a north-south line. The monarchs of Portugal (João II) and Spain (Ferdinand and Isabella) accepted the Pope's authority, with the stipulation that discoveries by either carried the responsibility of converting native peoples to Christianity.

---

68 Codignola: "This does not mean that the pope was always in control. In fact, the little evangelical action that was taken in the course of the sixteenth century and the early seventeenth century came independently of the Holy See" (1995, 199). Corroborating Oré's picture of Vatican politics playing out in the Americas is Codignola's quote from the Chilean lawyer Juan Luis Arias who warned in 1609 against "'English and Dutch heretics, instigated by the devil . . . sowing with great zeal and speed the infernal poison of their heresy, infesting thus those millions and millions of good people who dwell' in Florida, New Spain, New Mexico, the kingdom of Quivira, the Californias, Virginia, and Bermuda" (1995, 196).

The spiritual power of the Pope was superior to the kings' secular power, yet it reinforced it and authorized it—recall the metaphor of the two swords (the secular sword would remain sheathed until released by the Pope). Later in the sixteenth century this precedent for the Pope's authority, then, was invoked—not by theologians, as Solórzano states, but principally by canon lawyers, who insisted that conquest included the obligation of evangelizing. According to Spanish lawyers, neither England nor France met that demand.

THE JURIST AND THE MISSIONARY: SOLÓRZANO AND ORÉ

There is no evidence that Oré's *Account* had any direct influence on Solórzano's legal thinking. Solórzano was a civil servant and not a cleric. Although they were contemporaries and led parallel lives in Peru and Spain, their professional fields were different. But Oré's narrative of missionary service, the detail with which he testifies to the formation of a Franciscan bureaucratic system, duplicates Solórzano's emphasis on the role of the Catholic Church in not only legitimizing but also structuring the monarch's authority in the Americas. The Mexican historian Silvio A. Zavala has pointed out in his *Las instituciones jurídicas en la conquista de América* (1988) how discoveries and pacification, as soon as news of America arrived in Spain, were envisioned as jointly to be carried out by temporal and spiritual forces. Although Oré does not specify a readership for his *Account*, his language—which mentions several Spanish monarchs, carefully referring to them as "Our Majesty" or "king of glorious memory"—emphasizes the Crown's commitment to missionary endeavor.

Oré's *Account*, then, valuably testifies as to how the Catholic Church's governing structure functioned in the late sixteenth and early seventeenth centuries. In the face of societies where Catholicism's claims and authority were being challenged, Spain was using the presence of the Church's men on the ground in America to press its right to be there. The Church's delegates were establishing new posts in remote areas and absorbing new charges into a seemingly universal belief. Its officials—some missionaries but others in parishes in towns and cities (bishops, priests, nuns) struggling to coordinate their work with civil government—maintained contact with headquarters by means of a paper trail. This paper bulk, in its turn, helped to reinforce a network that non-Catholic (or competing Catholic) societies were refuting and challenging with their similarly packaged treatises on international law. Within the Church, at the same time the rules of global governance were breaking down, Oré's story of Franciscan martyrdom in its paper format brings to the fore the idea of self-sacrifice in the service of the Roman Church. Beyond a wake-up call to Vatican theologians evaluating the rules for sainthood, Oré's depiction of confrontation between European powers in the Americas asks whether "evangelization" could continue to be made part of Spain's expansion when "colonization" sufficed for other powers.

Conclusions

Rather than an inconsequential moment in US historiography, often based on English-language sources and a view of the United States as just its land mass, La Florida's early history is increasingly being seen as part of what has come to be known as Atlantic history. Following this geographical redefinition, scholars mainly interested in the region's economic and political history have seen La Florida in terms of Europe's first imperial projects, proxy wars between those powers, and the area's relationship to a lawless piratical trade. As a result material narratives have largely omitted the theological and legal dimensions behind the several landfalls. The beliefs of Calvinists and French Huguenots, who came mostly with ministers prepared only to serve those small pilgrim communities, have seldom been scrutinized; governance has been reduced to politics, and "La Florida" has been narrowed to "Florida." English-language scholars have acknowledged the theology of New England's Puritan founders but largely ignore French and Spanish ideological motivations for their arrivals.

For example, Francis Parkman's *Pioneers of France in the New World* (1865), which could have yielded information about French attempts at settlement in La Florida, has largely been discredited. Parkman has been called an apologist for the Anglo-Saxon Protestant policy of Manifest Destiny; he has been thought to have colored the Spanish-French conflict as a kind of chivalric face-off and belittled the native population with florid stylistic phrases like "the terrified wretches" with their "hideous war-cries."[69] Nevertheless, Parkman's history, popular when it was published, continues to be read and admired by literary scholars as a significant work in the romantic tradition. Looking into the work anew, one finds that, although the author evidences a strong anti-Catholic sentiment—perhaps deriving from the story he is telling of Huguenot fears and hatred of the dogmatic Catholicism they are fleeing in

---

69 Parkman's principal critic is Jennings (1975), who largely took issue with Parkman's depiction of Indians.

France and encountering again from Spain in the Carolinas, but also perhaps because of the writer's personal biases in favor of an original English culture in the United States—Parkman usefully draws evidence from archival sources (both French and Spanish) from both sides of the conflict. In the case of Spain, he quotes liberally from letters written by Menéndez de Avilés, from eye-witnesses Gonzalo Solís de Merás and the chaplain Francisco López de Mendoza, and from the eighteenth-century historian Andrés González de Barcia Carballido y Zúñiga (1673–1743). Additionally, Parkman importantly demonstrates the religious dimension of the French/Spanish conflict, calling it a war between "brother Catholic kings," each of whom claimed rights to the region (1996 [1865] 136, 142). Like Solórzano, Parkman is sensitive to the way a previously respected world order was breaking down. Kings no longer uniformly accepted the Pope's edicts, and men were rewriting international law.

A general lack of interest in La Florida among US historians is perhaps related to the seeming primitiveness of its Indian culture. Bit by bit, however, historians are reevaluating the evidence. Research into a mounds culture extensive in the eastern part of the country, and into the language excellence and league organization of the Iroquois and the Plains Indians, is causing them to rethink the achievements of those peoples. From the vantage point of the Spanish American empire, David J. Weber has helped to reclaim La Florida's early history by concentrating his research into its frontier areas, which exploration and colonization belatedly reached after initial pushes into the Caribbean basin, Mexico, and Peru. Spaniards, going from the coast into the inland areas of Mexico and Peru, encountered high civilizations and rich natural resources. Yet as they penetrated later into the heart of North America, expecting to find equal fortune, they were disappointed. However, Weber states in *The Spanish Frontier in North America* (1992) that the Mississippian culture, when first seen, was economically viable and satisfactorily organized but that exposure to European disease and Spanish slavers soon depopulated and degraded the region. As a result later reports made it seem that those groups were, as he states in a second book, *Bárbaros: Spaniards and Their Savages in the Age of Enlightenment* (2005, 180–82), in a more primitive stage of development.

Weber's narrative in *The Spanish Frontier in North America* covers some of the same material as Oré's and helpfully enlarges incidents that Oré tells piecemeal. Weber explains the politics behind Philip II's wavering support of La Florida's various expeditions as that area demanded investment (1992, 68). Constrained by wars in Europe and the Mediterranean, Philip began to rely on private money for help in the Americas; indeed we have seen that Menéndez de Avilés was one of those who put up some of the cost for La Florida's exploration. Weber quotes Menéndez's opinion that the Indians along La Florida's coast were "warlike," so in 1572 Menéndez urged the Crown "to permit 'that war be made upon them with all vigor, a war of fire and blood, and that those taken alive shall be sold as slaves, removing them from the country and taking them to the neighboring islands'" (1992, 74). As Oré relates, in the last years of the sixteenth century, experience with the high civilizations of Peru and Mexico had begun to affect European thinking about the Americas, so La Florida's less-developed cultures and seeming lack of mineral wealth made the area unattractive. Indeed, Oré seems to conclude that La Florida's real value seemed to be its strategic position; its Indians demanded conversion by different means than previously employed.

Oré's work looks like ecclesiastical business, from which social scientists in the past have extracted data for their material studies but then often just cast aside. Literary scholars, on the other hand, can see in this reportage more than testimony to be taken literally; they can read in it rich evidence of the writer's cultural formation, the rhetorical boundaries within which he worked, the silent demands imposed by his targeted readers. His minimal style and often elliptical storytelling, his careful narrative, and his concentration on bureaucratic detail can be seen to reveal inhibition, as if he were biting his tongue in trying to communicate to Franciscan superiors and civil authorities the needs of the friars in La Florida while not offending those in the court who were supporters of a more aggressive path to pacification and conversion. Sensitive to the needs of the native population but also indoctrinated in Spanish and Franciscan values, he limited his document to what was expected of him as a religious functionary.

Like the *cartes édifiantes* that French Jesuits sent back to superiors from Canada, India, China, and Japan in the seventeenth and eighteenth centuries, Oré's *Account* is a linguistic bridge between *langue* and *parole* (to borrow Ferdinand de Saussure's concepts), testing the novel American experience against European-invented language. The cartes édifiantes had this same problem in their reporting. However, those Jesuit authors' commitment to "edifying"—in the sense of "instructing" and "satisfying" readers unfamiliar with the foreign world and curious to know more of it—perhaps allowed them to choose observational words that did not necessarily carry the freight of the business of religious conversion. Instead those Jesuits in China were more interested in describing the sophisticated court culture they found and the technological accomplishments of that geographically huge empire.

Both Oré's *Relación* and the Jesuits' letters resemble hagiography, though the portrayal of saintly lives in that genre often supposes a lay readership looking for pious inspiration. Yet Oré's emphasis on martyrdom suggests he was also presenting readers at official levels of society with tough theological problems that needed to be addressed. Just as he had done in preparing a brief to be submitted to the Vatican for Francisco Solano's sainthood, Oré here collects the testimony of participants and witnesses for readers—many of whom, as "devil's advocates," would challenge the purity of the martyrs' sacrifice. Oré's *Relación*, then, points to the usefulness of bureaucratic literature to get beyond what seems to be neutral reporting.

However, another kind of writing seems to fit Oré's *Account*. By the end of the sixteenth century and the beginning of the seventeenth, Spain had gone far in formulating its overseas organization; one can appreciate in Oré's *Account* of Franciscan governance not only how far but also the degree to which Spaniards with long tenure in the Americas and criollos, writing from the Americas, were rethinking their instructions for imposing order. The 1567 document, *Gobierno del Perú*, written by Juan de Matienzo (1520–1579) to describe the Real Audiencia of Lima and Charcas,[70] outlines in astounding detail what can only be an imagined government for the viceroyalty. He draws civil and ecclesiastical offices and then shows how these two lines of authority would dispatch their duties; provisions are made for tax collectors, for prison officials, for interpreters, for the maintenance of black slaves, and so on. Periodically *visitadores* or inspectors would come, charged with seeing that written orders had been implemented and directives obeyed. Matienzo was appointed oidor (judge) and lived in the town of Charcas—today's Sucre[71], the constitutional capital of Bolivia—where he later died. Although he was educated in Spain, his experience in Peru shaped his administrative thinking and the verbal framing in this missive to the king. There Matienzo

70 The Royal Audiencia and Chancery of Lima (Audiencia y Chancellería Real) was a superior court in the New World empire of Spain, located in Lima, capital of the Viceroyalty of Peru. It was created on 20 November 1542, as was the viceroyalty itself, by the Emperor Charles I (or V of the Holy Roman Empire). The Audiencia began functioning in 1543 and initially had jurisdiction over the entire area of the viceroyalty—virtually all territory controlled by the Spanish crown in South America and Panama. Later other *audiencias* were established. In 1559 part of the territory of the Lima Audiencia was separated and given over to a new Audiencia of Charcas, and in 1563 an Audiencia was established in Quito with jurisdiction over the northern territories of the Viceroyalty of Peru.
71 Also called historically La Plata and Chuquisaca.

says that he knows Spaniards in the Conquest period were guilty of the ill treatment of Indians but that now, years later, proper government has corrected those wrongs. Under good government Indians were supposedly freed not only from abuses by those early Spaniards but also from the domination of their own caciques. Matienzo's paper fabrication of a society overlaid by rules and regulations, which must have been imagined to function as an ideal but also as an indirect indictment of realities, forces readers to work to understand its several meanings.

Oré, then, writing almost sixty years after Matienzo, ends his story of martyrdom in La Florida with the suggestion that Church governance, now established, promises a bright future. That area, we have read, had foundered in imposing ecclesiastical structures onto the Floridanos. But now, Oré's final words tell, their conversion and acceptance of a new way of life in the parishes assures law and order. The men's exemplary lives and deaths, the unexplained miracles, seem to have been more instrumental as communication tools in persuading natives to accept the new faith than any coercive means. One can only guess how much Spain's military and civil administration might have aided the religious; given Oré's complaints of military force and civil corruption, that omission can be read as erasing the importance of those sources of authority. What is clear is that the commitment to paper of the structure of the friars' mission posts, their election of a superior, reified the framework of organization; paper seemed to settle any questions of unrest and gave credit to the Franciscans for the Indians' conversion. The fact that Oré's work saw print, rather than remaining in manuscript like much of the documentation that characterized Jesuit reporting from the field to headquarters, suggests some desire on the part of his Franciscan superiors to extend his message, to keep La Florida for Spain and Rome.[72]

Oré, Matienzo, Solórzano, Guaman Poma, and El Inca Garcilaso are all examples of post-Conquest writers calling for good government in the Spanish Indies, along with Vasco de Quiroga in his several writings in the sixteenth century on utopian communities in Mexico and Juan Rodríguez Freyle in his 1636 work, *El carnero*, an appeal for ending corruption in the area of today's Colombia. Their work represents a shift in the direction of literary production—writers mostly writing from the Americas, directing their missives both to readers from their home areas and from the metropolis, correcting imperial

---

72 On manuscripts v. printing, and on readership in the Jesuit world, see Hsia 2009, 9 and 17.

policies, recommending reforms, and beginning to call for administration for the increasing Spanish populations instead of the pacification previously thought to be adequate for the native population. Unlike the blueprints that Europeans first drew up for their American discoveries—many of which were designs for islands where boundaries were delimited according to Thomas More's *Utopia*—these latter-day reports of actual administrations are beginning to show the defects of idealism and the failures of legislation.

La Florida is unique among Spain's American possessions. Partly an extension of Antillean geography, the region challenges those in North America who have been content to divide the US land mass into Anglo and Hispanic spheres, describing the latter in terms of "border studies" and thus using their European invaders and their respective Indian groupings to demarcate divisions. La Florida does not lend itself to these two categories; its history shows multiple European influences, a Hispanic presence beyond the Southwest and California, and a native way of life unlike those in other parts of the territorial United States. Fortuitously, in Oré's *Account* La Florida has a paper trail that opens up its history to an understanding of the special character of its early governance. Spain, its first invader, was at that moment itself undergoing huge changes in its Counter-Reformation struggles. Therefore, Oré's view of the presence of Catholicism in an area where several European powers contested for conquest and colonization provides a unique perspective on the breakdown in the Western world of a seemingly universal Christianity, on division in Europe as new legal codes, new arguments for human rights, and new sources of authority disrupted belief. The internationalism implicit in Oré's work—the theological, political and legal questions he opens up—are new material for scholars to examine in this instance of early American conquest and development.

This Edition

This translation of Oré's *Relación de los mártires que ha habido en las provincias de La Florida*[73] is based on the copy in the José Durand Collection at the University of Notre Dame's Hesburgh Libraries. Sara Weber made available a digital version of the original Spanish text, which provided the working copy for Raquel Chang-Rodríguez's modernized and annotated edition in

---

73 Modernized spelling of title.

Spanish (2014) and the basis for this translation into English. Atanasio López's Spanish version (1931) and Maynard Geiger's English translation (1936) were consulted, as well as Father Geiger's *The Franciscan Conquest of Florida* (1937) and *Biographical Dictionary of the Franciscans in Spanish Florida and Cuba, 1528–1841* (1940).

THE UNIVERSITY OF NOTRE DAME'S COPY OF THE *RELACIÓN*

Notre Dame acquired Oré's *Relación* in 1995 at the death of José Durand, distinguished professor of Spanish at the University of California, Berkeley. Durand's research focused on the life and works of El Inca Garcilaso de la Vega, and he surely acquired the *Relación* knowing of the relationship between the two Peruvians. It is not known where Durand bought the book or from whom. There are no signs of previous owners, except a handwritten note on the verso of the folio that mentions *La Florida del Inca*. Although part of the note was lost on account of the tight binding and the pages having been trimmed, it is possible to reconstruct its contents, adding the names of the six martyred Jesuits according to information from Garcilaso, as was noted earlier. Previous editors of the *Relación*—López and Geiger—offer no information as to the editions they employed. However, Geiger states, "On the one known copy in existence in Spain no date appears" (1937, 286). Because López and Geiger were both Franciscans, it is likely they both used the same edition. A search to locate copies in Spanish libraries has not been successful.

The Notre Dame text bears the catalog number F.314.074 1617z. It is bound in modern parchment, and the title appears on the spine in black ink, reflecting seventeenth-century custom. The imprint consists of thirty-two folios, the last one with the verso of the last leaf blank. As already mentioned, the volume is lacking the title page, so printer, place of publication, and date are unknown. Language on the first folio, which must serve as our only source of knowing Oré's intent for his work, follows:

> Relación de / los martires que a avido en / las Prouincias de la Florida; doze Religiosos de la Com / pañía de IESVS, que padecieron en el Iacan y cinco de / la Orden de nuestro Serafico P. S. Francisco, en la Prouin / cia de Guale. Ponese assi mesmo la discripcion de Iacan, / donde se an fortificado los Ingleses, y de otras cosas tocan / tes a la conuersion de los Indios. Hecha por el P. F. Luys / Hieronymo de Orè,

Lector de Teologia, y Comissario / de la Prouincia de Santa Elena de la Florida / e Isla de Cuba[74]

In the Notre Dame copy small portions of the text have been lost due to damage from humidity; some text has been restored by means of bleaching. However, on some folios, spots obscure letters and words as well as the folio number on the upper-right margin (particularly on the last five folios). In regard to numeration, the sequence is lost after folio 26v; from there the number skips to folio 28r. There is no folio 27; from 28v it jumps to 30r; folio 30v is followed by 29r. Spotting makes it impossible to distinguish numbers in following folios. The last folio shows the number 32 on the lower-left margin and with a different type face; it could be that the number was added later. In spite of the odd foliation, lacunae or transpositions in the narrative do not occur. The binding of the thirty-two folios measures 20.1 cm × 15.6 cm. The watermark appears in all folios. The mark is a cross inside an oval with a pointed bottom. On the second page, the lower part of the watermark has three straight lines; the middle line is two lines at the foot of the cross, and on either side two lines forming a 45 degree angle. It has been impossible to photograph this mark owing to its location on the lower part of the page and to the tight binding. A very similar but not identical watermark appears in Edward Heawood's *Itinerarium* (1969, plate 144, number 967, Amsterdam, 1623, J. V. van Linschoten).[75]

CRITERIA FOR MODERNIZATION AND TRANSLATION

Considering the value of the text and the necessity of making it accessible to specialized readers as well as the general public, we provide here an English translation with annotations and revised punctuation. Since in the original the sections are not numbered, the number of each part or chapter has been added and placed in brackets. In an effort to make the vocabulary and syntax intelligible, convoluted sentences have been collapsed while, in other cases,

---

74 "An Account of / the Martyrs / in the provinces of Florida; Twelve Religious from the Com / pany of Jesus, Who perished in the Jacan and five from / the Order of Our Seraphic Father Saint Francis, in the Provin / ce of Guale. Here is also recorded a description of the Jacan, / which the English have fortified, and other things relat / ing to the conversion of the Indians. Drafted by Father Friar Luys / Hieronymo de Oré, Reader of Theology, and Commissioner / of the Province of Santa Elena in Florida / and the Island of Cuba."

75 Thanks to John O'Neill, curator of Rare Books and Manuscripts at the Hispanic Society of America, New York, for this information.

letters or words have been added. When unable to decipher a sentence or a word due to the loss of print we have resolved the addition of the missing vocabulary by referencing Atanasio López's edition. In chapter 7 the names of the Franciscans who arrived in 1596 appear in bold type, and the added numbers are within brackets; in chapter 8, Father Ávila's report is included preceded by a caption to note the change in narrative voice. Double indents underscore the change of voice in chapters 9 and 10 to highlight the discourses of Father Friars Francisco Pareja and Martín Prieto. Documents from the Archivo de Indias have been quoted following the original spelling, with the exception of the name of the province of Santa Elena, where the *H* has been omitted for the sake of uniformity.

In carrying the *Relación* to English, we have corrected previous interpretations, updated language usage, and added explanatory notes. For help with ecclesial terms, we have relied especially on Geiger's 1936 translation. We have reduced the courtesies, formulae, and legal redundancies of sixteenth- and seventeenth-century language. For some problematic usages, we have consulted the 1726–1737 *Diccionario de autoridades*. When Oré uses *reducir* or *someter* to describe the process of Christianizing the Floridanos, the English cognates of these words—such as *reduce* or *submit*—introduce connotations of Spanish superiority and Indian inferiority, and forced change. Although they may offend modern readers, we have retained their English equivalents since they betray period usage and etymologically they connect accurately with understandings of the English terminology then and now. *Someter* in its transitive sense was indeed connected to imperial aims. But *reducir* had wider applications, among them being "to persuade" or "to attract by means of reason and argumentation." Even *pacification* is not an adequate equivalent of that process the friars wanted to achieve by means of their personal example and mental and spiritual exercise, rather than through coercion. With no intended derogation we have retained the term *Indian* the Spaniards in the period employed to refer to the native Americans—so as to emphasize that historical usage. *Indian* designated where the original Spaniards thought they had landed: the Indies.

However, we have sought other ways to translate Oré's use of the Spanish word *infiel* than with its English cognate *infidel*. In addition to calling the natives *infieles*, Oré also called Indians who were unbelievers "pagans" and "Gentiles," or described as "apostates" those who departed from their Christian instruction—thus recalling the language of Bartolomé de las Casas who, earlier in the sixteenth century, had tried to explain American identity by means of parallels with Roman Catholicism's Others in the Mediterranean. We have retained some of these usages by Oré; however, we have also used *heathen*, a term preferred by contemporary historians. Interestingly, the Franciscan seldom calls the Floridanos "barbarians," "idolaters," or "savages," and does not call them "sinners," preferring to explain their viciousness as the devil's influence. When Oré describes their spiritual leaders as *hechiceros*, his choice of words is again significant; he does not call them *curanderos* or healers. However, dictionary usage, which defines *hechiceros* as "witch doctors," "shamans," or "magicians," seems inadequate. *Hechicero* misleads in suggesting a person who casts an *hechizo* or spell over another—a practice that Oré never apparently witnessed or says anybody else witnessed. So even that Spanish usage, as well as the English terms that dictionaries commonly accept as equivalents, do not do justice to the Indians' pre-Conquest belief systems. Lacking a good English equivalent for *hechicero*, we have retained "witch doctor," though with this cautionary explanation.

An Account of the Martyrs
in the Provinces of La Florida

(Relación de los mártires que ha habido en las Provincias de La Florida)

Contents

An Account of the Martyrs in the Provinces of La Florida—Twelve Religious of the Compañía de Jesús [the Society of Jesus], Who Perished in the Jacán, and Five of the Order of Our Seraphic Father Saint Francis of the Province of Guale . . .

In addition a description of the Jacán, which the English fortified, and a record of other things relative to the conversion of the Indians. The account compiled by Father Friar Luis Jerónimo de Oré, reader in theology and commissioner in the Province of Santa Elena de La Florida and the island of Cuba.

IN THE YEAR 1513 JUAN PONCE DE LEÓN[1] WAS THE FIRST SPANIARD TO discover the coast and mainland of the kingdom of La Florida. Ponce de León was a well-born native of León; previously he had been governor of the island of San Juan de Puerto Rico. Because he discovered La Florida on Resurrection Sunday, which that year fell on 27 March, he named his discovery Florida because among Spaniards this most holy day is called "Pascua Florida" (Flowering Easter), connoting the flowering of spring.

---

1 (1474–1521), born in Santervás de Campo, in the present-day province of Valladolid, kingdom of León, to a noble yet impoverished family. Although he is known as the "discoverer" of La Florida, a territory he named on his first expedition in 1513, other Spaniards, without royal authorization, had arrived in the area prior to him.

Ponce de León located La Florida sailing from the north of Cuba. He was satisfied with just touching land there, in the same way as in other parts of the world at that time discoveries were being made of different islands and lands. This was the case of the island of Madeira, which Prince Henry,[2] son of the king of Portugal, was instrumental in having discovered. Henry was an educated man and a great mathematician, and by means of his studies he had knowledge of other lands. From the coastline in Portugal he commanded ships to sail to Madeira, and from that refueling station to venture to other islands where, in his role as a pious prince, he promoted the preaching of the faith of Christ in the years around 1490.

All this Portuguese activity awakened the interest of Cristóbal Colón [Christopher Columbus], who two years later set out from Spain, dispatched by the Catholic kings [Ferdinand and Isabella]. Columbus discovered Hispaniola,[3] which he called Fernandina;[4] he founded the city of Santo Domingo; he went on to discover Puerto Rico, and the islands of Cuba, Jamaica,[5] and those in the Windward group.[6] After their discovery these islands were conquered and populated with Spaniards; they were inhabited by innumerable Indians who in all parts of these islands had quickly been annihilated.

Some years afterward Ponce de León returned to La Florida, charged by the Catholic kings to conquer and govern. When he landed the Indians resisted and fought him fiercely, routing his men and killing almost all of them.

---

2 Reference to Prince Henry of Avis and Lancaster, also known as the Navigator (1394–1460). Thanks to his cartographic endeavors in 1420 the Archipelago of Madeira or Madera was discovered (by João Gonçalves Zarco and Tristão Vaz Teixeira). The date offered by Oré is an error, as Prince Henry died in 1460.

3 Today it is home to the countries of Haiti and the Dominican Republic.

4 In the *Diario* of Columbus, entry of 15 October 1492: "And entering the gulf between these two islands, it should be known, that on the one island of Santa María and the other larger one, which I named Fernandina, I found a man alone on a raft that passed from the island of Santa María to Fernandina" (Colón 1989, 35). It was the third island discovered by Columbus, today Long Island in the Bahamas. Cuba was originally called Juana, in honor of John of Aragon and Castile, the crown prince; later it was renamed Fernandina to honor King Ferdinando (Arrom 1980).We have found no records of Hispaniola receiving this name.

5 Columbus arrived in Jamaica on his second transatlantic voyage, on 5 May 1494; its first Spanish settlement was called Sevilla la Nueva. The island, mainly a supply base, remained a Spanish possession until 1655, when the English admiral William Penn and the general Oliver Robert Venables took it for Britain.

6 Today the northern islands of the Lesser Antilles. They were originally named thus because of the winds' orientation from east to west that provided navigable routes from the Old World to the New. The transatlantic currents and winds (from Barlovento and not Sotavento) that produced the fastest route through the ocean carried the vessels to these islands in the southeast of the Antilles, then allowing them to continue the voyage to the larger Caribbean islands or to North America.

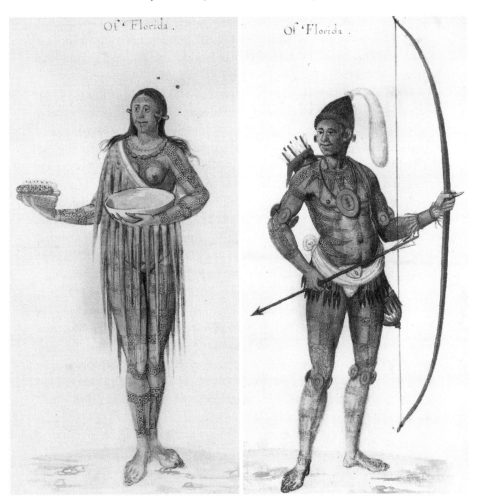

FIGURE 11 The Timucuan wife of a chief of La Florida. Watercolor by John White after a lost original by Jacques Le Moyne de Morgues. Le Moyne was part of the French colony in northern Florida (1564–1565). The British Museum purchased the watercolors from its founder, Sir Hans Sloane, in the mid-nineteenth century, and notice of them appeared for the first time in Laurence Binyon's *Catalogue of Drawings by British Artists and Artists of Foreign Origin working in Britain preserved in the Department of Prints and Drawings in the British Museum*, vol. IV, London, 1907. Courtesy of the Trustees of the British Museum.

FIGURE 12 A Timucuan chief from La Florida. Watercolor by John White after a lost original by Jacques Le Moyne de Morgues. Courtesy of the Trustees of the British Museum.

Only seven escaped, among them Juan Ponce.[7] Afterward [stain] a pilot named Miruelo,[8] owner of a caravel, arrived. But because a storm hit that coast, he was prevented from marking the landfall and taking its latitude, as he was supposed to do as part of his job.

At that same time Lucas Vázquez de Ayllón,[9] judge [oidor] of the Audiencia Real [jurisdiction under royal protection] of Santo Domingo and appeal judge who had been on the island before the Audiencia was founded, fitted out two ships, together with six partners. The ships went among the islands to hunt for Indians to work in the gold mines for a business these men had set up. As the result of a storm the Spaniards arrived at the cape they called Santa Elena[10] because it was that saint's day, and they landed at the river, which they named Jordan[11] because the first mariner who saw it was called by that name. Then Indians came to see the ships and were frightened to see things they had never seen before and that were strange to them. But the Spaniards and the Indians dealt with one another in a friendly way and the Spaniards invited the Indians to board the ships to see what they carried. More than 130 Indians climbed aboard. But once seeing them below deck, the Spaniards raised anchor and set sail for Santo Domingo. One of the two ships was lost; and the Indians who were held on the other, although they reached Santo Domingo, died of sadness and hunger because they refused to eat. They were filled with anger over what had been done to them and how, under the pretense of friendship, they had been deceived.

---

7 In his third expedition (1521), Ponce de León and his people were attacked by Indians of the Calusa ethnic group; the discoverer of La Florida died in Havana from wounds suffered in this second voyage.

8 The pilot Diego Miruelo who in 1516 explored the bay of Pensacola.

9 It probably refers to the 1521 slave raiding expedition commanded by Pedro de Quejo and Francisco Gordillo, sponsored by Vázquez de Ayllón (c. 1475–1526). It arrived at Winyah Bay at the opening of the South Santee River, in modern-day South Carolina (Milanich 2006, 59). Gordillo and Quejo returned to the area in 1525. Ayllón later commanded (1526) a large expedition to these territories; it departed from Puerto Plata, Hispaniola, and ended in Winyah Bay. Upon encountering native hostility and lacking food, they marched south, probably by land and sea, and established San Miguel de Gualdape (1526). Even though its specific location has not been established, current research has placed the settlement in the territory belonging to the Guale group, in the area of Sapelo Bay, modern-day Georgia. The founding took place thirty-nine years before Saint Augustine's and eighty-one before Jamestown. Subject to attacks, disease, and hunger, the colony was abandoned after three months. Only 150 persons returned to Hispaniola.

10 The presidio by the same name was established there later and expeditions left from this fort to go inland, among them Juan Pardo's. Pardo founded San Juan (1567–1568), in the domain of the Joara, in modern-day North Carolina (Geiger 1936, 10n18).

11 Called Río de las Corrientes, San Juan, and today St. Johns.

In the year 1524,[12] the judge Lucas Vázquez de Ayllón, whom the emperor Charles V had honored with the regalia of the Order of Santiago as well as the title of governor of the province of Chicoria[13] (the one discovered by the pilot Miruelo who had failed to demarcate the land and measure the sun[14] so as to take its latitude), fitted out three ships in Santo Domingo. One ship was lost in the River Jordan, but reaching the coast with the other two, he arrived at a peaceful spot. The judge commanded two hundred soldiers to land, and they penetrated into the interior toward the settlement of the Indians, which was at a distance of three leagues. The Indians reassured the Spaniards with festivities and dances for three or four days, and then one night they suddenly massacred all of them. In that way they retaliated for the trick that the Spaniards had played on them when they carried off their comrades to work in the gold mines.

In the year 1539, on the order of Antonio de Mendoza, viceroy of New Spain,[15] Captain Juan Vázquez Coronado[16] set out to reconnoiter further in La Florida. But having discovered and seen much and very good land, he could not bring colonists there because of many obstacles [stain]. Almost at this same time Pánfilo de Narváez[17] arrived in La Florida and made discoveries; but he was lost with all the Spaniards he had with him. The only ones to escape were Álvar Núñez Cabeza de Vaca[18] with three Spaniards,[19] to whom God in his mercy granted the opportunity to perform miracles in the

---

12 It could reference the *capitulación* (royal decree) authorizing Vázquez de Ayllón's exploration and settlement of this area issued in 1523; the ill-fated expedition departed in 1526 from Puerto Plata in Hispaniola.

13 Mythical land in the southeast Atlantic coast where it was believed, from reports provided by sailors and the testimony of Francisco "El Chicorano," a native from the region who had been taken away as hostage to Spain, copious mineral wealth was to be found. Paul E. Hoffman (1984) denominated this collection of information the *Chícora legend* (Milanich 2006, 59).

14 That is, Miruelo did not precisely identify the site.

15 He was viceroy from 1535 to 1550 in New Spain, and later in Peru for ten months (1551–1552).

16 Reference to Francisco Vázquez de Coronado (1510–1545) who explored the southwest of the United States in search of Cíbola and the Seven Mythical Golden Cities. He had previously sent Friar Marcos de Niza and Esteban or Estebanico, a North African slave and a surviving member of Pánfilo de Narváez's expedition, to search the region; the first assured him of having seen a magnificent city—although he did not enter it—and the sea to the west, the Pacific.

17 (1478–1528), named governor of Florida by Charles I of Spain (V of the Holy Roman Empire) he led a failed expedition that sailed from Sanlúcar de Barrameda in 1527 with over six hundred persons.

18 (c. 1490–c. 1560), surviving member of the Narváez expedition, who crossed the continent with three companions and wrote *Relación* (1542) about his experiences, and known as *Naufragios* after its reprinting in the eighteenth century.

19 In reality two Spaniards, Alonso del Castillo Maldonado and Andrés Dorantes de Carranza, and a North African slave, Esteban or Estebanico. Another survivor, Juan Ortiz, remained captive in La Florida and was rescued during the expedition of Hernando de Soto, in which he served as an interpreter.

name of Christ among those faithless peoples. Father José de Acosta[20] in his book *Natura novi orbis*[21] considered at length these journeys, as well as other writers.

In the same year, 1539, Adelantado Hernando de Soto went to La Florida. De Soto was a resident of Cuzco, one of the first conquerors of Peru who had accompanied the marquis Pizarro[22] in Cajamarca when Inca Atahualpa was taken prisoner.[23] Because de Soto was the first Spaniard whom he saw and with whom he spoke,[24] Atahualpa, a very powerful king, took a special affection for him. Although Atahualpa was being held prisoner in his own homeland, the Inca ruler admired the audacity and valor of the few Spaniards, and gave de Soto rich expensive gifts. With these, together with the portion the Spaniard claimed as a result of Atahualpa's ransom, and the spoils of war after Atahualpa's defeat, de Soto returned to Spain and to his home, Villanueva de Barcarrota,[25] with 100,100 ducats. He was tremendously wealthy because up to then there had never been in Spain as much gold and silver as the amount he brought.

Not content with his deeds in the conquest of Peru and desirous of undertaking similar exploits, de Soto petitioned the emperor Charles V, of glorious memory, who at that time was holding court in Valladolid, to grant him the right to the conquest of the kingdom of La Florida. He wanted to do it at his own cost and risk, expending in the effort his own property and putting in danger his personal security in order to serve His Majesty—his petition was granted. Then he left in the year mentioned, 1539, with seven galleons and 950 men,[26] with priests, clergy, and friars from the Orders of Saint Dominic and Saint Francis and one Trinitarian.

---

20 (1540–1600), Jesuit scholar who pursued several missions in the viceroyalties of Peru and New Spain, recognized for his descriptions of the flora and fauna of the Americas, and his ethnographic commentary on the Indians of the Andean highlands.

21 The first work (Salamanca, 1588) about America by Acosta was later translated into Spanish and incorporated in his fundamental *Historia natural y moral de las Indias* [Natural and Moral History of the Indies] (Seville, 1590).

22 Reference to Francisco Pizarro, conquistador of Peru, under whom Hernando de Soto served. The king rewarded Pizarro for services rendered with the title of Marquis.

23 (1497–1533), the sapa Inca or ruler of the empire upon the Spanish arrival. He defeated his half-brother Huáscar in a bloody war that pitted royal family groups against one another.

24 Hernando de Soto, by command of Francisco Pizarro, led the delegation that met with Atahualpa in the thermal baths near Cajamarca. There is no agreement as to how Atahualpa received de Soto. Nonetheless, various sources confirm that later the conquistador opposed the execution of Atahualpa.

25 According to recent scholarship, he was born in Jerez de los Caballeros, c. 1500.

26 Without counting personnel responsible for service and operations at sea, who were also a large number.

More people from the island of Cuba came on to join him, among whom was a well-born conqueror from the island named Vasco Porcallo de Figueroa,[27] whom de Soto named field master of his entire army. The fleet arrived at the bay of the Holy Spirit,[28] at the land site that the Indians call Pohoi.[29] From that point began the discovery and conquest of the extensive provinces of the Apalache and Acuera,[30] Auinu, and others. Through them de Soto entered [stain] Apalache, and after long day marches he reached and conquered provinces as far as the Río Grande [Mississippi River], where he died. Tearfully and with great emotion his men buried him in the middle of the river in a tree trunk carved out as a coffin. They covered it with wood and with a heavy limb from an oak threw it to the depths, fearing that the Indians might desecrate his body and bones out of revenge.

The captain whom de Soto had named before his death,[31] together with other troop leaders and soldiers, then set out across unknown lands toward Mexico City. The men divided and some ended up in different parts of that kingdom [New Spain]. And, although they went through great military skirmishes, difficult labors, hunger and weariness—all of which are worthy of honor and the perpetual memory of Spaniards as well as Indians who in that part of Mexico are extremely fierce warriors of indomitable spirit—it was not God's will that, despite the fact that they represented a large number of infantrymen with their horses, they should settle those regions and spread civilization. Instead, de Soto's men continued on discovering new vast provinces, heavily populated with Indians.

When it was known in Spain that the explorer Hernando de Soto had died, in the year 1549 the emperor Charles V sent out a religious from the Order of

27 Conquistador recognized for his cruelty. He was related to the House of Feria and was a distant relative of the Cuzcan author El Inca Garcilaso de la Vega (1539–1616). He was named to this post to replace Nuño Tovar who, during the transatlantic voyage, had an affair with Leonor de Bobadilla, a lady in waiting to Isabel de Bobadilla, de Soto's wife. The mestizo son of the new field master with a Taíno woman, Garcilaso de la Vega—namesake of the chronicler—also joined de Soto's expedition.

28 South of present-day Tampa Bay.

29 Inhabited by the Tocobaga Indians.

30 This native group peopled the lands west of the Jordan River or Saint John River, in the area of the Oklawaha River (Milanich 2006, 48).

31 Reference to Luis de Moscoso (1505–1551), who in 1543, after much foot travel and navigating the coasts of the Gulf and the Mississippi River, arrived, with a diminished group of fellow explorers, at the Panuco River to later enter Mexico, capital of the New Spain viceroyalty.

Santo Domingo, Father Luis Cancel,[32] as superior of other religious from that order, who offered to preach and reduce those Indian populations to the obedience of the Church and to His Majesty. When they arrived in La Florida, they jumped ashore and began to preach to the Indians who, having learned by experience with Spaniards earlier,[33] without waiting to hear their sermons, killed Father Luis and two others of his companions; the rest fled to the ship and returned to Spain giving testimony of the fierceness of those barbaric Indians.

In addition, some French vessels made entry into the kingdom of La Florida, anchoring in the bay of San Mateo.[34] They signaled their ownership with a post[35] made of a tall tree, and on it they placed the coat of arms and the fleur-de-lis claiming it for the king of France.[36] When His Majesty learned of this, he ordered the governor of Havana, Diego Mazariegos,[37] to send someone to remove the post; for this purpose, a gentleman from the kingdom of Toledo named Hernán Manrique de Rojas[38] went to La Florida.

32 Luis Cáncer de Barbastro (?–1549), a Dominican follower of Bartolomé de las Casas, who sought and received permission (1547) to evangelize the population of La Florida and to test out the viability of pacific missionary undertakings. In 1549 he sailed from Veracruz with other Dominicans (Gregorio de Beteta, Juan García, Diego de Tolosa, and the lay brother, Fuentes). In Havana the governor of Cuba granted them Magdalena, a Christianized native probably of Calusa origin, to serve as an interpreter. Once in La Florida, in today's Tampa Bay, Tolosa and Fuentes were assassinated and the interpreter disappeared. Juan Muñoz, a former soldier of de Soto's expedition enslaved by the Tocobaga natives, joined the group. Luis Cáncer was killed later, according to the eyewitness account of Gregorio de Beteta.

33 Probably a reference to the devastation caused by Hernando de Soto's and Narváez's expeditions.

34 Reference to the colonization attempts by France in Florida; Jean Ribault founded Charlesfort in 1562, on present-day Parrish Island, South Carolina; in 1564 René Goulaine de Laudonnière (c. 1529–1574) established Fort Caroline (near the modern-day city of Jacksonville) as a refuge for the French Huguenots fleeing from persecution in Europe. Led by Pedro Menéndez de Avilés, the Spaniards seized the fort and killed the French (except women and children) and renamed it San Mateo. Two years later Dominique de Gourgues retook the fort and annihilated the Spaniards.

35 A column with an inscription that records an event (DLE); in this case the post signals the taking of possession of that territory, claimed for the king of France. Portugal marked its territories along the coasts of Africa with a stone pillar.

36 An engraving of Jacques Le Moyne de Morgues in *Brevis narratio eorum quae in Florida Americae provincia Gallis acciderunt* (1591) shows the Timucuan chieftain, Athore, and René Goulaine de Laudonnière beside a column erected by Jean Ribault in 1562. This column is probably the "tree" that the Spanish sovereign ordered removed. However, the French seemingly erected two pillars or posts: one near the opening of the Saint John River on which Jean Ribault inscribed the French coat of arms and the other in the French establishment of present-day South Carolina (near Port Royal) (Geiger 1936, 13–14n42).

37 Governor of Cuba (1555–1564); he began construction on the Castillo de la Real Fuerza and a watchtower in what later became El Morro.

38 It occurred in 1564. By order of the governor, he sailed from Havana on the frigate *Nuestra Señora de la Concepción* on 12 May 1564; he destroyed Charlesfort, found the post or pillar, carried it to the frigate, and then shipped it to Spain, according to the report dated 9 July 1564 (Hoffman 2004, 212–15).

He cut down the tree, removed the symbols of the French king, and thus ended the hopes of the French to populate that region. All this happened in the year 1554.[39] Ten years later, when the French tried to defy the ban [stain] and enter and populate the area, what happened to them will be seen in the next chapter.

FIGURE 13 Lord Atore showing Ribault's column to Laudonnière. Attributed to Jacques Le Moyne de Morgues in Theodore de Bry, *Brevis narratio eorum quae in Florida Americae provincia Gallis acciderunt* (1591). Plate 8. Courtesy of the Special Collections Department, University of South Florida. Digitization provided by the USF Libraries Digitization Center.

39 According to the report given by Manrique de Rojas this all took place in 1564 (Hoffman 2004, 212–15).

CHAPTER TWO

Account of the Arrival of the Adelantado Diego Menéndez Valdés in La Florida, and the Things That Happened to Him There[1]

HIS MAJESTY THE EMPEROR HAVING BEEN INTERESTED[2] IN THE conquest and discovery of La Florida (as has already been related), his son, King Philip II of glorious memory, pursued the task with the same interest.[3] For that reason, in 1564, His Majesty sent Pedro Menéndez Valdés,[4] a nobleman who had been honored with the order of Saint James [Santiago], to La Florida with the title of adelantado of the provinces of La Florida, and also named him governor and captain general, giving him license for conquest.[5] Menéndez Valdés was also awarded the governorship and captaincy of the island of Cuba, and appointed to head the fleet of twelve galleons of the Convoy of the Indies [Carrera de Indias].[6] He was a person of such ability that by himself he performed all the duties of the offices for which now four persons are required.

---

1 Reference to Pedro Menéndez de Avilés (1519–1574), adelantado and governor of La Florida (1565) and later appointed governor of Cuba (1567).

2 Charles I of Spain and V of the Holy Roman Empire as of 1519.

3 Menéndez de Avilés accompanied Prince Philip to England (1554), when he married the queen, Mary Tudor. When the war with France, in which Spain and England were allied, ended, Menéndez commanded the fleet that brought King Philip II from the Netherlands to Spain (1559).

4 The correct name is Pedro Menéndez de Avilés.

5 For the details on the *capitulaciones* or the contract between the Crown and Adelantado Menéndez de Avilés, see Lyon 1976, 38–70.

6 A trade monopoly between Cádiz and American ports. It was also called the Treasure Fleet.

The adelantado lost a son who was sailing on another ship in the fleet,[7] and he went to look for him, taking with him a few vessels along that coast. He landed at a port called San Mateo, twelve leagues distant from San Agustín,[8] and he found at the entrance some French ships whose men had already built a fort a league from the sandbank. The French general was Juan de Ribao[9] whose forces they had encountered before, admitting defeat. The two argued about which one should gather his sails,[10] but agreed to postpone the challenge for the following day because the adelantado considered the French to be superior. The Spaniards then set sail that night for Havana, and entered the port of San Agustín where the next day they sighted the enemy, which had set out in search of them. But they let the French ships pass, and with a few friendly Indians who were familiar with the area they went back to the French fort. At dawn, they assaulted it without losing any men. They sacked it and proclaimed themselves victors and owners of the fort and everything in it.

When the French armada arrived near Cape Canaveral,[11] thirty leagues away from San Agustín, a huge wind storm came on, making their headway so difficult that they landed and turned back north in search of their fort. The adelantado calculated that his enemy would have been shipwrecked as a result of the storm, so with his infantry he crossed the bar of Matanzas, five leagues before getting to San Agustín. Turning south he found Juan de Ribao and the greater part of the men of his fleet. The adelantado sent out a messenger to tell the French to surrender because he had taken their fort, as proof of which he sent the keys to the fort and a hat belonging to the French general. Ribao, seeing certain signs of his loss, surrendered. But when the French forces were passing the Spaniards in a small boat, the Spaniards beheaded all of them (though sparing Ribao); those who retreated inland later suffered the same fate.

With the success of this victory, the adelantado returned to San Agustín along the beach, leaving Ribao, the French general, in the hands of a captain named Bayona. However, he instructed him to kill Ribao along the beach

---

7 The vessel, in which his son Juan and other relatives formed part of the crew, was part of the fleet that carried the treasure of the Indies. Commanded by Menéndez de Avilés, it was lost in 1563 in the Bermuda Channel; the governor searched for the ship upon his return to La Florida, where he encountered the French in Fort Carolina, which he took and renamed San Mateo.

8 On 28 August 1565 Menéndez de Avilés entered this bay, calling it San Agustín; he established a fort there and founded the city with the same name.

9 Jean Ribault (1520–1565).

10 Although it refers to the action of gathering the sails on a ship (*DLE*), in this case it symbolizes the lowering of a flag in taking possession of a territory.

11 During the first half of the sixteenth century the Spanish explorers called it Cabo Cañarreal; in the expedition of Francisco Gordillo (1521–1522) it was called Cabo Cañaveral (Stewart 1945, 11–13).

where he would find a dagger;[12] and that is what he did, stabbing him with it. Because the French were killed at that site, the Spaniards called the place Matanzas [the Massacre].

When the adelantado [Menéndez de Avilés] had fortified the fort at San Agustín, he returned to Havana where he notified His Majesty of what had happened. Within eight months *urcas* [heavy cargo ships][13] came on carrying supplies, munitions, and other gear. The ships also brought the fieldmaster Sancho de Arciniega,[14] with support troops of almost one thousand infantrymen. By order of the king he fortified four presidios˙ with them, from the inlet of Carlos[15] as far as Santa Elena.[16] And because every year ships were lost along the coast of Matacumbe,[17] owing to the fact that the pilots were unfamiliar with the Bahama Channel[18] and remembering the fact that Indians killed Spaniards who sought refuge on the beaches, they called that place Mártires [Martyrs]. Some, it is true, were true martyrs, dying as Catholics at the hands of heathen. The Spaniards who were stationed in the forts that were distributed in different parts, made some sallies, as a result of which they had some encounters with bellicose Indians. All along that coast, the Indians are warlike, particularly those of Santa Elena and its surroundings. There many people died, suffering hunger, much discomfort and great labors, particularly in defense of the forts of San Agustín and Santa Elena.

12 Short lance, ancient symbol of infantry captains (*DLE*).

13 Large barques, very thick at the middle, that served to transport grain and other crops (*DLE*); their use was frequent on the Carrera de Indias.

14 He arrived in San Agustín in June 1566 with a fleet of seventeen vessels and 1,500 men (Geiger 1936, 18n12).

15 Bay in the lands of the Calusa natives, in southwest Florida.

16 The second of the newly founded Spanish settlements, located on present-day Parris Island in South Carolina and established in 1566 by Menéndez de Avilés following the agreement with the Spanish Crown. It became the capital of La Florida until, due to poor administration and conflict with the neighboring natives, it was abandoned in 1576.

17 Key toward the southern end of La Florida peninsula, between Key West and Tortugas.

18 Navigational passage through which ships steered going and returning from Spain to Havana, and then transiting to Mexico, Panama, and La Florida. Due to keys, atolls, inlets, the high seabed, and changes in the tides, the route was considered dangerous.

CHAPTER THREE

About the Discovery of the Jacán and the Martyrdom of Twelve Clerics of the Compañía de Jesús

AROUND THE YEAR 1570, WHEN ADELANTADO PEDRO MENÉNDEZ WAS governing the presidios of La Florida, a ship circling to the north at latitude 37½ degrees, set out from the port of Santa Elena and put into a large bay that the Spaniards called Madre de Dios. From among the Indians who came on board, they seized a young chief and took him to Spain.[1] After catechizing and baptizing him, they named him don Luis;[2] the king decreed that the Indian be given all the necessary sustenance during the time he was in Spain and that he be sent to study with the fathers of the Compañía de Jesús [the Society of Jesus].

Around the year 1577[3] the adelantado brought fifty settlers to La Florida, dividing them between the two forts of Santa Elena and San Agustín. The

1 The year was 1561 and the bay the Chesapeake; the vessel belonged to the expedition captained by Ángel de Villafañe (Geiger 1936, 25n1) and was the Spanish caravel *Santa Catalina*, whose captain was Juan Velázquez (Wolfe 2014).
2 His name was Paquiquineo, and he likely was the son or brother of a local chieftain. There are several versions of his capture (1561). He was taken to court, protected by the king, and introduced to Spanish culture by the religious. Later he returned to New Spain and, very ill, was baptized in Mexico with the name of Viceroy don Luis de Velasco (1550–1564). The pious behavior of the youth inspired trust among his Jesuit protectors, who believed that his desire to evangelize his people was genuine. After several failed attempts to return to his homeland, he accompanied the Jesuits in the mission to Santa María de Jacán or Madre de Dios (1570). See the version cited in the "Preliminary Study" by Bartolomé Martínez, who resided in La Florida at the time (Vargas Ugarte 1940). Garcilaso, in *La Florida del Inca*, offers another account of the capture and agency of the youth (see 1956 [1605], book 6, chapter 22).
3 There is confusion surrounding this date. Menéndez died in 1574; he governed La Florida from 1565 until his death. The event above took place in 1570–1571, before the date indicated by Oré.

following year, 1578,[4] eight religious from the Compañía [Jesuits] came on to convert the natives, and they were assigned to the city of Santa Elena. Two went to the province of Guale,[5] fourteen leagues away, between San Agustín and Santa Elena, so as to instruct the natives; one went to a northern stretch of territory to a province that they named Escamacu.[6] This Jesuit took in his team a boy ten years old named Juan de Lara,[7] who was the son of a settler, so that he might have access to the language—Juan de Lara lives now in San Agustín. After spending a year and half with the natives and considering the little success he was having with them, this lone Jesuit returned to Santa Elena to join his brothers.

Father Álamo, one of the religious from that congregation, went back to Spain to give an account to his superiors of the conditions and qualities of the natives, and of the land and the little success that the Jesuits were having in their work. It seemed to the fathers that their failure to baptize anyone in all that time was owing to the resistance and toughness of the Indians. However, it happened that the young chief don Luis, now educated so that he read and wrote the Spanish language and was expert in other fields of knowledge he had studied, was then in the Jesuit house in Seville. When he heard the Jesuit's story of failure in trying to convert the Floridians, he said to the rector and to others that he would volunteer to return to his homeland in the company of some priests, and with the help of God and his good efforts he would bring those Indians to the faith.[8]

His words stirred in the religious a great desire and zeal to save souls, and with that determination they offered themselves to the king and petitioned for a license and the necessary resources to go to La Florida, taking with them don Luis. When the king granted them a license and approved their request, they sailed and arrived safely at Santa Elena. From there Adelantado Menéndez de Avilés gave them a ship and supplies for a year, and so they took off with Captain Vicente González. In all, there were

---

4 The first Jesuits arrived in 1567. There were three of them: the Fathers Pedro Martínez, Juan Rogel, and Brother Francisco Villarreal. Others followed in 1568 and in 1570 (see Vargas Ugarte 1940; Cushner 2006, chapter 2).

5 One of the first four provinces (Apalache, Guale, Mayaca-Jororo, and Timucua) into which the territory of La Florida was divided for the evangelization of the native population. It included the coast and islands of the modern state of Georgia, where the Guale tongue was spoken (see Milanich 2006).

6 Name of the area inhabited by the Escamacu group, from the Eastern part of modern-day Georgia and South Carolina.

7 It was common to take Spanish youths to the missions so that they might learn the local language and assist in mass. Others have indicated his name as Alonso de Olmos (see Wolfe 2014).

8 Oré's version differs much from the historical record (see Wolfe 2014).

twelve priests[9] and religious, and a boy named Alonso de Lara,[10] an older brother of the other previously mentioned [Juan de Lara], both sons of a settler in Santa Elena.

When they arrived at the bay of Madre de Dios or the Jacán,[11] they went up the river twelve leagues where the chief don Luis and two brother leaders had their villages. There the Spaniards were well received and given shelter with a demonstration of great joy. Seeing the natives' good disposition, they disembarked with their stores and lodged in a house that they made out of palm branches, with a little corner at one side so that they could say mass until they might build a more comfortable church. From there the ship went back to Santa Elena to inform the adelantado where it had left the religious. But inasmuch as the enemy of humankind [the devil] always tries to thwart deeds like this aimed at saving souls, he urged the chief don Luis, who was now back among his own kind, to give himself over to vice so wildly and shamelessly that Father Juan Bautista de Segura,[12] superior of those religious, rebuked him severely. Following that, with charitable and religious language, the father admonished, exhorted, and pleaded with don Luis, reminding him that the Spaniards had come because of his promises of protection, made in Spain. If don Luis persisted in providing such a bad example, they could not make him the means by which the Gospel was preached, because the sacred word had to be conveyed by ministers and interpreters whose lives were pure.[13] With these and other soft words that he and the rest of the religious said to don Luis, they failed to change him; rather, they caused him to become more hardened in sin. The devil reigned in his heart just as in Judas's, bringing about treason. And wanting to escape from the eyes of people who were scolding him, he said that he was going to a nearby village to look for chestnuts and other nuts and that he would return in a few days.

---

9 They were eight, as indicated in an anonymous handwritten note in the left margin of folio 5v, drawing on Garcilaso's *La Florida* as a source and confirmed by modern historians such as Vargas Ugarte (1940). Garcilaso de la Vega confirms this number in *La Florida del Inca* (1956 [1605], book 6, chap. 22, 446–47). Vargas Ugarte likewise indicates that there were eight martyrs; only the young Alonso de Olmos—who accompanied the Jesuit clerics Juan Bautista de Segura and Luis de Quirós; lay brothers Gabriel Gómez, Sancho Cevallos, and Pedro de Linares; and preachers Cristóbal Redondo, Gabriel de Solís, and Juan Bautista Méndez—survived (1940, 12–14).

10 Alonso or Aloncito helped as an acolyte in mass and devoted himself to learning the native languages (Milanich 2006, 99–100).

11 They arrived in the fall of 1570. For more details about the location of the mission, see Lewis and Loomis 1953.

12 Vice-Provincial of the Jesuit Order in Havana (see Vargas Ugarte 1940).

13 He highlights the central part of exemplary missionary labors, an idea put forward in his *Símbolo católico indiano*. See Cook 1992b.

The holy fathers let him go. But seeing that he did not return on the day he said he would, they wrote him a letter, begging him for the love of God to return, for without an interpreter they could not carry out their conversions. There was no dealing with the apostate chief: he did not come back, nor did he respond. So they determined to send a respected father who was a preacher, and a companion, to where they thought [don Luis] was, to urge him to return with them, presuming that this personal contact would win him over. But because the devil had already taken over his soul, as soon as the two emissaries arrived, he killed them. On the eve of the Purification of Our Lady,[14] the same day as that of the Illustrious Martyr Saint Ignatius[15] in whose heart the name of Jesus was found inscribed, the blood of the two blessed martyrs was spilled, and [don Luis] left to kill the remaining Jesuits. When he arrived at the place where the other Jesuits were, he told them that the two had stayed behind with the Indians who would come on in the morning with the chestnuts and other nuts as gifts. And since the following day was the feast day of Our Lady of the Candlemas [Nuestra Señora de la Candelaria], he wanted to go with all his Indians to cut wood to construct a church in honor of the Virgin. He asked that mass be said in the morning and that all the machetes, hatchets, and other tools be turned over to him so that he could distribute them.

14 The Purification or the day of Nuestra Señora de la Candelaria. It is one of the oldest Marian celebrations in Catholicism, commemorated on 2 February. Its iconography is based in the presentation of the Christ Child in the Temple of Jerusalem, according to the law of Moses, and also the purification of the mother, who carries a candle in her hand (Luke 2:22–40).

15 Reference to Saint Ignatius of Antioch. He was persecuted and martyred in the time of Trajan, thrown to the beasts. The Dominican Vincent de Beauvais, asserted, centuries later, that Ignatius had Christ's name in golden letters on his heart, supposedly discovered when the pieces of his body were collected and preserved as relics. From the twelfth century until 1969, his feast day was put at 1 February in the General Roman Calendar. This could explain how young Luis departed on 1 February, on the eve of the Feast of Nuestra Señora de la Candelaria. Currently the feast day of Saint Ignatius of Antioch is celebrated on 17 October by Catholics and on 20 December among the Orthodox.

CHAPTER FOUR

How the Indians' Treachery and the Death of the Religious Were Discovered

AFTER A YEAR HAD PASSED THE SAME CAPTAIN, VICENTE GONZÁLEZ, went to take supplies to the religious. Within sight of the town he saw on the beach persons dressed in cassocks and other religious garments; so it appeared to him that they were the priests. He waited until one of them came on board. But when a canoe approached with some Indians, through sign language he asked why the fathers were not coming on to meet him. He wrote a letter to them, saying that he was Vicente González. But when he did not get an answer, he grew suspicious; and when the Indians returned to the ships, he seized two. The rest threw themselves into the water; and within a short space he saw that many canoes full of Indians were coming toward him. Immediately he set sail, returning to Santa Elena.[1]

The Indian prisoners he had taken confessed that all the religious were dead but that one person had escaped: a boy called Alonso de Lara. At that time His Majesty recalled the adelantado, ordering him to return to Spain. Before leaving, however, he offered to return from Santa Elena[2] by way of San Agustín, where he had two new frigates that were just being completed. Because it was the month of July, leaving the port of [San Agustín] for Spain, they stopped in at Jacán where the frigates were completed. At the insistence

---

1 According to Geiger, it first sailed to Havana (1936, 31n2).
2 He arrived in Santa Elena on 22 July 1572.

of the religious who had remained in Santa Elena, he [Menéndez] went on to rescue Alonso de Lara. From the two presidios he took 150 soldiers, among them being Juan de Lara, the younger brother of the captive; they all left in four ships.

When they arrived at the bay they found two Indians loyal to the cacique who had protected Alonso de Lara from the fury of don Luis. The cacique had gotten him out by night with the help of his niece so that her uncle would not be killed by him [don Luis]. The ships anchored; when two Indians approached, Juan de Lara inquired about his brother Alonso. They answered that he was in the hands of a cacique, a day's march away. Adelantado Menéndez de Avilés told them to say that the boy was his son and to send him back, sweetening the request with some gifts. The next day he sent Captain Vicente González with a *patache* [scout boat][3] carrying thirty soldiers to the village of don Luis, on the chance that they could apprehend him. When they got to the edge of the village, the captain ordered the soldiers to hide below deck; and when the Indians saw only six men, seventy came on in canoes. They wore the patens[4] from the chalices as necklaces; being naked (which is Indian custom throughout the area), they covered their private parts with the corporals.[5] The captain invited them to eat cane syrup and a honeyed biscuit of the finest quality that the Spaniards had with them. When they were enjoying themselves, the soldiers suddenly emerged from below deck and seized thirteen high-ranking Indians. They killed more than twenty and then returned with their prisoners to the bay where the adelantado had stayed behind. Within two days, two hundred Indians then came on and delivered over Alonso de Lara. He was naked in the Indian fashion; it was he who provided a long and true account of the martyrdom of the fathers whose story has already been told.

The adelantado sent one hundred soldiers, and his son-in-law don Diego de Velasco,[6] to take Alonso de Lara and his brother to assess that land, which

---

3 Or *pataje*. A war vessel intended to accompany fleets to carry messages, scout the coastlines, and protect the entryways into ports (*DLE*).

4 Gold, silver, or metal dish in which, in Catholic liturgy, the Holy Wafer is placed during mass, from the conclusion of the Pater Noster to the moment of consumption (*DLE*).

5 Fine cloths on which the consecrated elements are placed in the celebration of the Eucharist (*DLE*).

6 He was the illegitimate son of Juan de Velasco, and grandson of the constable of Castile. He accompanied Menéndez de Avilés on his first voyage to La Florida, where he was governor and captain general between 1571 and 1576; later he was the principal bailiff of Mexico and Gentleman of the King's Household. The missionaries reprimanded him for his ill treatment of La Florida's native population. "Avilés. Familia del Adelantado Pedro Menéndez de Avilés." Álvarez, Mellén: http://www.euskalnet.net/laviana/gen_astures/aviles.htm, accessed 15 July 2012.

they said was very rich, and to speak with the cacique who had defended Alonso de Lara. They returned with little or no information regarding what the Spaniards wanted to know, because the Indians had fled to the mountains. The adelantado interrogated the thirteen prisoners that Captain Vicente González had brought him, and he proposed that they bring to him don Luis—either dead or alive. One Indian dared to say that he would do so; a time limit of ten days was fixed so that if he did not return by then, his companions would be hanged. So he set out but he never returned although a few more days passed beyond the agreed-upon time. The adelantado then commanded that all be put to death, but first he asked them if they wanted to become Christians. They said yes and accepted baptism willingly, after which a religious instructed them in the basics of the faith, and they were hanged on a yardarm of the ship. When that was done, the adelantado returned to Spain on 24 August 1572. He sent Alonso de Lara, together with a religious, on a patache to Havana.

Adelantado Pedro Menéndez returned to Spain because he was recalled by His Majesty to ready the fleet at Santander. But he died there, and his body was taken to the town of Avilés, where he was a native.[7] In the parish church they placed his body in a crypt of honor, covering the tomb with a big slab emblazoned with the cross of Santiago and an epitaph in which his deeds were written in gold letters, together with the title of adelantado. In Florida his son-in-law don Diego de Velasco was left to govern; he had married Menéndez's youngest daughter, doña María Menéndez.[8] The adelantado had explored the coast of La Florida from Cape Canaveral, at latitude 28 degrees, as far as the bay of Madre de Dios of the Jacán (which now the English[9] have fortified and populated), at latitude 37 degrees. He also explored the coast of the Bahama channel, from Cape Canaveral right up to the inlet of Carlos.

7   He died in Santander on 17 September 1574, at the age of fifty-five, and was buried in the church of San Nicolás, in Avilés.
8   This daughter was illegitimate. María and Diego de Velasco, her husband, moved to La Florida in 1571 and traveled on the same vessel as María de Solís, the wife of Menéndez de Avilés. "Avilés. Familia del Adelantado Pedro Menéndez de Avilés." Álvarez, Mellén: http://www.euskalnet.net/laviana/gen_astures/aviles.htm, accessed 15 July 2012. About the family and their affairs throughout various time periods, see Bushnell 1978.
9   The English populated the area in 1607, when Jamestown, capital of Virginia until 1699, was established. This detail helps to confirm that the *Relación* was written after 1607.

CHAPTER FIVE

Regarding the Rebellion of the Indians of Santa Elena and Guale

AT THE SAME TIME THAT THE ADELANTADO RETURNED TO SPAIN AND left governance of the presidios to his son-in-law, don Diego de Velasco, the Indians of Guale and Escamacu were living in such peace and tranquility that only one soldier was required to go from one village to another to trade and deal with the Indians. It happened then that one of the most important caciques of the Guale territory became a Christian, together with his wife. But because one of his subjects then lost respect for him and became disobedient, the [Christian] Indian lord surrounded his village; a nephew of this disgruntled cacique then shot [the Christian lord] with an arrow, killing him. Following that, the wife of the Christian Indian lord went to Santa Elena to complain to the governor. She asked for protection and justice for the homicide because her husband had been a Christian. To satisfy her request, the governor called together all the principal leaders of the province of Guale with the assurance that nothing bad would happen to them and requested that they deliver over to him the murderer. With this promise of safety, they came and brought the Indian who had done the deed. Although the governor attempted to placate the wife with gifts and flattery, she was not happy; when she saw in front of her the man who had killed her husband, with even more insistence she demanded justice, protesting that if she did not get it, there would be many killings. The governor, in order to avoid greater disturbances, pronounced the sentence that the Indian be decapitated. The sentence was executed in view of all the caciques. But seeing that the governor's word had been broken,[1] the caciques returned home, indignant and angry, swearing to avenge this injury. They joined in a confederation with the Indians of Escamacu, their neighbors to the north, and they sent them presents along with the news of the Spaniards' betrayal. They asked them to kill any Spaniards who might visit them. These Indians of Escamacu were held in high esteem for their valor, and even feared.

At that time some Indians fled from service to the Spaniards, taking away their masters' clothing, so twenty-two soldiers set out to look for them. When they arrived in Escamacu, the Indians treated them well. But because the Indians' hearts were heavy, they sent their women and children away—a sure sign of battle. When the Spanish ensign asked why there were no women around, the Indians answered that it was because the soldiers appeared to be set for war with *escaupiles* [protective gear][2] and fuses ready to be lit. The ensign, so as not to disturb the peace, ordered his men to disarm; and he posted a guard on top of a *bohío* [hut].[3] But at dawn, a soldier went into the bushes to relieve himself, and at that moment he saw a whole band of Indians approaching the camp. Luckily, the post sounded the alarm but, when the fuses were lit, the Indians slaughtered with their arrows many of the soldiers. The man in the bushes, who was unable to get to his weapons, ran where fortune led him toward Santa Elena. As he looked back, he saw coming toward him Alonso de Lara (whom they had rescued in the Jacán) and another soldier. Both were badly wounded and they got near enough to tell him that all their comrades were dead. But realizing that immediately behind them, all the Indians were coming on, the soldier said: "I am alive and healthy and you are badly wounded. Good-bye, brothers." So he jumped into a lake until he saw the Indians pass by, dancing merrily over their victory, with the heads of Alonso de Lara and his companion.

As soon as it got dark, he climbed out of the lake and headed south, staying away from the road. A day later he arrived at the island of Santa Elena, and he was forced to swim across the bay. When Juan de Lara and other youths saw a naked man crossing the swamp, they all ran to see who he was. They found it was a man called Calderón, who told them about the deaths of all their

---

1 Apparently they interpreted the man's death as one of their own having been harmed after they had been assured of safety.

2 Quilted protective piece of clothing made of cotton, used by the Mexicas and adopted by the conquistadors to defend themselves from arrows.

3 In the Caribbean, a type of cabin made from palm leaves; it had only one door.

companions. Then they went to the town where, once everyone heard the news, there was great lamentation for the loss of brothers, children and husbands.

At the same time three soldiers were in the province of Guale for the purpose of a rescue. However, an Indian woman warned them to go back to Santa Elena, saying that the Indians planned to kill them. So that night, without the Indians knowing it, they got away. However, four leagues from there, at a narrow opening where hardly a canoe fit, Indians from Escamacu, who were bringing twenty heads of dead Spaniards to the caciques of Guale, found the three soldiers and returned them to Guale where they were killed. In that way the whole area of Guale rose up in rebellion.

At that time His Majesty sent Hernando de Miranda[4] as governor and captain general of the provinces of La Florida,[5] according to all the legal capitulations, to replace Adelantado Pedro Menéndez de Avilés, who had died. Miranda was a son-in-law of the adelantado, married to doña Catalina Menéndez, her father's designated heir. When he arrived in Havana from Spain, he found waiting for him the *situado*,[6] money that had been brought from New Spain to pay for the expenses of the soldiers in La Florida. So when [Hernando de Miranda] went on to San Agustín, he made his first payment there since it was the first port. From there he traveled on with three ships to Santa Elena where the adelantado's wife was. Crossing the bar, they were facing into the wind and several of the royal officials asked to be left behind. So ten men were put in a *chalupa* [small boat] for their trip to town. The weather then grew calm for a long stretch, and the general [Hernando de Miranda] raised sail leaving the royal officials ashore. The next morning, the men set out in search of their general. But not finding him where they thought they had left him, they went along the coast as far as the bar of San Mateo, from which point one goes by narrow waterways to Santa Elena without having to venture out to sea. They reached an Indian village in the territory of Guale and clambered onto land, without knowing that the population was in revolt, while four men stayed behind in the chalupa. When they entered the bohío, these royal officials and the soldiers

---

4 First husband of Catalina Menéndez de Avilés; governor of La Florida for a few months in 1576. Her second husband was Hernando de Alas. "Avilés. Familia del Adelantado Pedro Menéndez de Avilés," Mellén Álvarez, http://www.euskalnet.net/laviana/gen_astures/aviles.htm, accessed 15 July 2012. Also, see Bushnell 1978.

5 Upon Adelantado Menéndez de Avilés's death, Catalina Menéndez de Avilés and Hernando de Miranda claimed the titles of Governor, Captain General, and Adelantado of La Florida.

6 The rent to cover the salaries and expenses in La Florida, an unproductive dependency. On the topic, see Bushnell 1994.

who accompanied them were immediately killed by the sudden addition of more Indians who later killed the men in the chalupa.

When General Hernando de Miranda reached Santa Elena and was informed that the Indians had risen up, he dispatched a detail of thirteen soldiers to search for the royal officials. When they arrived in the area it was late so they stationed themselves at the opening of a narrow river, very near the village of Guale. From there they saw the Indians building great fires and as a result there was a lot of smoke—which among Indians is a warning sign. Within an hour, twelve canoes filled with warriors arrived in the village, prepared to offer aid to the Guale people. The search party then understood that the royal officials and the soldiers who accompanied them were dead. The Indians called on the Spaniards to come on shore, promising them chickens and women. With this understanding, they returned to Santa Elena with one soldier less, whom they left behind as a spy. As a result the death toll was upped to thirty-seven. The soldiers arrived back at night to a place very near to the fort, and because the tides were against them they left their patache in the river and went by land toward the fort. Before they had gone a quarter of a league, they saw torches and a great number of Indians dancing. They concluded that the fort was being besieged. They reached the fort, however, with the news that the royal officials and those who were with them were dead, as a result of which there was much confusion and crying and demonstrations of grief on behalf of the dead men.

The next day the general sent Captain Solís with nine soldiers to survey the island and flush out any Indians who might be hidden in ambush. When one Indian came out and skirmished with the soldiers, the others emerged, and the soldiers killed them all. The remaining Indians surrounded the fort and for forty-four days they attacked twice daily. When General Hernando de Miranda realized that the noose was tightening and the Spaniards lacked fuses for the muskets, which had to be made out of sheeting, he agreed that all the fort's inhabitants who were not engaged in fighting should embark immediately for San Agustín. He stayed behind with sixty men and burned the fort.

Then he made use of a stratagem to escape. Pretending to be asleep, he had the women put him on board ship as if he did not know he was being moved (a scribe from the same region in Spain as General Hernando de Miranda gave testimony to that effect). When the soldiers were standing at the mast deciding who was going to stay, from the stern of the ship the governor said they had forcibly put him on board and that all should come on board. So hastily they set sail, leaving behind their possessions for the enemy to sack. Hardly had they lifted anchor when a huge crowd of Indians descended on the fort, tearing it to pieces and disabling all the artillery. The Spaniards arrived in San Agustín where Governor Miranda left in his place Gutierre de Miranda.[7] He then departed for Spain to give an account to His Majesty of what had happened and to ask for aid. He was carrying seven boxes of the annual subsidy. When he arrived home, they seized him and subjected him to an examination as to why he [Hernando de Miranda] had left and permitted the fort at Santa Elena to be destroyed.

At that time a French galleon called *El Príncipe* (*The Prince*)[8] arrived at the bar of San Agustín. This ship had been badly damaged by the fleet commanded by don Cristóbal de Eraso, and it sat for three days at half a league from the bar. Knowing that Santa Elena was depopulated but that the artillery had been left behind, the ship went for repair in the bay. But a league away before getting to the bar, it struck a shoal and was quickly lost. The men were not able to get anything from the wreck, not even food. When the Indians were out hunting, they found them and assaulted them. When they surrendered they were divided as slaves between the Indians of Guale and Escamacu.

---

7 Governor of La Florida, 1576–1577.
8 It was shipwrecked off the coast of Santa Elena in December, 1576; its crew was killed by Indians; the survivors were enslaved (Geiger 1936, 40n11).

CHAPTER SIX

Regarding the Entrusting of the Government of La Florida to Pedro Menéndez Marqués, and Also Telling about the Religious of Saint Francis who Went to Convert the Natives and Events Related to the Jacán

AROUND THE YEAR 1577 HIS MAJESTY ORDERED PEDRO MENÉNDEZ Marqués,[1] nephew of the adelantado, the latter of whom was at that time admiral of the fleet of galleons of the Carrera de Indias, and *contador* (accountant) for La Florida,[2] to go with his infantry to rebuild the fort at Santa Elena in the capacity of governor of La Florida and its provinces. So the general went, and he tried to restore the fort, with the help of one hundred soldiers. They had many encounters with the Indians until the fort was built and they could leave from it to burn the Indian villages and inflict whatever harm they could. In one assault they killed or took captive 120 persons. In the province of Guale they set fire to all the villages in such a way that the Indians, feeling themselves pursued, killed, and imprisoned, submitted to and became confederates of the Spaniards. They asked the religious to instruct them in the lessons of Christianity so that they could be baptized. Thus they were pacified. [And] the first villages of Christians were Nombre de Dios[3] and San Sebastián, near San Agustín.

---

1 First interim governor (1577–1578) of La Florida and later permanent (1578–1594). Although Oré uses Marqués as his surname, the majority of the subsequent references are to Marquéz. Following Eugene Lyon, the first spelling is preferred and maintained in the text.

2 See Bushnell 1981.

3 A fourth of a league away from San Agustín; at a distance of "two musket shots," according to period documents. (Geiger 1936, 54n3). It was ruled by the clever female chief doña María, married to the Spanish soldier Clemente Vernal; it was destroyed by the flood of 1600 (http://www.kislakfoundation.org/prize/199901.html, accessed 10 July 2015).

Around the year 1585 news circulated that the English were coming to populate the Jacán[4] coast. Having an order from His Majesty, General Pedro Menéndez Marqués set out for San Agustín in a frigate; and he sailed toward Jacán to reconnoiter and to find an interpreter so as to communicate with the Indian population there.[5] In 1587, drawing near, he encountered a storm so fierce that he had to seek land. With great risk he succeeded in getting to Havana. He then returned to San Agustín in July, agreeing with the field commander Juan de Tejeda to put the fort of Santa Elena under the control of San Agustín. When he arrived there, he made that change.

In 1586 the pirate Francis Drake (Francisco Draque)[6] had burned the fort at San Agustín with his powerful infantry and cannon in a land attack. The presidio had only a few men and inadequate defenses—plus the fact that a bugler had gone over to the enemy and revealed information about the fort. However, in the time that he was there, Drake suffered much damage. Some of his launches were sunk, and Englishmen were killed—particularly one who was a high-ranking person, struck by a bullet from a soldier, Luis Fernández. This Spanish soldier lives still today, very old and poor, with children. All of this inflicted so much damage on Drake that he shot off a signal to lift the siege; the English sailed away and Drake returned to his life as a pirate. More damage would have been done to him and more resistance would have been shown if the Spaniards had not had to attend to the rebellious Indians of Icaste and Cazacolo inland.[7] The latter were attempting to rebel and capture the women and children of San Agustín, who had hidden in the bushes, with the idea of claiming them for themselves. Knowing who these women were, the Indians in their parleys had even apportioned them out according to the status of various Indian lords. His Majesty considered it prudent to listen to the advice given him, taking into account the harm done and the expense that afterward would have to be sustained to reconquer the Indians. The fact that the infantry remaining in the presidio was so reduced also made the king realize that it would be impossible to resist the

---

4 Probably a reference to the lost colony of Roanoke. It was established by Sir Walter Raleigh's associates in 1587, on the island by the same name, located at the mouth of Albemarle Sound, in present-day North Carolina. The reasons for the disappearance of its inhabitants are still unknown, whether they were murdered or enslaved and assimilated by local ethnic groups.
5 Probably by kidnapping an Indian.
6 Francis Drake (1546–1593), known as Draque or Draco (in Latin, "dragon"). He arrived in San Agustín on 6 June 1586 and burned the village, including the fort and the church. He assaulted Santo Domingo in Hispaniola and Cartagena de Indias in the same year.
7 In the area of the Cumberland Islands, present-day Georgia.

enemy's superior forces in a fort constructed of wood and sand, without the possibility of any additional relief.

In December of 1587 Father Friar Alonso de Reinoso[8] of the Franciscan Order[9] came on from Castile, together with other religious for the conversion of the Indians. They were distributed among the towns of Nombre de Dios and San Sebastián, in San Antonio[10] and its surrounding lands, in San Pedro and San Juan,[11] and in other places belonging to his jurisdiction. Some years before Father Friar Reinoso had come to La Florida with companions at the request of General Pedro Menéndez Marqués; and these men had busied themselves with conversions in the Guale region, in Tolomato, Topiqui,[12] Santa Elena, and San Agustín. Everywhere their efforts at preaching and exhortation had borne fruit. A great number of Indians were Christianized and baptized. However, from the beginning these Christian Indians felt themselves to be resented by those who were not Christians [stain obscures meaning], not because they had been forced to be Christians but because they had freely chosen to convert. In most of the towns where the Christians were persecuted, they were outnumbered by the non-Christian Indians who insulted them, holding them to be renegades, betrayers of native loyalties; as a result the Christian Indians suffered a great deal. This persecution went on for some twenty years during which time there were always bands of Indians camped around the town, lying in wait to ambush any soldier who carelessly went out for firewood, to fish or hunt, or for any other purpose. Any soldier who ventured out was then killed, as has been reported in earlier chapters. The Indians assiduously tried to stamp out any evidence of a Spanish presence, even extending to seed and cattle from Spain.

It was God's will, though, that little by little these difficult conditions were eased so that today the Indians consider it a great honor to be Christians. In fact they pursue those who are not and insult them, so the religious are now

8 We follow Geiger's spelling of his last name. Member of the Province of Santiago in Spain; on three occasions (1584, 1587, 1590) he brought missionaries to La Florida. In spite of his efforts, toward 1592 there were only five Franciscan missionaries in La Florida (Geiger 1940, 91–92). They are mentioned by Father Friar Alonso de Escobedo in *La Florida*, his epic poem about the region (c. 1600). See Sununu's edition of complete poem (2015).

9 As Geiger points out, they were not the first Franciscans to arrive in La Florida. In 1573 a group arrived in Santa Elena. However, shortly after Pedro Menéndez de Avilés's death and with no support from the local authorities, they abandoned the area (1936, 56n7).

10 Possibly present-day Georgia, west of Cumberland Island and under the jurisdiction of San Pedro Mission on the same island (Geiger 1936, 57n8).

11 Saint John of the Port, north of San Agustín, on Saint Johns River (Geiger, 1936, 57n8).

12 Both are on the coast: Tolomato, opposite Sapelo Island; Topiqui, on the southern part of St. Catherine Island. See Milanich map of missions.

faced with defending these *hanopiras*. This term means "red man" because the heathen Indians, for the most part, go around painted with a red tint extracted from the bixa plant; lacking that paint they cover themselves with soot or coal dust. In this the Indians of La Florida are like the barbarous Indians of the highlands of Peru, [as] both are expert in the use of the bow and arrow. But in Peru they go about clothed, or at least less naked than the ones here. The Floridians have the advantage in that they are more warlike and they do not have the vice of drunkenness that is notable in all the Indians, from New Spain to Peru.

The next year, 1588, in the month of May, Captain Vicente González set out from the port and presidio of San Agustín. In his company was Sergeant Major Juan Menéndez Marqués with thirty soldiers and sailors. They departed in a long boat from Sanlúcar,[13] which had come from Havana the year before carrying dispatches, and which had been purchased for the purpose of running along the coast as far as the bay of Madre de Dios del Jacán so as to seize interpreters and gather information about the population and fortifications of the English. Sailing along the coast, they arrived at Santa Elena, where they found the Indians to be peaceful, and the same situation at the port of Cayagua,[14] which they judged favorably. Following the coast and having passed the cape of San Román,[15] they spoke with some Indians whose language the interpreters they had with them did not understand. Continuing on, they passed Capes Trafalgar[16] and San Juan and two other natural harbors, after which they reached the bay of Madre de Dios del Jacán in June 1588. This port is almost three leagues wide at its mouth,[17] without any shoals or reefs, and more than eight fathoms deep as one enters—at a point that runs from northwest[18] to southeast. It forms a large round gulf. Between its entryway and the place where one touches land, going in a circle from west to northeast, and from east to west taking into account the bay's opening, it must be about three leagues. On the mainland there is a good port whose entrance measures three fathoms deep. In addition, at a distance of less than two leagues there is another port just a little toward the northwest. There Captain Vicente González said he had set on shore the religious of the Society of Jesus, whom

13 Sanlúcar de Barrameda, port in Seville on the Guadalquivir River.
14 Modern-day Charleston Bay, South Carolina (Geiger 1936, 58n15).
15 Cape Romain, South Carolina (Geiger 1936, 58n16).
16 Modern-day Cape Hatteras, North Carolina (Geiger 1936, 59n17).
17 Norfolk, Virginia (Geiger 1936, 58n20).
18 The mouth of York River or Mobjack Bay in Virginia (Geiger 1936, 58n21).

don Luis and his accomplices martyred, as has already been told. He also said that in a flat place beyond a ravine where some pine trees were clustered, he had commanded there be erected an altar where mass could be said. From there he exited toward the east, where on firm land in that area and within the bay, near some little islands and a small cove, the adelantado was waiting and putting finishing touches on the gunwales of two frigates in which he sailed back to Castile.

They left from that harbor and, sailing along the coast within sight of the mainland as they went north, they found another port that looked to be good with a deep harbor and on whose shores there were big rocks. At its northerly point there was a tall rock that could serve as a lookout. These three harbors can be seen at one glance from the mouth of the bay, although this last one is almost hidden. As they continued north the land on the eastern side seemed to be jutting into the bay. As they went on, it grew narrower such that at its narrowest point, from the coast and bank on the western side toward the eastern bank, it probably measured two leagues. Pressing on, they discovered creeks, coves and rivers along the western side. Then they came to a big river, fed with fresh water, whose mouth where it entered the bay was more than six fathoms deep. Along its northern bank they saw that the land was very high, cut by gullies, without trees and flat—a green field very pleasant to behold. On the south side of this river there is a beach and a bank lined with small pebbles; going up the river from there along the south side, there seemed to be a valley filled with trees and land favorable for raising cattle and cultivation. This river was discovered at latitude 38 degrees, and it was named San Pedro.[19] Toward the north along the west side, they made nightfall at a small creek, under the shelter of a shady tree surrounded by high terrain. Another day many Indians came to the shore, and the one who seemed to command the most respect was wearing a string of beads around his neck that looked to be made of fine gold. There they took captive a young boy of about fifteen.

Continuing on, they discovered many other harbors and rushing rivers along the western side, which entered the bay until, at latitude 35 degrees, they began to discern very high lands that sloped southwest from northeast. They also discovered more rivers. But then there appeared in the middle of the bay a small island. To the west of it they determined that the depth was

19 Potomac River (Geiger 1936, 59n24).

diminishing in such a way that they could not push forward and it was necessary to go around to the east where from that spot, facing the island, they saw that again the land rose tall and that it was gullied but also heavily wooded. Near the island, on the eastern side, there were shoals of greater or lesser depth, but hugging close to the mainland, on the east they found a very deep channel. Continuing north, they found the woods fenced off their vision in a circle, with the mouths of rivers and coves emerging at different points. This circle where the bay ends must be as wide as the bay of Cádiz. More than two or three leagues before reaching the terminus of the bay, they found that the water was fresh. And that afternoon they arrived at a point where a river, running from west to northeast, opened up amid great forests and huge rocky formations.[20] At its mouth, at full tide it measured three fathoms deep. Because it was nightfall, they anchored about a quarter of a league away. At daybreak it was low tide and almost miraculously they found that the ship was lodged between some rocky cliffs with the river on either side. With great risk and orders shouted to turn the rudder this way, and then that way, they got out to the mouth of the river, which was clear. There they saw a small shad. However, because it was dead and floating on the water, it was of no use to them as food. Yet in a small stream that was flowing down from the rocks, they spotted some small trout, such as they knew from the mountains. That day was the eve of St. John's Day[21] and, out of devotion, they named the river San Juan de las Peñas. They climbed up into the woods and from the top on the other side they saw another river [stain], as well as more forests and tall mountains with their ranges folded onto one another. Below, on the slope of the forest, was a valley whose tree growth was pale green and whose land seemed to be fertile and open to cultivation.

From that marking of 38 degrees as far as the end of the bay there is a large quantity of chestnut trees and tall oaks. There are many wild grapevines bearing plump grapes. That same day they left that river and went along the riverbank toward the east, where they discovered a lovely cove covered over with trees, where there were many deer. From there they headed north until they could go no further. Then they jumped on land at a welcoming beach below some slight slopes where they found a peaceful, pleasant valley with luxurious trees without bushes—and again with many deer. They succeeded in killing one, with which they celebrated the glorious day of

---

20 Susquehanna River (Geiger 1936, 46n30).
21 The feast of Saint John the Baptist is celebrated on 24 June.

San Juan. Captain Vicente González and his pilot Ginés Pinzón measured the sun and found they were at a latitude of 40 degrees. They also took the reading at their first stopping-off point on the mainland after having been in the bay, and they found that they were at 37 degrees and a few minutes.

On that same day of St. John when they left the end of the bay and headed south, and along the whole western front, no Indians appeared—despite the fact that they had taken one youth from there as has already been told. Until the day of the apostles San Pedro and San Pablo,[22] when in the morning they crossed the eastern part of the river and arrived at the small islands that are in view of the mouth of the bay, they stayed on board and were only able to jump onto land then. From there and a little further on, within sight of the bay where the adelantado had remained, they finally reached a spot where the ship could anchor and they could definitely land. However, because the sea bed was shallow, they could not bring the ship close to shore. And when many Indian men and women came to the beach and approached the ship, with the water reaching up to their knees, the Spaniards seized one and then set sail. That afternoon they sailed out of the bay and all that night they headed south with a strong wind from the west, and still another day until sunset. Because the wind kept blowing hard, they pulled down the sails and, with a great effort, made it to shore by rowing. They crossed a small bar of little depth and once within the bay they found a big cove, which at low tide left its southern part almost dry. Toward the north there was a big stretch of water that promised an extension toward the northwest. There the tree growth was very thick. Along the shoreline, toward the north, there was another mouth of the bay better than the one from which they had entered. The strip of shoreline, around a league from one bar to the other, is low and stripped of sand. But going inland a little further they found where they could dock. They located the spot because small canoes were to be found there, and also wells made of English barrels[23] and debris left by what seemed to be many persons.

Another day they set out, measuring the latitude of that landing spot and finding it to be 35½ degrees. They continued sailing toward the south and passed the three capes previously mentioned and the port of Cayagua,

---

22 The martyrdom in Rome of the apostles Peter and Paul of Tarsus is celebrated in the Catholic calendar on 29 June.

23 In Spanish, *pipas inglesas*. The *Diccionario de autoridades* (pipas, 3, 1990 [1726–1737]) gives two meanings for *pipas*: fuses for bombs or grenades (pipe bombs), and vats for transporting liquids such as wine or beer. Geiger (1936, 48 and 60n41) translates the phrase as "remains of English barrels." In the area wells were lined with stacked barrels.

Santa Elena, and the whole spit of land of Guale, until they arrived at the island of San Pedro.[24] This last spot was thickly populated with native Indians, and there they found Father Friar Baltasar López,[25] who was beginning to have great success with conversions. He had already baptized many, and these new Christians received the arrivals well, furnishing them with the supplies so badly needed. When they passed by the bar of that island, they continued on to San Agustín where they arrived in July of 1588.

All this navigation and discovery, setting out and returning, was accomplished in little less than a month and a half, according to the very reliable and detailed account of Sergeant Major Juan Menéndez,[26] who at present is His Majesty's treasurer in San Agustín. I have relayed his description of the bay of Madre de Dios and the log of its landing spots in such detail because of its usefulness to His Majesty until he deems it necessary to cleanse the area of those thieves[27] who have occupied the area and fortified it over the last thirty years. The pilot Pedro Díaz Franco,[28] sailing out of Havana, took notice of the same situation and communicated it. On two trips, at that latitude of 35½ degrees, where the dumps of English barrels were seen, he saw evidence of English settlement, and he counted a population of some three hundred men and some twenty women.

He was asked why he had not seen the village because he had been with his ships in that area of the English remains before, and he concluded that it could not be seen because it was ten leagues upriver from the mouth of the bay—as well as because of the fact that the English had tried to conceal the settlement until they could penetrate the area further for purposes of discovering good land for colonization and fortification. David Glavid[29] said the

---

24 Present-day Cumberland Island in Georgia where a mission dedicated to evangelizing the Timucuan ethnic group was established. The natives called it Tacatacoru.

25 From the province of Burgos in Spain. He arrived in La Florida around 1587 and devoted himself to evangelizing the Timucuans, whose language he came to know. He spent almost the entirety of his stay in La Florida among the Timucuans. He built a church in the mission that was consecrated in 1603, in the presence of Governor Méndez de Canzo (Geiger 1940, 68). He also wrote to the sovereign relaying the state of the missions in the area. See López 1931, and AGI, Santo Domingo 25, "El Comisario . . . ;" 1 folio, 15 May 1616).

26 Apparently Oré took advantage of the official report by Juan Menéndez Marqués to account for that territory whose retrieval he saw as fundamental for Spain's project of colonization.

27 Meaning the English.

28 A pilot captured by the English commanded by Sir Richard Grenville (1542–1591), known as Richarte Campoverde, en route to Spain and later taken to Roanoke (Geiger 1936, 61n47).

29 An Irishman captured in 1584 by the English led by Sir Richard Grenville; he was brought to Jacán and from there went on to England with Francis Drake. He returned to Roanoke, but since the English made the return voyage through Puerto Rico, he was able to escape. He served as a soldier in San Agustín from 1595 to 1600 (Geiger 1936, 62n49).

same thing. He had been brought to the presidio of San Agustín from Havana, where he had been taken as a galley slave by the English. And Glavid revealed more: he said that when the English had gone up river many leagues, they had found a great deal of gold dust. David Glavid, who provided this information, was an Irishman.

Having received this account of the voyage of the captain and sergeant major Vicente González, as well as the version from the pilot Pedro Díaz Franco, General Pedro Menéndez resolved to go back to Castile. He left in his place captain Juan de Posadas, his brother-in-law, and he took with him Sergeant Major Juan Menéndez, his first cousin. But at sea he encountered rough weather, which blew him within sight of Bermuda, Puerto Rico, and Santo Domingo; without being able to touch in at any of those ports, he finally arrived to La Yeguana[30] in dire necessity. But wanting to continue on and enter the ocean at Cape San Nicolás,[31] he found little breeze, so he was forced to double back by Point Maisí[32] and then by the old channel[33] to Havana. From there he returned to San Agustín, where he set out again for Castile on 18 May 1589.

He arrived at the port of Sanlúcar on 5 July of that same year; in his company were Father Friar Alonso de Reinoso and the sergeant major. He traveled to the court and informed His Majesty of their discoveries. It was understood that he would return to Havana with four supply ships with loads of infantry, provisions, stores, and munitions. From there he would take the galleys and frigates that he judged to be necessary to go to San Agustín and draw from there the experienced soldiers that he needed, leaving behind raw recruits. The ships were to proceed to the area in question at 35½ degrees. Because the entrance to the bay was shallow, they were to enter with the frigates and galleys, and send the supply ships to the bay. Then they should destroy the enemy and return to the bay to join up with the supply ships. And after reconnoitering the land, they were to erect a fort in the most suitable area and provision it in the best possible way, with three hundred infantrymen. At a propitious moment the governor of the fort or his lieutenant was ordered to set out and

---

30 Better known as La Yaguana, a port in Hispaniola, southwest of Port-au-Prince, present-day capital of Haiti, where the city of Léogâne is located today.
31 In northwest of modern Haiti.
32 The easternmost point in Cuba.
33 Maritime passage that permits navigation across the Greater Antilles; it is a strait off the northern coast of Cuba and the Sabana-Camagüey Archipelago and south of the Great Bahama Bank. It is approximately one hundred miles (161 km) long and fifteen miles (24 km) wide. It was considered very dangerous as sea captains had to find their way among low-lying keys and shoals of the southern Bahamas. It was used before and after the Bahama Channel became popular. Our thanks to Eugene Lyon for this clarification.

gather information about the disposition of the land, seize an interpreter, and through him learn if there were [gold or silver] mines.

But this resolution was never realized because another decree was issued. Instead General Pedro Menéndez was ordered to go to Tierra Firme [probably Panama] with two vessels[34] to escort to Castile the silver, gold, and pearls belonging to His Majesty—which he did. He left the bay of Cádiz on 16 May 1590; he returned with the treasure, entering the port of Viana de Camiña[35] on 4 September of that same year. Sergeant Major Juan Menéndez carried the news of its arrival to His Majesty, of glorious memory, at El Escorial, while the treasure was taken to the mint at Segovia.

In 1591 General Pedro Menéndez was placed in charge of the fleet of frigates belonging to the Carrera de Indias, and with transporting all the silver from Tierra Firme and New Spain. Having gone to Nombre de Dios,[36] he returned to Sanlúcar de Barrameda in January of 1592. The following year, 1593, His Majesty was informed of an insurrection in the presidio of San Agustín; the soldiers refused to obey the governor Gutierre de Miranda, who had been ordered to his post by the king, in the absence of General Pedro Menéndez. Also Rodrigo de Junco, who had come to govern at the orders of His Majesty, had drowned at the bar of San Mateo; and Captain Juan de Posadas, who had come to replace the treasurer Juan de Cebadilla who had died, had also drowned. When His Majesty received this information, he ordered General Pedro Menéndez to go to San Agustín to put down the rebellion. But while he was being dispatched, he was taken sick and he requested a replacement. Thus Captain Domingo Martínez de Avendaño[37] was appointed governor and captain general of La Florida; Sergeant Major Juan Menéndez, treasurer; and Bartolomé de Argüelles, accountant.

The Indian who had been captured on the eastern side of the bay died of apoplectic rage at the port of San Pedro. The one who had been abducted previously went to Castile; the general [Pedro Menéndez de Avilés] took him with him, but on the return voyage the Indian died in Viana, ill from smallpox but already Christianized. So they buried him in the convent of Santo Domingo.

---

34 In Spanish *galizabras*, vessels of lateen sail of about one hundred tons, common in Mediterranean navigation (*DLE*).

35 Ports of Portugal, probably Viana do Castelo; at the time both crowns (Spain and Portugal) were joined. They were ruled by the Hapsburg dynasty (Philip II [Philip I of Portugal], Philip III [Philip II of Portugal] and Philip IV [Philip III of Portugal]) from 1580 to 1640.

36 Port on the Isthmus of Panamá, not the mission by the same name in La Florida.

37 Governor of La Florida, 1594–1595.

He was a *ladino*, meaning that he spoke both his native tongue and Spanish. He talked a lot about the bounty and potential for development of his homeland, and about its gold that in his language was called *tapisco*.[38]

Some years later, around June of 1609, Governor Pedro de Ibarra[39] sent Captain Francisco Fernández de Ecija in a small vessel with infantry, some seamen, and an experienced pilot from La Florida named Andrés González, to reconnoiter the English[40] settlement, supposedly located on the bay with extensive fortifications and many soldiers and colonizers. This expedition entered the mouth of the bay. But when they sighted a large ship within the bay at one of the anchorages afforded by the islands, they turned around without accomplishing their mission and returned to San Agustín with this report.[41]

In June of 1611, don Diego Molina, together with his ensign named Marco Antonio and an English pilot, entered the bay with their caravel, passing by the presidio [of Roanoke]. The three had no sooner gone on shore when the English seized them. They said that an English pilot had been sent with the idea of introducing the caravel into the bay, which they had understood was the first good landing site in the bay. However, the Portuguese mariners who remained in the caravel seized the ship, apprehended its English pilot, and immediately sailed off to Havana, leaving the three behind. The English settlement was so heavily fortified and populated that it would have required a great force of arms to destroy or dismantle it.

According to the opinion of someone who has personally seen the bay that we have here described, it would be necessary to enter it with three sturdy galleons and a patache, two galleys, and two long boats constructed with care and light in structure so as to be able to come and go easily within the various parts of the bay. All these crafts should be well provisioned with artillery, arms, and munitions, with up to one thousand soldiers, artillerymen, the necessary seamen, and an engineer. The men need to have body armor, made of heavy sailcloth and cotton—well stitched—to deflect arrows. With all this cautionary preparation it will be possible to accomplish with some certainty the reconnaissance of the fortification, civilian population, and military force of the enemy. Then, with the galleons and galleys it will

---

38 Algonquian word; Geiger assigns its root to mean "metal" (1936, 63n69).
39 Governor of La Florida: 1603–1610.
40 Present-day Virginia; the pilot Andrés González traced the course of the journey. http://www.armada.mde.es/html/historiaarmada/tomo3/tomo_03_23.pdf.
41 According to Ecija's report, the voyage lasted from 21 June to 24 September 1609. By then the English had been settled in Jamestown for two years (Geiger 1936, 63n61).

be possible to interfere with the enemy's commerce and trade with England. By land, since there are many sites where we can construct forts, it will be possible by means of ambushes and skirmishes to harass the enemy and diminish its strength. All this will assure stopping that thieving power's reach at that site, as well as at another site at latitude 33 degrees where they are erecting fortifications on the island of Bermuda.[42]

Arriving from England as if they were coming to secure coasts, without anybody offering any resistance or interference with their designs, the enemies' ships sail from these two ports of the Jacán and Bermuda. They then run along the coasts of the islands of Cuba, Puerto Rico, Jamaica, and Santo Domingo and rob what they can without anybody punishing them because, with their booty of cowhides, wine, and whatever else they can lay their hands on, they quickly seek escape in the Bahama channel in whose navigation their pilots are as familiar as those who have made ten or twelve trips to the Indies. They then return to these two safe havens, which are really like animal lairs,[43] and from there return to England wealthy as a result of what they have been able to pillage. These robbers are rich as a result of what they have been able to pillage but they leave behind poor merchants whose goods (hides, wine) and money they have taken. Their activity ruins the womenfolk[44] who have waited for monies from the legitimate sale of the hides. But most of all, the English shamefully damage the reputation of the Spaniards who have kept silent, suffering over so many years the attacks of these corsairs. They have entered areas with no defenses, to take whatever they could, trading solely by the force of men and arms. All this means that without a fleet and superior galleons it is not possible for Spanish frigates and ocean-going ships to sail securely for fear of marauders. Only in the wintertime, when weather restricts the English to their two hideouts, do the Spaniards feel free of these thieves and dare to run the risk of setting out in their ships.

---

42 Oré is conscious of the harm the English can cause to Spanish vessels from these two locations: Chesapeake Bay and Bermuda.

43 In Spanish, *guaridas*, refuges; but in Spanish also a place where animals hide (*DLE*). Oré here criticizes the Crown for allowing these territories to become a safe haven for the enemy—and the English, whom he apparently equates to animals.

44 In Spanish " . . . sin remedio a algunas doncellas que le esperaban, de la venta de los cueros" could also allude to the inability of women to marry because they lacked monies for their dowry, as "remediar" is to bring a woman to matrimony (*DA* 1990 [1726–1737] 3, 564). Since according to the Church, matrimony was the ideal state for a woman, if understood as noted, Oré would be indicating that the actions of the English have an impact on the economic as well as in religious life of the Spanish La Florida.

CHAPTER SEVEN

Account of the Death of Five Martyrs and of a Confessor—All Religious of the Order of Our Father Saint Francis in La Florida

IN 1595, AT THE COMMAND OF HIS MAJESTY KING PHILIP II, OF glorious memory, at the request of Captain Domingo Martínez de Avendaño, Father Friar Francisco de Arzubiaga, commissioner general of the Indies of the Franciscan Order, sent twelve religious to proceed with the conversion of the Indians in La Florida by teaching them the doctrine of the Christian faith—which had already begun, as has been said previously. The men, all chosen from the province of Castile, set sail from Spain on 14 July, the day of the glorious doctor San Buenaventura.[1] Father Friar Juan de Silva,[2] preacher and a very religious and prudent man, was named superior and commissioner. His companions were the following:

[1] **Father Friar Blas de Montes,**[3] priest and confessor, was a very spiritual religious, given to incredible feats of penance. He fasted during all the

---

1 Cardinal General of the Franciscan Order, also known as Seraphic Doctor. With the reform of the liturgical calendar by Paul VI his feast day became 15 July.
2 With a group of twelve Franciscans, Silva departed from Sanlúcar de Barrameda, Spain, on 14 July 1595 (Geiger 1940, 108).
3 A native of Albacete, he belonged to the Franciscan province of Castile; he arrived in San Agustín on 23 September 1595, after a layover in Havana. From San Agustín he tended to the spiritual necessities of the local natives. When the Guale rebellion broke out in 1597, he accompanied governor Canzo and collected the personal items belonging to the murdered Franciscans. On the long journey from San Agustín to the north of Georgia, he grew ill. A deed from 1 July 1598 authorized his return to Spain due to the fragility of his health. Nonetheless, in 1602 he continued as custodian of the Floridian friars (Geiger 1940, 77). The father-commissioner could accompany the friars to America, or take them to the departure port. The names of the Franciscans are indicated in bold script and numbered, enclosed in brackets.

days[4] related to the day of our Father San Francisco, as well as the three days of Lent and every Saturday throughout the year, when he only took bread and water. During the vigils of Our Lady and those of other saints of his devotion, he fasted without eating a bite (not even bread, or fruit or anything else) and only drank water when thirst overwhelmed him. He fasted during all of Holy Week, apart from only three small breaks. On Sunday and Holy Tuesday he took bread and water; on Holy Thursday he ate whatever the community gave him. He never had his own cell or bed; instead he lived in the choir. After ordination, the only clothing he wore was his habit, without a tunic, and a hair shirt underneath. Whenever he went on a journey, as he left town, he took off his sandals and put them in his sleeve, even though the roads were covered with snow a half-yard deep. This happened many times because, since he was such an exemplary religious, he was frequently sent out to help the needy. He was of good build and enjoyed even better health and fitness. He radiated a spiritual happiness that consoled people around him; everyone loved him. In La Florida he endured many corporal and spiritual difficulties caused by a certain person who, because of the advice he gave that person in his confessions as he tried to thwart the man's dishonest designs, the person sought revenge by bringing ridiculous testimony against him. As a result he fell ill. Knowing of his need and familiar with the priest and his saintliness, the Duchess of the Infantado[5] wrote to him to return to Spain. She secured an order from His Majesty and a release from his prelate so that he could return to Albacete, his place of birth, and see if there his long illness would find some relief. But there the saintly man died, and was buried in the church where he had been baptized. His tomb is now an object of veneration.

[2] **Father Friar Pedro Bermejo,**[6] priest and confessor, was a native of the village of Tendilla, a religious who was very well thought of for his

---

4 Liturgical period in which they prepared to celebrate Saint Francis's feast day, 4 October. There is a secondary feast day commemorating the day Francis received the stigmata on 17 September.
5 Reference to Ana de Mendoza y Henríquez de Cabrera (1554–1633), the sixth duchess of the Infantado from 1601 to 1633. She belonged to the Castilian aristocratic family of the House of Mendoza (http://www.cyclopaedia.es/wiki/Ana-de-Mendoza-y-Enriquez-de-Cabrera, accessed 26 July 2015).
6 He was born in about 1553 and belonged to the province of Castile. He occupied several posts in Franciscan convents in La Florida: in 1602, confessor in Nombre de Dios; in 1605, guardian in San Agustín and custodian of Santa Elena; in 1609, guardian in Moloa; between 1609 and 1612, definidor (member of the definitorio or governing body of the order); and in 1616, guardian in Bayamo (Cuba) (Geiger 1940, 34).

saintliness and fervent expressions of charity for the sick. As a result they made him a caregiver in Guadalajara. He fasted throughout the year, and on many days only took bread and water. He was very observant of the rules of the order, particularly of holy poverty. This I personally observed when I visited the convent in Bayamo[7] where I found him to be the guardian of that house. There he only used a few things that were absolutely necessary, and everyone agreed he was a saintly and apostolic man. He has always been drawn to and practiced in mental prayer.[8] He has been of great benefit to the Indians of La Florida. Because of his doctrinal teaching, but more because of his exemplary life,[9] he has brought many of the unfaithful to knowledge of the true God.

[3] **Father Friar Miguel de Auñón**,[10] preacher from the province of Castile, was a native of Zaragoza. He was of noble birth and his ancestral home was known by all. He had a great spirit, and a grace about him, particularly in the use of his voice. He was beloved by everyone who knew him. He had strength and a natural gift for dealing with people so that his will prevailed over others—whether religious or secular. The Indians loved him very much, as will be seen later when his martyrdom is told. The convent of the city of Havana called for him to preach there, so he set sail. Normally the trip there is short taking only six to seven days, as I know since I made it twice. But he tried for forty days and could not even go around the cape they call Canaveral, which in itself only takes two or three days. Seeing this, his ship returned and the preacher said, "God did not send me to the city of Havana but to this land to teach doctrine to the Indians. So I intend to remain here until I die because here I will receive God's favor. I do not think it was by chance that I did not succeed in my voyage." Thus he prepared himself to go and work with the Indians.

---

7 Village on the eastern side of Cuba. A change of narrative voice to the first-person singular is noted; it will appear in other chapters of the *Account*.

8 The Franciscans practiced it methodically from the sixteenth century.

9 It is important to underscore Oré's concern for the good conduct of the missionaries, as key to converting the native population.

10 Another member of the Castilian province who sailed on 14 July 1595 and arrived in San Agustín on 23 September 1595 (Geiger 1940, 28). He began his ministry on the island of Guale (Saint Catherine, Georgia). When, in 1597, a portion of the Guale natives rebelled, Father Auñón and Brother Antonio de Badajoz were murdered.

[4] **Father Friar Pedro Fernández de Chozas,**[11] preacher from the province of Castile, was a religious of great soul and energy in his labors with the Indians. The whole time that he was with them, he taught through his preaching. He concerned himself with the Indians' spiritual needs as well as with organizing their lives with plans for them to raise cattle and to cultivate the soil. He also taught them the art of singing, for which he was much esteemed. Considering all this, he made an attempt to go inland, to the peoples of the province of Latama,[12] where he was also very well received. When he returned from that assignment, he was sent to Spain with the news that the religious had suffered martyrdom. Since then he has served honorably as *custodio* or provincial representative for Castile, and he took this title with him when he went to Rome in 1612. He returned as commissioner general of Jerusalem, charged with soliciting bequests for the Holy House there. Later he was guardian in Madrid.

[5] **Father Friar Pedro de San Gregorio**[13] was a saintly religious who was what we would call a *recoleto* [recollect].[14] He came from the retreat house and holy convent of Castañar in the province of Castile. He was a man of great devotion and mortification in his appearance as well as in his inner life. He was a native of the town that they call part of the House of Uceda. He took sick in Puerto Rico as he was traveling with his companions, and he stayed on the island to recuperate. When then he could not find passage to La Florida, he returned to Spain.

[6] **Father Friar Pedro de Auñón**[15] was a preacher and a native of the village of Auñón in the province of Castile. He grew ill in Sanlúcar and

---

11 He was assigned to San Pedro (Cumberland Island, Georgia), where, among other things, he trained the Indian flock in singing. Along with Father Veráscola, he went on an expedition to the area of La Tama or Latama. Upon his return to San Pedro, specifically the northern portion of Puturiba, he received news of the Guale rebellion and there found several of the rebels, including Asao's chieftain, who continued on northward. By Father Chozas's agency, Governor Méndez de Canzo learned of the rebellion. Soon after, he was sent to Spain and later to Rome (1612), where the General Chapter of the Order voted in favor of placing the Custody of Santa Elena under Franciscan jurisdiction. In Madrid he occupied the post of guardian and commissioner for Jerusalem. He never returned to La Florida (Geiger 1940, 52).

12 Area in the northern center of Georgia called La Tama or Latama by the Spanish. Its inhabitants did not belong to the Guale group and spoke a dialect of Hitchiti, from the Mosqueguanan linguistic family. The governor Gonzalo Méndez de Canzo and the Franciscan superior Father Friar Francisco Marrón authorized this trip (see Geiger 1936, 80n17).

13 Another of the friars who departed from Sanlúcar de Barrameda with Father Silva.

14 A strict observant of the Franciscan rule who lives a secluded, meditative life.

15 Another member of the Franciscan province of Castile, native of Auñón in Guadalajara.

thus remained in Spain to his own great sorrow and that of his companions.

[7] **Father Friar Francisco Pareja**[16] was of the same province in Castile, also a native of Auñón. He was a man of great saintliness and incredibly devoted to saving souls, which is attested to by the works he composed and printed in the Indian language—a feat in which he surpassed all his brother friars. At first the Indians inflicted on him many offenses, but he answered them with a great deal of patience and persevering in remaining among the natives. He tended to their needs, teaching them the law of Christ and defending them from the insults and attacks of the Spanish soldiers. By this means and the good example he always set, he overcame the cruelty and harshness of the Indians, and turned them from wolves into lambs. Thus because of the virtue that shone in him, he was given the positions of guardian, *definidor*[17] or internal judge, and custodio. In the visitation I made to celebrate the first provincial chapter of this province, I found him to be a saintly man and worthy of his election[18] to be provincial and exercise, as he does at present, the office with sanctity and integrity despite his advanced age in traveling along the roads of La Florida.

[8] **Father Friar Pedro Ruiz,**[19] priest and confessor, was a religious person who has always set a good example for Indians and Spaniards, and on account of this he has been assigned to different posts as guardian, custodio, and commissioner of this custody [Santa Elena] before it was elevated into a province. Because of the great satisfaction [in discharging his duties] that he gave, the prelates of Spain gave him the title of father of this province; in this first provincial chapter whose founding

16 A native of Auñón, Father Pareja was assigned to the mission of San Juan del Puerto, founded in 1587 on Fort George Island, at the mouth of Saint Johns River (the coastal area of Jacksonville, Florida). Besides San Pedro, Cumberland Island, Santa María de Sena, on the island of Amelia, San Juan was part of the Mocama province. Father Pareja devoted himself to studying the Timucuan language, spoken by the Saturiwa people, one of the Mocama chiefdoms. *Cathecismo en lengua castellana y timucuana,* published in Mexico (1612), was a product of these efforts. He was elected provincial of Santa Elena when the chapter gathered (1616) in San Buenaventura de Guadalquini, as told at the end of this report.

17 Each one of the clerics, who with the superior authority forms the *definitorio* or governing body of the religious community. The gravest cases are reviewed and resolved by this group (*DLE*).

18 It took place in 1616, during Oré's second visit to La Florida. He met with the Franciscans of La Florida in San Agustín shortly after his arrival in 1614.

19 In 1602 he was in the mission of San Sebastián and Tocoy in La Florida; afterward he went to the mission of Santa Catalina (Guale Island, Georgia). He returned to Spain by 1610 and enlisted missionaries for La Florida, to which he returned to occupy other posts within the Franciscan Order (Geiger 1940, 100–101).

we are celebrating now, he was also named guardian of the convent of
Havana. He was from the province of Castile, native of the village of
Valdesoto, in the jurisdiction of the village of Uceda.

[9] **Father Friar Francisco de Ávila**[20] was a young priest from the province of Castile, native to the city of Toledo. He was a man of great
energy and capable of enduring great suffering, as we will see when we
deal with his captivity among the Indians.

[10] **Father Friar [Francisco de] Veráscola**[21] was a priest from the province
of Cantabria, a Basque from Vizcaya. He was a religious endowed with
a great capacity for kindness and simplicity; he inflicted on his body
many penances, which we will see later.

[11] **Father Friar Pedro de Viniegra**[22] was a lay brother from the province of Castile. He was very humble and inclined toward prayer without ever being remiss in fulfilling his spiritual and community
exercises. He was so interested in learning the Indians' language that
he understood it and acquired the use of it so well that he preached
with all the zeal and spirit of an apostle. He was a great believer in
holy poverty and fulfilled that vow with such perfection that he only
wore a poor habit without even a tunic underneath. Seeing his
humility and his gift for languages, and the grace and energy of his
preaching to the Indians, and that it was a shame that he was not a
priest so as to confess them and say mass (even though he had all
the attributes to be a priest and administer the other sacraments),
at the request of the fathers of this custodia the father commissioner
in New Spain issued a patent to ordain him. In this way he became

20 He catechized in various missions in modern-day Georgia (Tulafina, Ospo). As a consequence of
the Guale rebellion (1597), the natives tried to assassinate him, but the friar escaped. He was found and
captured by the Indians and he endured captivity for ten months, until his liberation in 1598. He left a
narration of this portion of his life in a now lost account, which was preserved in the Franciscan archives
of Havana where Oré read it and used it in his *Relación* (chapter 8). It must be noted that, as he was the
only Spanish survivor of the Guale rebellion, Governor Canzo encouraged him to relate the event;
however, Father Ávila made use of his cleric's immunity and refused to testify because he could cause
many deaths among the native populations (Geiger 1940, 29).
21 Francisco de Veráscola (we follow Geiger's spelling of his last name), because of his height and pro-
portions, was known as the "Giant of Cantabria" ["el gigante de Cantabria"]. He traveled to Florida in
1585 and was responsible for the mission of Santo Domingo de Asao in Georgia. Along with Father Friar
Pedro de Chozas he was exploring the interior of this territory when the Guale rebellion took place;
ignoring the circumstances, upon his return to the mission he was murdered by the natives (Geiger
1940, 114–15).
22 He was born around 1548 and arrived in La Florida with Father Silva, in 1595.

one of the best ministers to the Indians that have appeared in our times.[23]

[12] **Father Friar Francisco de Bonilla**[24] was a priest, a native of Talarrubias of the province of Castile. As soon as he arrived, they sent him with some messages to New Spain. He stayed there, distracted by events, until he came on here. By the time he entered our chapter, he was already advanced in years.

These religious were all received with great demonstrations of joy by the governor, by all the soldiers of the presidio, and by all the Indians. At that time the custodio and prelate of the religious was Father Friar Francisco Marrón,[25] a preacher already more than eighty years old. He died twenty-two years later [c. 1617] in this convent of Havana, and I personally buried him. When he was asked at the hour of his death how long he had worn the habit, he answered for more than eighty years and that he was over one hundred years old. He died like a Christian and a religious. He was one of the religious who gave accurate testimony of the martyrdom of the five religious whom the Indians killed. This testimony he gave compelled by obedience to Father Ávila, and it will be attached to this account, as God spared him to relate the martyrdom of his companions, telling the how, the when, and the cause of the killing.

There were seven[26] other religious of those who had come before with Father Friar Reinoso:[27]

23 After his ordination (c. 1608), he was assigned the mission of Nombre de Dios in La Florida; in 1609 he was vicar of the convent of San Antonio de Arapaha, and in 1610 guardian in San Juan del Puerto, La Florida (Geiger 1940, 116–17).

24 He arrived in La Florida in 1595 with Father Silva; from there he left for New Spain, returning in 1616 to participate in the chapter of Santa Elena province, which took place in San Buenaventura de Guadalquini, Georgia (Geiger 1940, 35).

25 Before arriving in La Florida, he was a missionary in Peru, Guatemala, and Mexico. Between 1594 and 1597 he was a priest vicar to the bishop of Cuba in San Agustín, Franciscan custodian, and guardian of the convent of San Agustín in 1597—the same year as the Guale rebellion in the Franciscan missions in today's state of Georgia (Geiger 1940, 71). He likely arrived in Florida in 1574, with the first Franciscan missionaries. Several of his letters, in which he describes the missionaries' situation, can be found in López 1931, *Relación histórica*, appendix 2, 5–10.

26 Oré gives the names of six.

27 They arrived in 1587. Alonso de Reinoso, from the Franciscan province of Santiago, brought missionaries to La Florida on three occasions: 1583 (eight Franciscans); 1586 (thirteen clerics, including Reinoso himself); 1589 (more than eight clerics). In spite of these efforts, in 1592 there were only five Franciscan missionaries. This has been attributed to Father Friar Reinoso's unruly personality as well as the hardship of the missionary lifestyle in La Florida. Traces of this Franciscan are lost in 1590, when he traveled to Yucatán (Geiger 1940, 92).

[1] **Father Friar Baltasar López**[28] was from the province of Burgos. He suffered a great deal among the Indians. He knew their language well. Three times the Indians condemned him to death but miraculously each time God delivered him. He lived on the island of San Pedro, which was the headquarters of the Timucua Indians whose territory is extensive. He had cared for their chief since the time when he was a child, and on that island almost everyone was a Christian.

[2] **Father Friar Pedro de Corpa**[29] was a priest and confessor from the province of Castile. He was stationed in the province of Guale and he knew that people's language well. He spent a lot of time with the Indians because, although the time had not yet arrived when they became proud of being Christians, with his good example and perseverance he was gradually pacifying them.

[3] **Father Friar Blas Rodríguez**[30] was a priest and confessor from the province of San Gabriel. He was a very good religious and well versed in the language of the Indians, which will be seen later.

[4] **Brother Friar Juan de San Nicolás**[31] was a lay brother from the province of Santiago. He was the hardest worker that was ever seen, even today in his old age and living in the convent in San Agustín. This man of great simplicity is very devoted to prayer. Everyone in the presidio was so impressed by his faith that they asked for his torn and worn-out undergarments as swaddling clothes in which to wrap their babies; they thought of them as holy relics. Everything that the brother learned as he was studying in the order he observes today as if he were still a novice. He is so oblivious of the things of this world that it seems as if he

28 He was one of the first Franciscan missionaries in La Florida. He arrived in 1587 with Father Friar Reinoso. Establishing the mission of San Pedro, on Cumberland Island, he catechized the Timucuans. During the Guale rebellion the Timucuans in San Pedro remained loyal to the missionaries, although Father López was not among them, but instead occupied in establishing another mission. He learned the Timucuan tongue very well and preached in it. In 1599 he went to New Spain due to illness; becoming sick yet again upon his return to La Florida, he then abandoned the mission of San Pedro to reside in San Agustín. In 1603 he was at his mission again and inaugurated a new church with the presence of Governor Méndez de Canzo (Geiger 1940, 68).

29 Another of the missionaries who arrived in the area in 1587 with Father Friar Alonso de Reinoso. He was in the mission of Tolomato (modern-day McIntosh County, close to Darien, Georgia) when the Guale rebellion started. He was murdered there by chieftain don Juan or Juanillo and his followers (Geiger 1940, 44).

30 Franciscan missionary who arrived with Father Friar Alonso de Reinoso in the 1580s and settled in the mission of Tupiqui, in the state of Georgia; after pronouncing mass, he was murdered on 16 September 1597 by cacique Don Juan or Juanillo and his followers during the Guale rebellion (Geiger 1940, 95).

31 He left Spain for Florida in 1584; San Nicolás was linked to the convent of San Agustín, where he labored as gardener and sacristan. He was still there when Oré returned to the area in 1616 (Geiger 1940, 105–6).

were not part of it. Two or three times the devil gave him a beating when he went out to trim the lamps; although his body suffered badly and he came out with his head broken open, with prayer he has defeated [the devil]. His spiritual exercise, after having worked since sunrise in the garden, and then fasting until sunset when he ate and carefully cleaned and trimmed the lamps, consisted of prayerfully watching over those who needed him among the living and the dead. He went among their graves praying and sprinkling holy water. He also performed a spiritual exercise by going through the streets with great devotion begging for bread. He never gave excuses for not performing this task; instead, obediently, he fulfilled it and any other tasks the guardian asked of him. In the practice of humility, he excelled to the extent that it seemed as though he were still a novice; in everything concerning virtue he was outstanding. He kept perpetual silence, but the few times he spoke his words were so edifying that they taught devotion to those who listened and conversed with him.

[5] **Brother Friar Antonio de Badajoz,**[32] a lay brother from the province of San Gabriel, knew well the language of the Indians of Guale, which we will tell about when we describe his death.

[6] **Father Friar Juan de Silva,**[33] together with all the other religious, prayed to God after having celebrated the feast of our father Saint Francis. They begged Our Lord to give each of them the fate he deemed more appropriate in order to secure the conversion of the souls they came to seek out from Spain so that he might be served.

Father Friar Francisco Marrón, guardian and custodio of the religious, gave to each one the place and district among whose peoples he was to work. The governor Juan Martínez de Avendaño[34] was also present. So the men divided up and set out from San Agustín, entering the ten villages where each had been assigned. They were separated from one another by three or four leagues. But some were further separated by many swamps and canebrakes that could not be traversed by land or by water. They attended to their

---

32 He arrived in Florida in the 1580s. He resided on the island of Guale with Father Auñón when the Guale rebellion broke out; although the Christianized and loyal Indians notified him on two occasions about the rebellion of cacique don Juan or Juanillo and his followers and of their intent to kill both him and Father Auñón, he paid no attention. Both were assassinated on 17 September 1597 (Geiger 1940, 30).
33 After gathering and bringing missionaries, he returned to Spain (Geiger 1940, 108).
34 His correct name is Domingo Martínez de Avendaño, governor of La Florida (1594–1595).

doctrinal teaching to the great advantage of the Indians, busying themselves with preaching, catechizing, baptizing, and administering the other sacraments.

Two years after their arrival in La Florida, in 1597, the Indians of Guale, at the instigation of the devil who subverts all good works, rose up in rebellion. This happened because a young Indian, a baptized Christian[35] who was heir to the chiefdom or *cacicazgo*, was told by the priest that he could not take a second wife. He was rebuked and told to live as a Christian and not as a heathen. A Christian could have only one wife—the one whom he had married.[36] So this cacique and two other Indians, who were deficient because, like their young lord, they were given to the same dishonest practice, without saying anything to anybody or seeking permission as they had always done, went inland among their fellow tribesmen. In a few days they came back at night, smeared with red paint[37] and with feathers in their hair (which in their culture is a sign of impending cruelties and killings).

The night they arrived neither the friar nor the village people realized the danger. In the morning when the friar opened his house, the renegade Indians went in. They found him in prayer. But without saying anything or waiting to listen to reason, they killed him, clubbing him to death with a stone axe they call *macana*[38] and in the language of the Incas from Cuzco is called *champi*.[39]

All this happened in Tolomato, headquarters for that area, and the religious who was killed was Father Friar Pedro de Corpa. When he was dead, they began to appropriate the women for themselves, using them for their detestable and dishonorable ends. They ordered that the head of the dead friar be placed on a pike set up at the landing place, and that two Indians take his body and hide it in the bushes so that the Christians could not find it. It has not appeared to this day.[40]

After that they sent word to the nearby island of Guale[41] that the cacique should order the killing of the two friars in his territory. But the native lord was very upset by the request and, rather than comply, with a heavy

---

35 Refers to don Juan or Juanillo, leader of the Guale rebellion.
36 For a review of the motivations behind the rebellion, see Francis and Kole 2011.
37 A type of red dye that, by mashing, is extracted from the seed of a small tree from the annatto family (*Bixa orellana*); it was used by the Indians to tint their bodies. Its use was associated with war.
38 Taíno word for designating a club like weapon made from hard wood edged with a sharp flint (*DLE*).
39 Quechua word; it refers to a palm-wood cane (*chonta*) topped with a copper or stone star that was used by the Incan armies (Tauro 2001, 4:592).
40 Friar Pedro de Corpa's corpse was never found.
41 Saint Catherine Island, in today's Georgia.

heart he warned the lay father [Friar Antonio de Badajoz], the interpreter, of what was happening. He advised him that he and the father commissioner [Miguel de Auñón] should go to the island of San Pedro.[42] He would give them a boat and people to transport them there, even at the risk of his own life.

But the lay friar did not believe him and refused to pass on the warning to the Father Commissioner Miguel de Auñón; the cacique did not say anything to him because he was ashamed and because he felt such affection for him. But again, on the second day, the cacique tried to warn the lay brother, but again he could not believe the Indian and responded in the same manner as the first time. On the third day the Indians of the conspiracy came to the cacique and told him that they had come for the purpose of ordering him to murder the friars. If he did not do it, they would have to kill him. The cacique said he would not do so, but if they would pretend to do it and let the friars go free, he would give them everything he had. However, the Indians were solidly in agreement that they had come to kill and they answered that were ready to carry out the deed.

The cacique then went to Father Friar Miguel and, in tears, told him what was happening and that he had been unable to convince the other Indians to let the Spaniards go free. He and his fellow Christians Indians were going to flee to the bushes and weep for the friars whom they considered their brothers. When Father Friar Miguel and his companion heard this, they knelt down to pray to prepare themselves for death. Friar Miguel said mass and then spent more than four hours in prayer. When the Indians arrived they sacked the house and gave the lay brother such a severe blow with a macana that he died. At first they did not dare to approach Father Miguel out of respect for his person until a heathen Indian came up and struck him with the macana, stunning him. When all the faithful in the village rallied to try to defend him, immediately another heathen Indian came from behind and hit him so hard that his brains spilled out. Within a few days this heathen Indian became so desperate that he hanged himself from an oak tree with the cord from his bow; and this seeming act of repentance impressed the villagers mightily. The Christians buried the body [of Father Friar Miguel de Auñón] at the foot of a very tall cross that the friar himself

42 Cumberland Island, in today's Georgia.

had erected; after six years[43] when the [Spaniards] went to look for his bones, they found they were still there as the [Christian natives] had said.

The renegade Indians then went to the town of Topiqui[44] that is near here, where Father Friar Blas Rodríguez was living and they told him, "We have come to kill you and you have no alternative but to die." Then the father begged them to first let him say mass and then they could do to him whatever they wanted. So he celebrated mass and the Christian women folk came crying, as well as a few men, to pray with him. Then he divided up with them the little he owned. Four hours after he had said mass, he then tried to reason with all his spiritual children (those whom he had baptized and taught the law of God). Seeing that they had rebelled against him, he said to them:

> My children, death does not bother me because the death of the body, even though you may not be the instrument of my death now, comes to everyone and each hour we should all await it. What bothers me is the harm which you are doing to yourselves and what the devil has been able to do to you by causing you to offend God, your Creator. It also weighs on me that you are so ungrateful for the work that I and the other friars have done to teach you the path to Heaven.

Then he said to them, now weeping copiously: "Look, children, you still have time if you want to abandon your evil intentions, because God Our Lord is merciful and He will forgive you."

But they did not take his advice and were not moved by his tears. Instead those sacrilegious Indians seized all the relics and ornaments of the church, as well as everything in the friar's cell. As a result of his requests, they held him for two more days so that he could prepare for death in the best way he knew how as a good religious and a Christian. When those days had passed, then they gave him a blow to the head with a stone axe, splitting his skull; and they threw his body to the birds because the Christian Indians did not dare to intervene and bury it. But the birds did not come on, and a dog that dared to touch it promptly died, events that everyone witnessed. Finally, an old Christian Indian stealthily took the body and

43 Both friars' remains were discovered weeks later, in November 1597 (Francis and Kole 2011, 52). However, Oré appears to refer to the year 1605, when the remains were transported by the Spaniards to San Agustín (see Geiger 1936, 85n49).
44 Three leagues north of Tolomato (Geiger 1936, 85n50).

buried it in the bushes. But since he is now dead, no one now knows where the bones are.

Father Ávila was at his mission[45] post when the renegade Indians came on to kill him. They arrived at night and since he had gone to bed, they knocked at the door pretending that they were bringing a letter from his prelate. He answered that they could give it to him in the morning because by that time he knew that they had killed Father Corpa and he was fearful. The Indians insisted that he open the door, and again he answered that he could not admit them until morning. They should go with God since he was already retired. Then the Indians violently tried to open the door, in which they succeeded. But the religious, seeing himself in danger, hid behind the door. Since there was no light, the Indians pushed in and sacked the few things that the poor man had. But in their greediness, they did not find the priest, who was able to flee and hide among the rushes. They searched carefully for him, however, and finally found him when the moon came out. They shot him with three arrows and left him for dead. One arrow pierced his right hand, another went through his shoulders, and a third through his thigh. Then an Indian approached him, pretending to act out of charity, and told him to take off his habit, saying, "Take off that habit which is soaked in blood and I will have it washed for you." So the Indian took it off, leaving the friar naked. But the Indian put it on himself.

However, this was to the friar's advantage because the Indian, who was a *caciquillo* [minor chieftain], diverted the others' attention and thus they did not kill him. He persuaded his fellow Indians to take him along with them— either to await a crueler death or to let him live, serving them in captivity, because, if he was left in the rushes, they figured he would die. They tied his arms and took him, under guard, to their heathen villages. It is incredible what this friar went through in the year he spent[46] as captive among those barbarians. Even in winter, which is as cold as Madrid, he was naked and had no one to cure his wounds, or cloths to bandage them. Instead God, miraculously and mercifully, restored his health.

After this the Indians determined to kill him by burning him. They tied him to a pillar that would serve as a torch, at the foot of which they heaped firewood that they collected for this occasion. When he was thus afflicted, an Indian woman came up to him who had a son who was being held as a

45 In Ospo, Jekyl Island, on the coast of modern-day Georgia.
46 In reality, ten months.

hostage by the soldiers in San Agustín; she had him removed from the pillar, saying, "I am claiming this man in place of my son because he will assure me of my son's freedom. If I free him the governor will not kill my son." So with this turn of events, he was spared and given a little more freedom. However, he was persecuted greatly by the children, who almost killed him or choked him because, when he taught them to read and to learn about Christian doctrine, he had sometimes whipped them. The Indians made him serve as a slave in the community house. He was hungry many times, but also it must be said that wherever he went somebody gave him something to eat because he asked for it for the love of God. They made him fetch firewood on his shoulders and stand guard over the fields when corn was planted so that the crows did not eat it first.

Although in this brief eulogy I have told of the death and martyrdom of four religious, as well as the great trials that Father Ávila suffered, it seemed to me appropriate to include here the account that he himself wrote in his own hand before he went back to Spain. The account stayed in the hands of Father Marrón until, at his death, it passed to the archive of the convent in Havana. In it, after having told briefly of the death of his companions, he went on to document his captivity, detailing minutely his own suffering. This account follows.[47]

---

47 The autobiographical version of Father Ávila has never been located. However, Oré reviewed it and offers the only available retelling.

CHAPTER EIGHT

An Account of the Great Suffering That Father Ávila Endured in the Year and a Half That He Was Held Prisoner by the Rebellious Indians, and the Death and Martyrdom of Father Veráscola, Who Was from Vizcaya in the Basque Provinces

[The following is testimony in the words of Father Ávila.][1]

RETURNING TO MY STORY OF HOW GOD FREED ME FROM INDIAN HANDS, I state that, although I hid among the reeds, they found me and shot me through with arrows. The Indians held me for an hour, leaving me with one of their guards during the time that it took them to sack and rob the church and our house. Then the same chief who had freed me came with three or four other Indians, and at that hour of the night they took me to their village, two leagues away, along a very rough road. But, since I was very badly wounded and I could only walk with difficulty, they urged me along, pretending that they were going to treat me kindly and cure me there. Finally, around twelve o'clock at night, they threw me on top of a pile of reeds and stationed guards around me in a small bohío until morning; I hardly made it through those hours.

When morning came, the chief returned and stripped me of my clothing so that only my underwear was left. He said that everything was bloody and he wanted to wash my clothes. In the meantime I was left with an old deerskin, which is how the Indians dress. In that manner I looked like an Indian on the outside, and thus I was an object of ridicule, so everyone laughed. The chief gathered all the children and women and said: "Come kiss our father's hand,

---

1 Father Ávila later indicates he was captive for a period of ten months.

receive a blessing." And because we had taught them this custom as a sign of good upbringing and education, the chief commanded that this gesture be used as a way to ridicule me. When the Indians had entertained themselves by making fun of me, the chief had my hands tied with a rope. I was then taken to Tulufina,[2] which had been my first posting; it was six leagues away through swamps and mud up to our waists, which bogged us down.

The Indians did even more. They reminded me that I had said that the land of Tulufina was evil and that the Indians there were also very bad. "As a result," the chief said, "I want you to go there and they will treat you as you deserve." And so they took me there, without any pity for my wounds, displaying great cruelty. Because the trails were so bad at each step I got stuck in the mud and fell. They were so happy at my distress that they could not hide it, making fun of me with hand motions and showing their teeth, and tormenting me with slaps on the neck. If God had not given me the strength and relief to endure, the road would have killed me because I was so sick and in pain. But Our Lord, who wanted to free me from their grasp, gave me the strength to bear it. We arrived about four in the afternoon at a large village that was called Ufalage,[3] along the road to Tulufina. There many men and women came out to meet me; all were covered with bixa dye, making merry and ridiculing me. In this way they took me to their camp and made me sit on the ground with everyone around, laughing and taunting me. I was tired and I had not eaten, so I wanted to stay there that night. But they refused and they took me that same night to Tulufina because they said that there the Indians were waiting for me. That village was two leagues distant, along a worse road than the last one. In many spots the water reached our waists, but despite all this God gave me strength, so before night fell we reached Tulufina. A little bit before we arrived, there were so many Indians who had set out to intercept us, their bodies covered with bixa dye, and their faces all covered with red paint,[4] that they resembled innumerable devils.

These Indians also tormented me by making fun of me, and when I got to the door of their bohío, I found a big pile of dry palm branches, which they said was to kill me by burning me up. When I entered I saw they had erected a tall cross and at one side a whip, which was a green stick of many branches

2 Or Tolofian, a town in the province of Guale—an area called Ybaha by the natives—that encompassed the coast of present-day Georgia, from the Savannah River to Saint Andrews Bay.
3 Ufalague, whose chieftain was one of the allies of don Domingo against don Juan and don Francisco, the instigators of the rebellion against the Franciscans (Francis and Kole 2011, 57).
4 Dye from the fleshy fruit of the bixa tree.

that they customarily use so that the first lash draws blood. On the other side of the cross were a tarred club and a pine branch with the skin of the head of an animal. They had me sit at the foot of the cross and they tied my hands, although my arm was swollen from arrow penetrations on the hand and shoulder. Then they tied me by the neck to the cross so tightly that I almost choked. When this was accomplished, an Indian who was the leader in the hut said to me: "Do you understand what this is? This cross is your invention, and we are going to hang you on it. The tar club will be tied to your body and burn you. The whip is to scourge you, and the animal skin here is a sign that you are to die. Tomorrow all this will be done, as I have said."

Then an Indian emerged with a chasuble,[5] imitating mockingly how we say mass. Another came out and put a book in front of me. When I did not look at it, a bigger chief appeared and struck me in the face and on the head with it with such a blow that it left me senseless. I was naked because they had even stripped me of the animal skin I had had; and then another Indian came with a cord such as those that we religious tie around our waists, knotted and doubled, and hit me with it three or four times so hard that it seemed he had left me for dead. With all of this a chief came, bringing a hot coal, and applied it to my back. Because I was bound, I could not shake it off easily, so it burned and I felt great pain. Then the Indians began to dance around me; and whenever they felt like it, they hit me with a macana. In this way they danced for three hours, performing other devilments.

When they finally got tired of dancing, they sat down; and since there was a moment of silence, I begged them to help me for the love of God and release my arms a little because they were so swollen. Even though they were going to kill me, at least they could afford me this act of pity. But they did not do what I begged them to do. However, then they began to talk among themselves of showing a little leniency with me, recalling that in San Agustín there was a boy, the son of their chieftain,[6] and that perhaps if they did not kill me at some time in the future they could trade him for me.[7] Others said that persons who came into that bohío should not die; and still others that the daughter of the sun, who was a witch that they all recognized, had appeared to them and told them not to kill me.

5 Vestment that, in order to say mass, the priest wears over another robe.
6 The heir to the chiefdom of Tulufina?
7 This is was actually happened later: Governor Méndez de Canzo traded some captives for the Franciscan.

Finally, with all these demurrals, they agreed to let me live. One of their leaders got up and asked me, "Do you want me to untie you? Do you want to live or die? We leave it in your hands whether you survive; but I warn you that if we do not kill you, you must stay here with us, serving us by bringing us water and firewood, by digging at planting time, and by responding to whatever request we make of you." When the cacique had said this to me, I was half-dead and I answered: "Do with me whatever you wish. My body is in your hands. But if you do not kill me, when I am better I will do what you want because now I can scarcely move." This seemed all right with him and so he talked more calmly and then proceeded to untie me. They made me sit on the ground, propped against a bench. They gave me two ears of cooked corn to eat. But I was in such a state that even if it were good substantial food, I could not eat it. Nevertheless, so as to make believe that I was obeying them, I pretended to eat. I begged them to lend me a large reed mat on which to lie down and they obliged. They assigned me an Indian to help if I needed anything. But, how could I sleep on those knotty cane stakes when I was naked and wounded and had been so badly treated? I only answer that if God had not given me the strength, it would have been impossible for me to continue living. I stayed in the hut for ten days with the Indians dancing until midnight, without them attending to my wounds. But God, who is merciful, then brought about that in a short period of time and, without any apparent treatment, I got better.

There was a little good fortune when they allowed me to walk from one dwelling to another, although I always went naked even in the greatest winter cold. I was the source of entertainment at any gathering because, whenever there was a celebration, they sent for me and gave me denigrating names so as to enliven the party. They prided themselves on not having killed me so as to have a focus for their laughter and scorn. They made me dig and watch over the cultivated fields so that birds did not eat the corn. They all had control over me. Whoever wanted to could hit me, especially the young boys who pursued me like crazy, hitting me with sticks or with whatever they could find. I suffered much hunger and need because the Indians themselves did not have enough to eat. If they had anything, first of all they attended to their own needs rather than to mine. Many times I was forced to satisfy my hunger and needs with leaves of wild grape and sorrel because in this land, unfortunately, there are no better fruits.

They tried—and even forcibly tried—to make me break my vows and come over to their side by taking an Indian wife according to their ways.

I resisted this with great spirit, frustrating the Indians so much that they marveled at my force of will and the liberty with which I spoke to them and contradicted them. After that they tried to make me clean the house of the devil, as we call it, and they call a burial place. There they place food and drink for the dead, which in the morning they find gone and believe the dead have eaten. However, in this they have been persuaded that the dead do not eat the food but rather their witch doctors do, as we have taught them; indeed their own witch doctors have confessed to this, and thus we have made good Christians of them. I said that although they might carve me up in a thousand pieces, I was not going to enter that house except to burn it up. Thus, seeing me so resolute, they left me alone. However, when things were at that point, the Indians decided to give me the ultimate test by taking away my rosary *corona*,[8] and saying to me:

> You are not going to see any more Spaniards, nor they you. Abandon your vows and start being an Indian. Thus you will enjoy what we enjoy. You will have a wife, or more than one if you wish. You will have in the afterlife what you have in this life because we know that he who has been miserable by being reduced to nothing in this life, will be that way in the next. He who has many wives in this life will have the same number then. And so, believe us and stop thinking about the things you have taught us, for they are all lies. Here we bring you this young and beautiful Indian girl. Marry her; she will delight you and you will have a good life.

As they were saying this, the Indian girl brought dried palm branches [*guano*] from the bushes, which are like straw, and made a bed and called out that it was time to eat. When I saw that, I perceived the devil's hand persecuting me; he did not miss an opportunity to tempt me and take away any feelings of consolation I had. I turned to God on that occasion, weeping and asking him for the grace to resist such a diabolical temptation. In answer, God gave me so many arguments and provided me with such spirit that by

8 Reference to the Franciscan Crown Rosary consisting of seven decades with each decade describing a particular joy from the life of the Virgin Mary, a Marian devotion developed within the Order and established formally in 1422. The seven joys are (1) the Annunciation, (2) the Visitation, (3) the Birth of Jesus Christ, (4) the Adoration of the Magi, (5) the Finding of the Child Jesus in the Temple, (6) the Appearance of Christ to Mary after the Resurrection, (7) the Assumption and Coronation of Mary as Queen of Heaven.

means of them I convinced the Indians. Yet to assure myself that I was free of this temptation, I fled to the bushes where for four days I subsisted on roots and herbs. I did not return to that village but instead went to another, and from then on nobody bothered me with such talk. One day, when I had nothing to do, I went out to a flat grassland where some Indians were digging. However, the devil decided to come into their hearts, and six of them took some thick poles and hit me with them so badly that they left me for dead. In this way my old wounds returned and new ones were added. But, praise God, within a short time without any apparent treatment, they healed. I was ten months in captivity there, during which time Our Lord kept me free of worse dangers and gave me the health and fortitude that I needed—I have not enjoyed such bounties since then.

[Here the narrator, Father Oré, interrupts to provide additional information]:

On one occasion in which they attempted an attack on enemy tribes, they said to Father Ávila, "See, here we have ten arquebuses, but without gunpowder and without bullets. Make powder and bullets for us or we will have to kill you." Father Ávila excused himself by saying he did not know how to do that. But the Indians replied, "Yes, you do because your books talk and tell you how to do it." He then answered, "I do not have any books because you have taken them." They said, "We will bring them to you." They then brought him a *Suma*,[9] a book of prayers for the religious, some books of a religious nature by Friar Luis de Granada,[10] and a breviary.[11] All these were of great consolation to him in his solitude. So he hid them in a hollow of an oak tree, where he went to read them for spiritual comfort. However, he always carried the breviary with him in public, but the children tore it apart. When the Indians persisted in asking him for gunpowder and bullets, he asked them for materials he knew were not available in that land. Thus the Indians concluded that he did not oblige because he did not want to but because the materials were lacking. So they left him in peace for a while.[12]

---

9 Compendium of philosophy or theology.
10 Reference to the Dominican Friar Luis de Granada (1504–1588); it is not possible to determine which of his books he mentions here. However, the comment corroborates the circulation of his writings in the Spanish Indies.
11 It contains the ecclesiastical prayers for the entire year for daily recitations (*DLE*).
12 Here concludes the story of Father Ávila, according to Oré's reading. The report detailing the Franciscan's time in captivity is now lost.

Father Ávila did not write down this information about the gunpowder and bullets, but it was told to me by a religious who dealt with him, both before and after his time with the Indians. They talked a lot and this religious told me many other things that I will omit so as to avoid going on too long.[13]

Father Veráscola at that time was in the city of San Agustín where he had gone to obtain some things that were needed for his cell and to provide for the Indians who were under his care at the doctrine of Santo Domingo de Asao.[14] He was returning very happy, planning to distribute to his wards what he was bringing. But they, perversely betraying the faith, without the father having the least idea of their apostasy, awaited his arrival. As soon as he disembarked, two Indians seized him. The rest then came on and killed him, chopping him up with axes. Following that, they buried him.[15]

Then those Indians tried to wage war on their Indian enemies and to kill those religious who were working among them. It seemed to them to be a propitious moment because their enemies were careless as a result of the fact that the religious had accustomed them to peace. So, many got together and they named captains and charged others with other duties; they made bows and arrows and took all the preparations they could think of for war. They gathered more than forty canoes[16] to launch against the main town of San Pedro on the feast day of our father Saint Francis,[17] when they thought the inhabitants would not be expecting any trouble; they planned not to stop until they had killed all the Spaniards. The Indians were arrogant in this matter, as many Indians are.

But it happened that a brigantine had come to San Pedro, bringing two religious and supplies. The ship came in peace and with no armament, with only one soldier and the necessary sailors. It was God's will that for thirty days it could not leave port for lack of wind, either by sea or by the channel. Four times it had to return to the town. It was there then on the feast day of our father Saint Francis, when the Indians attacked at dawn. With more than

---

13 Perhaps he is referring to Father Marrón, who, in Havana met Father Ávila first and then Oré, or to Father Francisco de Pareja, the expert in the Timucuan language and the only member of the order present during Ávila's captivity, and in 1616, when Oré gathers the materials for his report.

14 Present-day Saint Simon Island, Georgia. It does not appear in the documentation until 1606, after the establishment of the new mission; theretofore the name of this mission was simply Asao (Francis and Kole 2011, 60n6).

15 His remains were never found.

16 Exaggerated statistic, according to Francis and Kole 2011, 61n8.

17 The feast day of Saint Francis of Assisi, founder of the order by the same name, is celebrated on 4 October.

forty canoes containing many heathens and rebel Christian Indians, they started at the head of the island, killing all the Indians in their homes. But when the attackers saw the brigantine, they were dismayed, thinking that it was filled with armed soldiers, and their arrogance evaporated. In addition, it so happened that the leader of San Pedro was warlike, and he set out with Indian archers and also warriors with arquebuses in their canoes in pursuit of the enemy. The attackers fled, but many of those who had jumped on land were captured. The rest, realizing that they could not get away, landed on the other side of the river, abandoning their canoes. But when they then understood that they were in enemy territory and there was no way they could get back to their lands, they hanged themselves with the cords of their bows from the oak and laurel trees. Thus was extinguished the pride of those persons who had dared to place their hands on the religious and who were accomplices [to the crime]. They all died a horrible death.

Governor Domingo Martínez de Avendaño died in the month of November, on the 24th, in 1595. Three months before his death His Majesty had sent the religious he had requested. Following his tenure, with a license from the king, Gonzalo Méndez de Canzo[18] came on; he had governed the presidio when the Guale Indians killed the religious [1597]. When he found out about the crime he swore to punish everyone in that province. So one hundred Spanish soldiers and two hundred friendly Indians entered the devastated villages. They found the houses of the fathers burned to the ground and many others ransacked. They encountered no Indians who might have stopped them from landing. Circulating through some of the other villages, they found out from one Indian whom they seized that all had fled with a father who had arisen from the dead (that is what they called Father Ávila who had been their captive). So with the good efforts of the governor, they were able to rescue him, freeing him from the miserable enslavement in which the barbarous Indians[19] had held him.

---

18 Gonzalo Méndez de Canzo, governor of La Florida (1597–1603), famous for introducing the cultivation of the American product, corn, to his native Asturias. He attempted to create another settlement, more favorable for agriculture in La Tama or Latama but was unsuccessful in that project. He punished the natives for the Guale rebellion (1597), freed Father Ávila from captivity (1598), and urged the chieftains friendly to the Spanish, liberated by the ethnic lord of Asao, to assassinate don Juan and his followers. By various means he succeeded in submitting to the Crown the lords of Potano, Timuena, Apalache, Cicale, Mosquitos, the lady of Yufera, the chieftain of Ocone (whose territory was near the region of Latama); he also got the chieftain of Santa Elena (in South Carolina) to swear fealty to the Crown. In San Agustín, Méndez de Canzo built and equipped at his own expense the hospital of Santa Bárbara.

19 He was rescued with the help of intermediary Captain Francisco Fernández de Ecija (Geiger 1936, 99n21).

Because all the Indians had retreated into the woods, the governor could not punish them or intercept them. As a result he decreed that their corn fields and other sources of food be burned (the Indians themselves had already burned their houses when they fled). Because of this and the fact that in the following years they had no harvest, as well as because of their being so far away from the ocean that they had no access to fishing or shellfish hunting, they suffered great hunger. The Indians tried to sow a few crops but as soon as the seeds came up, the Spaniards cut the sprouts. In this way they understood that this was God's punishment for the deaths of the fathers.

Finally, the Indians made an effort to come back into the jurisdiction of His Majesty by appealing to the governor. But he replied that he would not accept them until they brought him the head of the leader of Tolomato [don Juan], who was the one responsible for the plot to kill the religious. Because he was a cacique this idea upset many and caused great division, but finally the majority turned against him. Don Juan resisted their attempt with many men of his own, but finally his enemies' determination was such that they killed him and his supporters. Brothers did not pardon brothers, nor did they spare cousins, neighbors, family members, or friends. With this act, the land was pacified; and at the end of six years after the death of the religious, it was reduced to the service of Our Holy Church and Our Lord.

CHAPTER NINE

Telling How the Indians of the Province of Guale Were Pacified, and Many Other Events That Have Happened to the Religious in Their Conversion of the Indians of La Florida

PEDRO DE IBARRA[1] SUCCEEDED GONZALO MÉNDEZ DE CANZO AS governor. During his period of office, in the year 1604, His Majesty Philip III sent a good number of religious from the province of Los Ángeles[2] to continue the conversions that had begun in La Florida. Father Friar Bartolomé Romero[3] was in charge of these men, two of whom were sent to the province of Guale where they remain today to the great benefit of the Indians. They have learned the Indians' language and are now very proficient; they have been successful in reconciling with them and leading them to our Holy Catholic faith.

These two religious were Father Friar Juan de Guadalupe[4] and Father Friar Esteban de San Andrés,[5] who came as companions to Father Friar Pedro

1 Governor of La Florida (1603–1610). He sent an expedition commanded by Francisco Fernández de Ecija, Ávila's liberator, to find out about the English settlement on the bay of Santa María or the Chesapeake, and to advise as to the best route for attack.
2 Its convents are on Mounts Toledo and Sierra Morena, in Spain; they became a keep (1489) and then a province (1517).
3 Commissioner of the friars who arrived in La Florida in 1605; from there he traveled to the mission of Nombre de Dios. By 1609 he was definidor of the keep of Santa Elena and guardian of the convent of Buenaventura de Guadalquini, where he was in 1616 (Geiger 1940, 98).
4 Member of the province of Los Ángeles in Spain; he was sent to Guale to assist in the reconstruction of the Christian settlement. By 1609 he was guardian of the convent of Saint Catherine Island, in modern Georgia (Geiger 1940, 60).
5 He was born around 1574, another member of the province of Los Ángeles in Spain. Upon his arrival in Florida, he was also assigned to Guale; from there he became vicar (1609), guardian of the mission of Santo Domingo (1612) in Talaxe, modern-day Georgia. In 1612, he was definidor of the keep and in 1621 of the province of Santa Elena in Florida (Geiger 1940, 102).

Ruiz,[6] one of those who came with the martyrs. These religious spent a lot of time in gathering the Indians to civilization and Christianity because they [the natives] had all exchanged wives among themselves, and had had two or more children with them during the time of their apostasy. The Indians enjoyed living with these women more so than with their legitimate wives. This situation was so bad that it went on for six years without the friars being able to get them to agree to and follow Christian law. Worse, some Christian women had gone inland to live with the heathen and had borne them two or three children; the husbands they had left behind had taken up with new women by whom they had more children. But because these Indians had been married by the Church, it was necessary for the spouses to go back to one another and return to living as husband and wife. However, this task proved to be more difficult than converting them in the first place. The religious said to the Indian husband, "Leave that woman who is not your wife." But he answered: "Return to me the wife who has gone over to the heathens, and make her love me so that I can abandon this one." And if the religious replied, "In the meantime, while we bring her back, leave this woman," he said back, "If I leave her, I have no one to feed me and if I go back to the house where my children are and do not take food and firewood to them, they will perish."

The religious were heartbroken, as they could not respond to these objections, and turned to God to find a remedy. He favored them with an answer because little by little he drew some of the offending parties on to the next life so that the remaining husband or wife was free of the old marriage contract and could enter into a new one.[7] We have an example of this in the life of the principal cacique of the province of Guale. During the time of his apostasy he brought to his house as his concubine his sister-in-law, with whom he lived and who bore him three children; with his legal wife, the woman's sister, he had had four. Knowing that the religious were going to order him to get rid of the sister-in-law, the man took the woman's hand and said to the friars: "I recognize the evil I have done in committing incest with the sister of my wife. But if I tell her and the children she bore me to leave my

---

6 A member of the province of Castile, where he was a confessor. By 1602 he was in San Sebastián de Tocoy, La Florida. After the rebellion (1597), he worked in Guale and in the mission of Santa Catalina, present-day Georgia. In his post as custodian of Santa Elena, he returned to Spain in 1610 to recruit missionaries for those lands. In December 1612 he was guardian of Havana with the title of father of the province.

7 Some died and the widower or widow could remarry following Church doctrine. However, in the *Relación* it seems these deaths took place in response to the clerics' prayers.

house, they will perish. But if she remains in my house in my care, I do not have to have anything to do with her. If Indians gossip about this arrangement, remember that I have warned you." So the friars pretended it was all right. They did not want to put an end to the good relations they had with the cacique and determined that it was advisable to act in this way until a better occasion presented itself and so much might not be lost. Afterward they tried to correct the cacique and encourage him to remove his sister-in-law from his house and send her to her father's. They knew that keeping her there scandalized the other Indians and set a bad example. They realized that any reeducation in this regard would have to begin with his example. The most they achieved was to get him to send her to a separate house—an ancient custom among the caciques who kept their wives and lovers apart from one another, living in the various houses they had.

But the Indians did gossip. They said among themselves, "Until now the cacique had two women and the children he had by them in one house; now he has two houses with a woman in each as if he were a heathen." So the religious tried to persuade the man to marry her to another person. However, neither he nor she wanted to marry; and no one else dared to marry her because it was the custom that nobody married, or even dared to talk to, the wives or lovers of caciques. Finally, God intervened and carried away the cacique's wife, so the sister-in-law gathered her sister's children together with hers in the house where she lived. But the religious prohibited the cacique from entering the house that belonged to his sister-in-law and mistress. He answered crying that he would then die of hunger if that woman did not feed him as he had no relatives who could cook for him, and if he was prevented from seeing his children and could not take them food and firewood. The religious then said, "Take them to our house and we will see that they are fed and cared for there in exchange for seeing you turn from sin." With great sorrow, Father Friar Pedro Ruiz said to him, among other admonitions, "If you do not want to stop sinning and instead take our advice, it would have been better for you not to have become a Christian because a heathen would not have to endure so many torments as you will have to suffer now as a bad Christian. But I tell you now in the name of God that if you do not reform, I will bury either you or that woman in thirty days."

This sentence caused all the Indians to marvel and was the reason why many were converted. Sure enough, within twenty days, the sister-in-law died and the cacique cried at the door of the church on the day of the burial, saying, "Because I did not take the friar's advice, my sister-in-law has died as the father predicted. My heart is heavy and I grieve. Learn from my error, all of you, and leave the women you have stolen. Take back the wives God gave you through the Church. In order to help you do this, I will do everything in my power to assist the Holy Father so that God sees my effort to reform and forgives my sins." With this example almost all the Indians who had accepted Christianity were reduced to its laws.

Another married [Christian] Indian did not want to live with his wife because he had dishonest relations with a widow with whom he had a child. Yet because they both loved the child, there was no way to separate them. The father threatened him, saying, "God is going to take this child whom you love so much away from you because he is the cause of your remaining in sin." Just as the friar had predicted, that dire consequence happened. Then the couple parted, saying the same thing that the cacique had said at the door of the church, which had filled the Indians with such fear that they mended their ways and rejected the immoral habits that were common everywhere— among Indians as well as among Spaniards.[8]

One of the religious who contributed most to the conversion of the Indians has been Father Friar Francisco Pareja, who has dedicated his ministry to teaching the Indians. So as to be most useful not only to those of his own mission and district but also to those in the whole province who speak the Timucua language, which he knows because he has worked in the province for over twenty years, he wrote and had published *Doctrina cristiana, catecismo y confesionario* (Christian Doctrine, together with a catechism and aid to confessions).[9] In addition, he has written many devotional treatises that the Indians rely on so much that they always have them close by. As a result of his teaching with those books many Indian men and women have learned to read in less than two months, and they write letters to one another in their own language.

In this first chapter [of Santa Elena], Father Friar Pareja was elected provincial because of his outstanding virtue; and he put down in writing, and signed in his own hand, many of the things he experienced in working with the Indians. The main point and the most worthy of being told is the following.

---

8 Cautiously, Oré bundles both collectivities and notes the Spaniards' lusty conduct.

9 It can refer to several books by Father Pareja: *Catecismo en lengua castellana y timucuana* (Mexico City, 1612), *Catecismo y breve exposición de la doctrina cristiana* (Mexico City, 1612), or *Confesionario en lengua castellana y timucuana* (Mexico City, 1613).

Responding to questions that I [Oré] posed in writing to all the religious, asking if there had been success in their work with the Indians, if the Indians lived as Christians and confessed as such, and if there were any reasons for which they could be denied communion, Father Friar Pareja answered in the following words: [10]

Father Friar Luis Jerónimo de Oré, commissioner [11] of this province of [Santa Elena], while all the fathers of this province were gathered together, commanded us to place our hands on our breasts and swear according to our priestly obligation [*in verbo sacerdotis*] to answer questions he posed. In fulfillment of which I, Francisco Pareja, definidor of this province, said the following:

To the third question, if we recognized any success in our conversion of the natives, if they gave evidence of being Christian, I say that in my more than fourteen years of work the most advanced have gone forward in their faith. These are already receiving Holy Communion with great devotion. I experienced the same thing inland when, as custodio, I was asked by the fathers to examine some persons to see if they were ready to receive communion. Among those peoples there are Indians who have sufficient knowledge to give instruction to others, as well as Indian women who are teaching other women to be Christian. They attend masses of obligation on Sundays and feast days, where they also take part in the celebrations and sing. In some districts they have confraternities for the processions on Holy Thursday. On Saturdays they come from the mission stations to the main mission to hear the Salve, and then they sleep overnight to hear Sunday mass.

There are churches in all the villages, and each community takes pride in building theirs better than the others. The Indians go to church in the morning and evening to take holy water and pray; they gather in the community house to teach one another to sing and to read. Each time the custodio leaves the convent, either for some distant place like the presidio or for business reasons or that he goes away to attend to an illness, many Indian men and women ask him to confess them, saying, "I may die before Your Reverence returns." When

---

10 What follows is a summary of the report by Father Friar Pareja, in response to the questions and doubts of the order's authorities.

11 The official visitor to a Franciscan province who is charged with inspecting.

someone gets sick, they always send a message from the villages so that the friar comes to hear his confession and give extreme unction. Although some die in these mission stations, they give oral testimony and ask that they be buried where the fathers say mass each day (this would be at the headquarters for every three or four towns visited by a religious). Others who are indisposed ask to be brought in canoes so that a priest can confess them, returning then to their home or bohíos. They are respectful of the dead, not only remembering them on a general day of commemoration[12] by bringing offerings of pumpkins, beans, corn, or toasted flour, but also throughout the year by having mass said for them and bringing the above-said gifts. On Monday they turn out for the procession of souls and to hear mass. These all are the signs of faith I have witnessed, and numerous others I have not mentioned because the list would be too long. I will only add that they have rejected all the rites, ceremonies and abuses of their past life.

In response to whether they confess as Christians, I answer that indeed they have been sufficiently instructed. As a person who has visited the custodia [of Santa Elena] everywhere, I have taken care to look for this activity to judge the Indians' preparation for communion. I have not found any cause for denying them that sacrament. Rather I have found many Indian men and women who confess and receive communion tearfully and in such a way that they are superior to many Spaniards. I even venture to say from experience that they respond to the mysteries of faith better than Spaniards who never think upon these things. But the religious on a daily basis instruct the Indians and repeat to them the word of God. In everything related to faith and belief, God is the one who judges. Only by a person's deeds can we humans know who has the greatest faith.

With respect to the question whether there are causes for denying Holy Communion to many of them, I do not find any unless it is the scruple of some religious. Among the Indians I have known I have not found any trace of idolatry, or witchcraft—but rather of superstitions such as when they say, "With this you will be cured; or if this herb does not cure, you will die; if the owl cries, it is a sign that some evil is going to befall; do not cook fish in boiling water if it was the first to enter the

---

12 Commemoration of the Day of the Dead, 2 November.

fishing ground where no other fish go; do not eat corn from the plot where lightning has struck because you will get sick; when a woman gives birth, make a fire a little bit away from her and place a stick of laurel above the door so that the devil does not bang on it as he often does."

All these things and others the Gospel has cast away, so they do not remember them anymore. Rather, the young people who have been nurtured with the milk of the word of God make fun of the old people who once in a while carelessly repeat these superstitions. It is not necessary to talk of drunkenness among the Indians because their beverage does not cause drunkenness. Indeed even many religious do not find themselves without it. They take the leaves of a tree that is like an oak, and toast them in a pot until they are dry. Then they pour water that is neither very hot nor very cold over the leaves. The drink is taken without anything else, and is very good for warding off kidney stones and other bladder problems, and preventing back pain. The formula has been taken to Spain and New Spain.

As to whether they have constructed churches and installed baptismal fonts with holy water, I say that they hold their local church to be the best of all the others in the surrounding area. As it happens, some heathen come by from their villages to visit the Christian villages and receive the fathers' blessings. The Christians then ask them, "What are you looking for here?" And they answer, "We came to see the church, your house, and to visit our relatives." Among the Indians, everyone is related through their names or lineage, even at one hundred degrees of separation. Then, after a time, they come back to the Christian villages and say, "Father, now we have a house and church for you; come and teach us because the Christians have told us that this is what we must do to see Utinama,[13] who is above in the heavens. And since the caciques around here are more *orobisi*,[14] which means wise, and who have become Christian, tell us the same thing, we also wish to become Christian. We want to be guided by what they say and do because of your teachings."

Finally, with respect to whether they use bodily and honorific ornamentation, I say that because of their poverty they usually just gather together a few deerskins with which to buy wax to anoint their

13 The Omnipotent (see Geiger 1936, 110n14).
14 Wise, enlightened (see Geiger 1936, 110n15).

dead. In other parts of this land, with a few handfuls of rice and some pigs (which they call *machos*) they accumulate enough to buy some small bells.

For anything else, the religious save some of their food and drink, and the sackcloth that His Majesty provides for their clothing, so that the altars might be adorned. I certify that Father Friar Pedro Ruiz and I [Pareja] have made chalices out of lead, which we have used to say mass. Many times it was necessary for one religious to take the ornament [the chalice] so as to celebrate mass while the other had to fast and wait until he could use it in his turn. This happened until, through fasting, we saved enough to provide this necessity for sacred ministry. The lead for the chalices and the stones for the altar we bought from the poor ration that was given to us or from the alms that His Majesty's charity sent us.[15] Many times it seems that these alms are thrown to us as if we were dogs, while the soldiers are thought to be the necessary persons here. However, we religious are the ones who bear the *pondus diei et estus* [daily burden of the heat];[16] we are the ones who really are pacifying and conquering the land. It has been proposed frequently that, given our extreme penury, and since His Majesty the King already provides us with an *arroba*[17] and a half of wine for masses, he should also send on two arrobas of wax each year for candles. But no one has come forward to make that request.

---

15 They received three reales (8 silver reales = 1 silver peso or "peso de a ocho") for their maintenance. This fund arrived from New Spain and was known as *situado*. See Bushnell 1994.

16 "The weight and heat of the days." In other words, soldiers are credited with pacifying the land; however, the friars bear the worst burden and, with their preaching and mild behavior, are really responsible for pacification.

17 Unit of weight in the Spanish-speaking world; today is about 11 kilograms. In Spain at the time Oré is writing, it was the equivalent of 11.5 kilograms or 25 pounds. *Arroba* originates from the Arabic *er-rubun* and it referred to the fourth part of a *quintal* (one hundred pounds). (*DA* 1990 [1726–1730] 1:415).

CHAPTER TEN

About Other Things That Happened to the Religious in This Conversion Effort, and an Account of the Large Province of Apalache

I, FATHER FRIAR MARTÍN PRIETO,[1] DEFINIDOR OF THIS PROVINCE OF Santa Elena in La Florida, state that Father Friar Luis Jerónimo de Oré, commissioner of said province, having commanded me by virtue of obedience and my having taken the oath *in verbo sacerdotis* to declare what I know on certain points that His Paternity has indicated to me, write the following:

I state that I am from the province of Los Ángeles [in Spain]. I left the house of Our Lady of Los Ángeles to convert the natives of La Florida in the fleet that came in 1605, ten years ago. After we arrived I stayed in Nombre de Dios until the 10 April 1606, when I was sent to the province of Potano,[2] full of heathen Indians; there was only one Christian there who had been baptized in the city of San Agustín. One religious came along as a companion, and I began to build a church in San Francisco[3] where I ordered my companion to stay on. I then went on to three other towns in which there were twelve hundred persons.

---

1 He arrived in La Florida in 1605 with Father Friar Bartolomé Romero. He was assigned to the mission of Nombre de Dios and from there went to Potano, where he built the church of San Francisco and catechized the native populations of Santa Ana, San Miguel, and San Buenaventura. He brought about peace between the Timucua and Apalache, and thus began the evangelization of the area; however, for lack of missionaries this effort remained weak until 1633. In 1616 he was definidor of the province of Santa Elena. In 1617, he returned to the Timucuan area (Geiger 1940, 90).
2 In the locality of San Juan River.
3 The mission of San Francisco de Potano, some twenty-five leagues southeast of San Agustín.

I began to catechize, but after twenty days the Indians where my companion was began to rebel, and they wanted to kill him. One night he escaped fleeing to my little convent. But I told him to return to San Agustín for his safety. So for five or six months I was in charge of all the missions we had started, and life was so difficult that I would prefer to leave an account of that period unsaid. However, I will talk about it since obedience compels me.

Every day I said mass in San Miguel and by myself taught Christian doctrine because there was no one else in that whole area who knew anything about it. I used to go from there a league and a half to San Francisco where I explained doctrine and gave talks, with the help of an *atiqui*,[4] which is the Indian word for interpreter. I would return to Santa Ana where I did the same thing. Then I would return to San Miguel to sleep. For breakfast I ate a little bit of porridge made of ground corn because that was all there was to eat.

In San Miguel and San Francisco, they paid attention to the doctrine and very diligently learned the things about God that were taught to them. In Santa Ana only four or five Indians gathered to listen; the rest made fun of me. When I was talking, groups would come near me, pushing me and making so much racket that nobody could hear anything. But I persisted and told them that in the other two villages they wanted to be Christians and hear the word of God. At that time the witch doctor of that place, who acted as their priest, told me, "Father, our cacique is very old. He is in a house but he is so old he can hardly stand. As a boy he was a captive of Hernando de Soto and he suffered a great deal at the hands of the Christians. So he warned us never to become Christians and as long as he lives, no one in this village will."

When I heard this I headed for the house where the cacique was. When he saw me come in, he turned his face to the wall, telling the other Indians to throw me out. He was so angry, he was foaming at the mouth. He scolded other principal lords for having allowed me to come near. Then when I began to speak to him some words from the law of God, not only did he not want to hear, putting his hands to his ears, but he ordered them to throw me out. They pushed me so hard

4 Or *atequi*, probably a linguistic borrowing from the Creek tongue (Geiger 1936, 121n4).

that I stumbled out of the house. At that moment there was a loud thunder clap and a wind so strong[5] that everyone fell to the ground. Not a house or storage building was left standing—not any bohío or other building big or small such as they have in those parts. The only thing that stayed upright, by the grace of Our Lord God, was a cross and the church in which we had said a few masses. The terror that struck many was such that the cacique called on me to instruct him in Christian doctrine, and within six days I baptized him. When that was accomplished he died, giving his soul to God.

Everyone in that village then expressed a great desire to become Christian. I baptized there four hundred persons, including children and adults. In San Miguel I baptized two hundred; in San Francisco, half of the town, which amounted to some two hundred persons. The rest were baptized by Father Serrano,[6] whom the prelate sent to help me. He will tell in his statement how many there were. In another place that we call San Buenaventura, in the same province of Potano, where in times past the Spaniards had killed many people, Father Friar Pareja, who was the custodio, sent a religious who baptized everyone.

In 1607 I went many times to Timucua,[7] a province near Potano that was governed by the great cacique of Timucua.[8] This man was very esteemed and feared. Taking into account the whole land of La Florida, he ruled more than twenty districts. Over a period of two years I tried numerous times to persuade him to accept the law of God in his territories. But he delayed almost three years because his subjects were involved in a war with the Indians of the province of Apalache. But finally the word of God was more powerful than the deceits of the devil, and he went to San Agustín to ask the governor and the prelate to send religious to his territories. He became a Christian in that city,[9] and the prelate ordered me to return with him.

On the first of May, 1608, I arrived back at his place. After I had preached the law of God over a period of several days, he told me that

---

5 The folio numeration begins to falter, but not the narrative thread.

6 Alonso de Serrano. He arrived in La Florida in 1605 with Father Friar Bartolomé Romero. He was sent to Potano in 1606 to assist in baptizing the new Christians; later, in 1608, he traveled to the Apalache territory. In 1609 he was definidor of the keep of Santa Elena (Geiger 1940, 107).

7 Territory in the northern part of La Florida, ranging from present-day Florida State to the Apalache region; it included a part of present-day Georgia (Geiger, 1936, 120n6).

8 Reference to native lord Saturiba or Utina?

9 He was baptized on Palm Sunday in April 1609, in Nombre de Dios (Geiger 1936, 120n7).

he had been feared throughout his lands and that in all the ceremonies of the Indians he held high rank. He personally become a Christian and for his lands to be so distinguished, he wanted us to visit all of them and destroy all the idols in them. Beginning with the place where he was then, that now is called San Martín, we burned twelve images in the middle of the plaza. Then we went to four other towns and in each one we burned six. I went along to preach, and after I had finished the cacique took my hand and said that in all of his lands [stain obscures meaning] that unfailingly the Indians should end their witchcraft, and all should prepare to be instructed in the lessons of Christianity.

I baptized in San Martín the little boys and girls, probably some one hundred; the others were catechumens whom another religious baptized because I was indisposed and could not perform the ceremony. Three days after I arrived, they told me that a little boy four or five years old was dying. The cacique brought me to him to be baptized, almost despite his parents' wishes. The child was surely dying, and his parents and relatives were crying, even howling as is the custom of the Indians. At that point, the child came awake and got up from his death bed and said, "Do not cry for me, rather sing because I am the first one of this village who is going to see God and find peace. Cry for the unfortunate people who died without seeing this moment and who are now suffering." I told them to ponder his words, and that the child was not uttering them but instead an angel. His speech made such an impact on his parents and everyone who heard him that immediately they begged me to make them Christians. His parents since then have always distinguished themselves for their Christian faith and virtue.

Having made that visitation with the great cacique of Timucua to all his lands, and in view of the fact that there could not be peace there because of the wars that the Great Apalache waged on those peoples daily, I told the cacique that I was determined to go to Apalache to start a process for peace. I said that as a result of the fact that his people had sworn obedience to Our Lord and King, and the faith of Jesus Christ was starting to take root among them, Our Lord, who spilled his blood for everyone, would also permit me to go to Apalache to redeem those peoples. At first he enumerated all the difficulties I would face, but finally he said that if I went he would not stay behind.

So we left for the province of Apalache in the middle of July of 1608, and in six days march we got to Cotocochuni,[10] a big territory neighboring Apalache. I had in my company 150 Indians from the province of Potano and Timucua. From Cotocochuni, about twelve leagues from Apalache, I sent as messengers two captives I found there who were from Apalache to inform their people who I was and what I was coming for—to make peace, even a peace that would last forever. I brought the caciques from the towns where I had gone through, bordering on Apalache, so that, together with the great lord [of Timucua] and the lords from Apalache, we could appeal for peace.

When the messengers reached Apalache, the whole province, whose population extended some twelve leagues, gathered. Some seventy caciques then asked them what had they [the people of Timucua] had done in preparation for my visit,[11] and how I had been received there. They said that the roads along which I had traveled near the town had been swept. They had cleaned a stretch of more than three leagues before entering the town, opening up a wide road. Awaiting my arrival, they had prepared a lot of food such as cakes made of corn flour.[12]

When I arrived at the plaza of Ivitachuco,[13] I swear I found more than thirty thousand[14] Indians. I do not exaggerate. To those who have gone there since and have not seen so many, I answer that the Indians love novelty and that that was the first time they had seen a Spaniard in their lands.[15] Secondly, they were amazed that their enemies were coming to their homes. So the two sides sat down together. They sent the little children out to gather firewood, and each child came back with a stick so that they could make a pile. They provided food for the two hundred men that I had with me for over six days, and when we left two carts were not adequate to carry away the leftover wood.

Finally, in everything I say about this province of Apalache, I refer to the informational reports provided to His Majesty and the Royal

---

10 Name used during the first two decades of the seventeenth century for the Yustaga province, within the missionary province of Timucua (Worth 2007, 185n9).

11 The alteration in folio numeration continues.

12 Tortillas?

13 The second largest town in the Apalache territory, in the northeast portion of La Florida also called Vitachuco.

14 Exaggerated statistic?

15 About seventy chieftains from Apalache gathered, representing 107 villages. It is calculated that it assembled the largest number of natives ever congregated in the area (Milanich 2006, 121).

Council, which I attested to; and which were also given to Governor
Pedro de Ibarra;[16] no Spaniard or anyone else saw these things but
myself at that time. I gave the same information to Governor Juan
Fernández de Olivera,[17] together with the reports later provided by
other religious who from here went there [Apalache].

Seeing that the caciques of Timucua and Apalache were gathered
together, I introduced the subject of peace. All accepted the idea joy-
fully. The cacique from Ivitachuco, as the most respected, raising his
voice in the midst of the others, said with tears in his eyes, "When
did I deserve that such a happy day would come for me, that I might
make peace with my enemies and I might welcome them here, eating
with me in my plaza and my home? Now we will have food; now we
will have contentment; now, children of mine, we will have qui-
etude." And he said many other things supportive of the idea of
peace.

Then, ratifying this expression, all the caciques from Apalache
agreed to send the cacique from Inihayca[18] as their delegate to San
Agustín, and to declare in their name their obedience to the governor
of San Agustín, a person whom they recognized as representative of
the king. So the cacique came as far as San Buenaventura de Potano[19]
with me; the governor, who knew what was happening, sent two soldiers who met him about two leagues from San Buenaventura on his
way to San Agustín. The soldiers had orders that if I was with him, that
they should separate us and then proceed with him so that the governor would receive him, and thus claim the reward for which he [the
governor] had not labored. But we are poor Franciscan friars who only
hope for reward[20] in heaven. So I was happy that the soldiers took him
[the lord of Inihayca] and offered their protection as they saw fit.[21]

The people of Apalache are numerous. Twelve leagues are populated; half or more have a great desire to be Christian. It is a very fertile

16 Governor of La Florida, 1603–1610.
17 Governor of La Florida: 1610–1612. Although the *Relación* recounts this entry into the Apalache territory, the missionary work of the Franciscans in the area did not begin until 1633 (Geiger 1940, 8–9)
18 Or Anhaica.
19 San Buenaventura de Guadalquini? Or does he refer to San Francisco de Potano?
20 The numerical alteration continues.
21 Father Friar Martín Prieto highlights the great missionary labor of the Franciscans and how persua-
sion is more powerful than weapons. He alludes ironically to the rivalries between the Order and colonial
authorities.

land, producing great food supplies like corn, beans, pumpkins, but little else. The Indians all go about as naked as the day they were born. But there is great difficulty in getting food and sustenance for the religious who work there because it is almost one hundred leagues from San Agustín from where supplies are sent.

Everything that has been told above, I [Oré] have set down using the report that the religious Father Friar Martín Prieto provided, although I have had a longer account from Father Friar Alonso Serrano. He entered the area [Apalache] later, preaching and planting crosses throughout the huge region of Apalache. After his effort four or five other religious came on who also documented the [Apalache] Indians' desire to become Christian. But the assignment of the religious to permanent residences with them has not yet been determined because of the difficulty of supplying them from San Agustín, as well as the great distances from the presidio where the Spanish soldiers who back up the missionaries reside. In the event the devil causes the Indians to rebel, they [the soldiers] will be needed to avoid the mistreatment or death of the religious, and apply His Majesty's justice in punishing the offenders. This legal provision was established in a judgment that His Majesty and the Royal Council [of the Indies] delivered to Juan Álvarez Maldonado,[22] a citizen of Cuzco and leader of the expedition to the land of the Chunchos. The provision dealt with this point: The soldiers had to ensure the safety of the priests and other ministers and missionaries. If, however, they were killed by the Indians, the criminals had to be punished. In Apalache, however, it is not possible for the priests and religious ministers to make peace with the Indians because much quarrelling has to go on while the Indians' dishonest and awful vices are eradicated. However, nothing is impossible with the help of divine grace and the prudence of those who have had a calling and been sent here.

Because the multitude of Indians in this province of Apalache, in a district measuring only twelve leagues, is so great, the religious of noble spirit want to use all their resources in the conversion of those souls. Other priests have entered the area to work with the Latamas, another large heathen group;

22 Juan Álvarez Maldonado, a conquistador residing in Cuzco; he led the failed expedition to the rain forest and discovered the source of the Madre de Dios River, under Governor Lope García de Castro (1563–1569); the anonymous *Relación de la jornada y descubrimiento del río Manu* [An Account of the Journey and Discovery of the Manu river] is attributed to him (1567).

and still others came into Santa Elena[23] where the presidio was first located and where it was logical that more support should have been provided since some years ago Spaniards had to abandon it so shamefully.[24]

One cannot hope[25] for any temporal gain from the many thousands Your Majesty spends in sustaining the soldiers in the presidio, and the number of religious engaged in preaching the law of Christ Our Lord who daily add people to the faith of the Catholic Church, an enterprise worthy of the Catholic King, whom may God keep for many years. But the spiritual gain is very real. The religious, who like oxen are threshing the fields and gathering the harvest for Our Lord, do not eat free of charge. Rather they do incredible work. They solicitously attend to baptisms, to administering the sacraments to the sick who are gathered in small villages, often six leagues or more apart. If the governor should wish to consolidate three or four small villages into one, as was done in the *reducciones*[26] of Peru by order of the viceroy don Francisco de Toledo, the Indians would be better taught and the ministers relieved of the excessive work they have now. Presently these men also face great differences of climate—rain and snows in winter and searing heat in the summer, as the seasons are marked as we regularly have in Spain.

With these reports on the Indians of Apalache who desired to be Christians sent to the Royal Council of the Indies by Pedro de Ibarra, who until very recently was governor of La Florida, Father Friar Antonio de Trejo,[27] commissioner general of the Indies before he was elected general of the order, commanded me to go with the *patentes* [letters][28] of his commission to Old Castile

23 Spanish town founded in 1566 by Menéndez de Avilés on modern-day Parris Island in South Carolina. It was the capital of La Florida from 1567 to 1587. It was founded in order to expand colonization northwards. Continuous attacks by the surrounding natives along with administrative issues forced the Spanish to abandon it in 1587, and its residents moved to San Agustín. See Lyon 1984. "Santa Elena: A Brief History of the Colony, 1566–1587," http://scholarcommons.sc.edu/cgi/viewcontent.cgi?article=1184&context=archanth_books, accessed 29 July 2015.
24 Santa Elena had been temporarily abandoned when Hernando de Miranda was governor of the area (1576). About the incident, see chapter 5 in *Account of the Martyrs.*
25 The folio is numbered 29. From 28v it jumps to 30r; folio 30v is followed by 29r, turning back in the numeration. The sequence of the narration is not altered.
26 In theory, Indian communities set up under ecclesiastical authority to facilitate conversion. When established in the Andes, they destroyed the traditional way of life and became a burden to the Indians who had to support the priest, labor in the mines, and pay taxes to the Crown. See Mumford 2012.
27 He was born in Plasencia (1579–1635), in a noble family; in his post of Franciscan General Commissioner of the Indies he traveled to Madrid, where he became a friend of Philip III, who named him Bishop of Cartagena (1618) and made him responsible for the diplomatic negotiations in the Vatican for the approval of the Immaculate Conception dogma (see Nadal Iniesta 2008).
28 Document or dispatch that superiors give to clerics when they transfer from one convent to another, a license to go somewhere, or place them to certain posts (*DLE*).

to draw twenty-four religious from the [Franciscan] province of La Concepción, from the Recollet houses in Abrojo de Valdescopezo, Villasilos, and from others from which I took them. To the satisfaction of the president and oidores of the Royal Council, I took them to Seville where they embarked for La Florida in 1612.[29] Juan Fernández de Olivera was governor then and he received the [missionaries] with great contentment. These religious were more than sufficient preachers and spiritual leaders. They have been very useful in converting souls.

---

29 Year in which Inca Garcilaso and Oré met in Córdoba. As we know, Oré did not journey to La Florida on this occasion. Although it has been noted that the group departed from Cádiz, Oré tells here that he escorted the missionaries to Seville (29r).

CHAPTER ELEVEN

Regarding the First Provincial Chapter of This Province of La Florida, and of the State and Disposition of All Its Affairs

[*In this section the narrative voice often alternates between the third and first persons.*]

IN 1614, WITH THE PERMISSION OF HIS MAJESTY AND WITH A PROVISION from the Royal Council of the Indies, Father Friar Juan de Vivanco, commissioner general of the Indies, ordered Father Friar Luis Jerónimo de Oré, from the Province of the Twelve Apostles in Peru, to visit the province of La Florida, as well as the convents on the island of Cuba. He gave him all the necessary patents for this commission, which Oré carried out according to the order of his prelate general.[1] He visited the province, consoling all the religious and calling them together to form a chapter at the city of San Agustín. When he had succeeded in ordering things there relative to the conversion of the natives, he returned to Havana, where he provided that convent with the necessary religious to preach to the Spaniards and to attend to the city's other needs. After [Oré] spent two and a half years governing this province, he received new patents from his prelate general to visit the province once more and again call together the guardians and *definidores*, this time to hold a meeting and choose a provincial and guardians for all the convents of the province, as well as for Havana and the whole island of Cuba.

On 6 November 1616, Father Friar Luis Jerónimo de Oré entered the city of San Agustín in La Florida, along with some companions, to hold a provincial

---

1 The general commissioner's decree was signed on 12 June 1614.

chapter. The trip from Havana had taken him twenty-five days before he reached the bar at the entrance to San Agustín. Then storms and other contrary weather made his ship anchor a distance from the bar; a storm forced the sailors to cut down the cables and jettison two anchors, damaging the ship, and costing its owner more than 500 ducats. Oré was welcomed by the governor, Juan Treviño de Guillamás,[2] by the religious, and by the soldiers from the presidio with great demonstrations of joy. He stayed in the convent there for ten days, giving an account of his arrival to all the religious concerned with the conversion of the Indians inland, in the Guale and Timucua territories.

On 16 November he set out on foot to inspect the territory, in the company of three religious. Although the governor ordered that a horse be provided for him, and a soldier brought it, he preferred to walk in the company of the religious. He traveled in a canoe on the river Tocoy[3]—a river bigger than all the rivers of Spain, France, and Italy—whose banks are covered with pines and other trees, and whose waters have many good fish. Twenty leagues up the river he and his companions arrived at the Convent of San Antonio de Enacape. There he ordered [stain in right margin] the guardian of that house, the guardian of another convent [stain] called Avino,[4] the religious of both guardianships, and a definidor, to gather to meet him. When they were all together in the convent, he gave a spiritual talk and then held the visitation. After each man had acknowledged his faults,[5] he charged them to pray for the good outcome of the election that was going to be held at the provincial chapter house. This same charge was listed in the patent that had been sent throughout the province, together with the news of his arrival. It also ordered the fathers to recite additional prayers [*suffragia*][6] at vespers and matins so that the hand of Our Lord might guide the founding of this first chapter house and the election, without any taint of vice or worldliness, or apparent solicitation. For this intention the commissioner, together with the religious of those two guardianships, prayed and underwent discipline. As a result, the religious were very consoled.

---

2 Governor of La Florida, 1613–1618.
3 Another name of the St. Johns River, initially named River of the Currents by Hernando de Soto (see Corse 1942).
4 To the southwest of Saint Augustine and at a distance of thirty leagues? (Geiger 1936, 133–34n7).
5 In congregational meetings clerics choose their superiors, confess their faults and deal with other issues (*DLE*).
6 See http://www.catholicculture.org/culture/liturgicalyear/overviews/months/11_1.cfm.

He then moved on to examine the Indians in their knowledge of Christian doctrine and the catechism. He found that the greater number of the men and women knew it very well; and the boys generally, besides knowing the doctrine, also knew how to serve at mass. During the days he was there, he preached to the people. He visited the baptismal font and the oil stocks[7] for the Holy Office; and in all the villages he said additional prayers for the souls of the departed, in the manner the manual dictates. Most of the Indian men and women appear to be knowledgeable in Christian doctrine; to gauge such, he proceeded not only as the superior of the friars but also as inspector of the provinces for the bishop[8] who had given him this commission. Thus, he visited the Blessed Sacrament in the main church of San Agustín; he also made a visitation to the baptismal font in the church, and inspected the oil and the chrism. Then he [Oré] published an edict attacking the public vices that might be found among the soldiers in the presidio. With the agreement of the governor, he named an attorney and notary from among the soldiers. Without offending anyone he resolved everything that needed resolution and displayed the prudence and tact necessary for dealing with the soldiers so as to bring about the desired corrections [in a way that] should be hoped for.

The father commissioner [Oré] and his secretary departed on foot from the convent of San Antonio, headed for the convent of San Francisco de Potano. And, although the land is flat, because it is swampy in some parts and strewn with very tall pine trees and lakes, they arrived at the mission station of Apalo in two and a half days with some fatigue.[9] After recovering, they left and went by a lake[10] with many fish, surrounded by very tall trees; [the group] continued on, arriving at the convent of San Francisco de Potano, and from there to the convent of Santa Fe de Teleco, and to the convent of San Martín [de Timucua]. [Oré] preached to the Indians in all these towns and examined them in their knowledge of doctrine. In the convent of San Martín de Timucua, according to the instructions in the patent he had been given, he gathered together the guardian of that house, the guardians of

7 Cups or vessels where consecrated oils or balms are stored on Holy Thursday to anoint the newly baptized, the confirmed, and newly ordained priests (*DLE*).
8 The bishop of Santiago de Cuba was Alonso Orozco Enríquez de Armendáriz Castellanos y Toledo. In 1624 he was named bishop of Michoacán, in New Spain [Mexico].
9 Between Enecape and Lake George (Geiger 1936, 134n12).
10 Lake George?

Potano and of Tarihica,[11] and the religious from the convents of San Juan de Guacara, Teleco,[12] and Cosa.[13] When they were together, he exhorted all the religious to remain true to the service of Our Lord, to observe the rule of the order, and to be faithful to the mission of converting the Indians. To conclude the visitation, he called the religious in one by one to examine them in their faults. When this was over he conducted the rite that cleansed them of blame. Then there was prayer for the success of the chapter. He spent three or four days in each of these villages, making the visitation and taking down in writing the exact number of the baptized Christians, both alive and dead.

Considering the huge effort that it would take for the religious who had a vote and their Indians to hold a chapter meeting in San Agustín, as it would be necessary to carry there all their books and bundles of provisions, he consulted with the father guardians and religious who were present if it would not be more convenient to hold the meeting in the convent of San Buenaventura de Guadalquini.[14] There food for the Indians and fare for the chapter fathers would be available cheaper than in San Agustín because everything was expensive in that city. Additionally, they would be spared the work of coming together at a place far from their homes. The voters representing the two districts of Timucua and Guale (which they call *agua dulce* or fresh water,[15] and *agua salada* or salt water) could meet in the convent of Guadalquini, traveling by water in canoes from one province to another. Resolving to make this recommendation, [Oré] wrote to the governor of La Florida, also asking him to send on any order he had [received] from His Majesty relative to the doctrinal instruction and conversion of the natives so that the religious could begin to carry it out.

When he had completed these formalities, [Oré] left the convent of Timucua with his secretary to go to the convent of San Juan de Guacara, eight leagues away. Having visited that town, he then went on to the *guardianía* of Santa Cruz de Tarihica that five years previously, when the friars from the province of Concepción had arrived, had not even four Christian Indians

---

11 Mission of Santa Cruz de Tarica?

12 Mission of Santa Fe de Teleco.

13 According to Inca Garcilaso, a province beyond Apalache (*F* 1956[1605], book 3, chapter 21). When Oré was writing the *Relación* (c. 1617) there were no Franciscan missions there yet.

14 Around thirty leagues north of San Agustín (Geiger 1936, 135n21).

15 In general, Spanish grouped missions according to their relation to the sea or rivers: those closer to the sea were "salt water," while those near rivers were called "fresh water"; this was also regulated by their location above or below tidewater. For example, the natives of the Saturiba-Encape alliance were known as "fresh water" (Milanich 2006, 48). On the nuances of the topic, also see Bushnell 1994, 67.

[stain]. He found that through the diligence of those ministers [stain], there were now 712 living Christians in the town, which is distant from Guacara another eight leagues. He conducted his visitation there with greater care owing to the fact that these Indians had only recently been converted. But he found that they all were familiar with the doctrine and the catechism, and that some Indian men and women, at the advanced age of thirty to forty years, had already learned to read and write in those four years. He stayed on there a little longer to preach the rudiments of our Catholic faith and to familiarize them with the sacraments.

Because on the road to go to the convent of Santa Isabel de Utinahica the woodland was closed off with thick clusters of trees and chaparral, from there [Oré] determined to take a shortcut, which turned out to be arduous [because] it cut through an unpopulated desert stretching some fifty leagues. On the way he passed through some towns of heathen Indians, but they received him warmly, showing that they wanted to become Christian. The men arrived at Tarraco on the Day of Santa Bárbara,[16] naming the place Santa Bárbara.

After I took leave of those Indians, about a league away from their village, a messenger came to ask what saint's name they would have to give to [their] village once they became Christian, and asking if, in the meantime, an Indian Christian could be sent to teach them about doctrine and the catechism. So all this was put in writing to the religious in Tari, requesting that he attend quickly and carefully to the desire expressed by the heathens in that extensive district, and the good work it promised. The said religious knew the native language very well.

Continuing our journey we arrived at three or four other small towns whose Indians had not been exposed yet to the Christian faith. Although we were running short of food because it was Advent, Our Lord provided us with mushrooms that we picked along the road and that we ate in the shelters that we made for ourselves at night, so as to fend off the severe frosts and rains that drenched even our tunics and the papers we were carrying. In these labors Our Lord comforted us and gave us strength to go on to Santa Isabel, crossing rushing rivers so deep we could not wade across them; the only bridges were long, thick pine trunks that the Indians who were accompanying me ran over readily as if they had lost their fear when crossing these dangerous passages. In my case, however, I confessed first and then crossed,

---

16 Her feast day is celebrated on 4 December. After 1969 it no longer figured in the Catholic liturgical calendar.

invoking Our Lord's name, out of obedience to the prelates who had ordered me to go on this visitation and commission.

After visiting the convent and the religious of Santa Isabel, and having preached to the Indians and examined them in their knowledge of doctrine, we descended in canoes by a river larger than the Tagus in Spain, to the towns in the territory of Guale. There, we visited the villages and the six priests in the convent [stain] of San José de Zapala, where one of our five martyrs had been tortured, and, after the visit, the friar conducted an examination of faults. Later on he led prayers and discipline, as in the previous meetings, and having sent out several days before the patent and letter ordering him [Oré] to convene all the towns in his province, the father commissioner and the father guardians from the Guale territory went to the chapter house where the remaining voting priests, guardians, and definidores were waiting. We arrived there late and then all of us religious walked in procession holding up high a large cross and singing *Te deum laudamus*[17] until we arrived at the church where we gave thanks to Our Lord who had brought us together in His name to attend to things relevant to His service. The religious consoled one another because since I had come to[18] this province for the first time two years ago,[19] many had not seen one another because they had been dispersed in towns a distance apart. We rested that night, and the next day we discussed in the chapter *definitorio* or [governance] session the reasons for the visitation, and we held the chapter of faults. Finally, in order that in a chapter that was so poor but also very religious and filled with apostolic fervor there should not be anything worrisome or sad, once everything ordered by the general statutes had been attended to, [Oré] admitted, consoled, and qualified all the voting members for the election on the designated day.

On the fourth Sunday of Advent, on the Day of Expectation of Our Lady, December 18, 1616,[20] the father commissioner, the deacons and two father definidores sang the mass of the Holy Spirit; later they gathered in the chapter.

---

17 "Oh, God, we praise you." Traditional thanksgiving hymn and one of the oldest in the Roman Church, sung in moments of celebration.
18 Note the first person singular.
19 Reference to his first and short visit to the province of Santa Elena in 1614.
20 Traditionally dedicated to the Virgin Mary in some churches; however, it is not known today by this name.

Father Friar Lorenzo Martínez,[21] formerly a teacher in the Abrojo, preached a spiritual sermon filled with great devotion. After that, the father commissioner [Oré], the president of the chapter, asked all the voting friars to elect persons who, under God's guidance, might be the fittest to be provincial and definidores. His Paternity nominated witnesses and a secretary, all three being worthy individuals. On the first round of the voting, Father Friar Francisco Pareja was elected. He had been definidor during the last three years and had worked more than twenty-two years in the mission field for the conversion of Indians, to the natives' great benefit.[22] Four definidores were also elected according to canon rules and by order of the general [Franciscan] statute. The father commissioner [Oré], president of the chapter, then ordered the cross, the cloth [*manga*][23] and candles to be brought forward. He began singing the *Te deum laudamus* and ordered the procession to begin. He assigned the elected father provincial to march in first place, the elected definidores second, after them the definidores from the past three years, and finally the remaining chapter members according to their age. All this was accomplished with skill and speed.

They walked in procession to the church and after the *Te deum laudamus* was finished, the father commissioner and president ordered the provincial and the elected definidores to acknowledge their faults. Then he confirmed them [in their posts] with a brief talk, recalling David's instructions to Solomon in his last will and testament, when David recommended that Joab and Shimei[24] be punished but that Solomon also seat at his table those who had been faithful and loyal friends. He [Oré] exhorted the father provincial to seat at his table of preference and honor the good and the worthy, but also to have the courage to punish the unworthy.

And in order that the friars might return to their mission stations by Christmas, His Paternity ordered that they should gather together immediately in governance session to apportion the offices of guardians, and also

---

21 Recruited by Oré for the Floridian mission, he left Spain in 1612; he was elected custodian of the province of La Florida (1616) and returned to the Peninsula for the General Chapter of the Franciscan Order. Upon his return to America, he occupied the post of preacher in Cuba, and later in 1633, that of provincial of Santa Elena. In this same year he departed for the Apalache territory to create a Franciscan mission there (Geiger 1940, 72).

22 The number 32 appears in the lower left-hand margin of the folio and it has a different type. It was likely added after the printing.

23 Fabric ornament that, using rings forms a cylinder shape into a cone; it covers part of the cross's shaft in some parishes (*DLE*).

24 Reference to the recommendations from David to Solomon (1 Kings 2:1–9) about the treatment owed to friends and enemies. He advises him not to forget tradition and to castigate enemies.

that the other voting members should gather for a meeting in the *discretorio*. These latter were to propose what seemed fitting with regard to the statutes and ordinances of the provinces, and present it to the definitorio for consultation. Thus, the schedule and the statutes of the province were completed in just four days. And because the next chapter meeting was close to the meeting for the general chapter, for which there had to be an election of a custodian, according to the general [Franciscan] statute of Barcelona and Toledo, His Paternity ordered that they should take the opportunity to elect that custodian. Father Friar Lorenzo Martínez was then elected, a choice that pleased everyone, and he was confirmed.

And to attest to the truth of all this and of what was said and done, we all signed our names to this report from this provincial chapter to our reverend fathers, the Vicar General of the Order and Commissioner General of all the Indies. [Signed:] F. Luis Jerónimo de Oré, commissioner of La Florida; F. Francisco Pareja, provincial minister; F. Lorenzo Martínez; F. Bartolomé Romero; F. Juan de la Cruz; F. Alonso Pesquera; F. Francisco Alonso de Jesús; F. Pedro Ruiz.

Bibliography

Editions of *Relación de los mártires . . . de La Florida*

c. 1619. *Relación de los mártires que ha habido en las provincias de La Florida.* ¿Madrid?

1931. *Relación de los mártires que ha habido en las provincias de La Florida*, published under the title *Relación histórica de La Florida, escrita en el siglo XVII.* Edition, prologue, and notes by Atanasio López, OFM. Madrid: Imprenta Ramona Velasco.

1936. *The Martyrs of Florida* (1513–1616). Translation, bibliographic introduction, and notes by Maynard Geiger, OFM. New York: Joseph F. Wagner.

2014. *Relación de los mártires que ha habido en las provincias de La Florida.* Preliminary study, chronology, modernized edition, notes, and bibliography by Raquel Chang-Rodríguez. Lima: Fondo Editorial. Pontificia Universidad Católica del Perú.

Other Works by Jerónimo de Oré by Date of First Publication

1598 [1992]. *Symbolo Catholico Indiano.* Edited by Antonine Tibesar, with studies by Luis Enrique Tord and Noble David Cook. Facsimile edition. Lima: Australis.

1606. *Tractatus de Indulgentis.* Alessandria, Italy: s.n.

1607. *Rituale, seu Manuale Peruanum, et Forma Brevis asministrandi apud Indos sacrosancta baptismi, poenityentiae, eucharistiae, matrimonij & extremae unctionis sacramenta.* Naples: Giacomo Carlino and Costantino Vitale.

1614 [1998]. *Relación de la vida y milagros de San Francisco Solano.* Edition, prologue, and notes by Noble David Cook. Lima: Fondo Editorial, Pontificia Universidad Católica del Perú.

1619. *Corona de la Sacratísima Virgen María Madre de Dios Nuestra Señora.* Madrid: Tipografía de Cosme Delgado.

Manuscripts, Archivo General de Indias (AGI, Seville)

AGI, Contratación, 5538, Lib. 2, ff. 125v–26v. Catálogo de Pasajeros a Indias, Fray Luis Gerónimo de Oré, franciscano, a Venezuela. 1613-06-20 (2 folios).

AGI, Contratación, 5538, Lib. 2, f. 128r/v. Pasajeros a Indias. Fray Luis Jerónimo de Oré, franciscano, a La Florida con Fray Francisco de San Buenaventura. 27 de junio de 1614 (1 folio).

AGI, Santo Domingo 25. Peticiones y memoriales de la Audiencia de Santo Domingo. 1608–1616.

AGI, Santo Domingo 25. El Comisario General de Indias, de la Orden de San Francisco, Fray Juan de Vivanco, solicita a su Majestad le mande dar licencia para que Jerónimo de Oré pueda pasar a los conventos de Florida y La Habana. La resolución del Consejo es de 12 de junio de 1614 (1 folio).

AGI, Santo Domingo 25. El Comisario General de Indias, de la Orden de San Francisco, Fray Juan de Vivanco, solicita a su Majestad que los gobernadores de La Habana y de La Florida favorezcan a Fray Francisco Hurtado. Consejo, a 15 de mayo de 1616 (1 folio).

AGI, Santo Domingo 25. Fray Luis Jerónimo de Oré, comisario y procurador de los religiosos de La Florida, suplica a su Majestad se sirva enviar a aquella tierra un número de religiosos para proseguir en las labores de conversión. Consejo, a 20 de febrero (Missing year) (1 folio).

AGI, Santo Domingo 235, ff. 71–72. Carta de los religiosos de San Francisco suplicando a S. M. les haga merced se provea en el gobierno de dicha provincia a Juan Menéndez Marqués. San Agustín de La Florida, 14 de enero de 1617 (2 folios).

AGI, Santo Domingo 235, ff. 69–70. Carta de los religiosos de San Francisco solicitando a S. M. varias cosas, entre otras que se junte a los indios para facilitar su conversión, que se aumente el número de religiosos, que al prelado se le deje libremente gobernar su provincia, etc. San Agustín de La Florida, 14 de enero de 1617 (2 folios).

AGI, Santo Domingo 235, ff. 73–76. Carta de los religiosos de San Francisco con relación del estado de las doctrinas que administran en La Florida, de las injustas calumnias que contra ellos se han vertido por el tratamiento que dicen se hizo a los indios, y de las dificultades que han tenido en la conversión de los naturales. San Agustín de La Florida, 17 de enero de 1617 (4 folios).

AGI, Santo Domingo 235, ff. 77–78. Carta de Fray Luis Gerónimo de Oré, refiriendo sus servicios en la conversión de La Florida, que después de haber visitado la provincia se vino al Capítulo General de la Orden a Salamanca. Suplica a S. M. que se envíen frailes para continuar con las conversiones en La Florida. No date or place of provenance. It contains a resolution of the Royal Council of the Indies dated 23 July 1618 (2 folios).

Dictionaries and Encyclopedias

CatholicCulture.org. http://www.catholicculture.org/culture/liturgicalyear/overviews.

Catholic Encyclopedia New Advent. http://www.newadvent.org/cathen.

Catholic-Hierarchy.org. http://www.catholic-hierarchy.org.

Catholic Online. Saints and Angels. http://www.catholic.org/saints/saint.

Covarrubias, Sebastián de (*T*). 1979 (1611). *Tesoro de la lengua castellana o española.* Madrid: Turner.

Cronología histórica. La conquista española de América y el Pacífico. http://cronologia historica.com.

Diccionario de autoridades (*DA*). 1990 (1726–37). 3 vols. Ed. facsimilar. Madrid: Gredos.

Diccionario de la lengua española (DLE). 2015. 23rd ed. Madrid: Real Academia de la Lengua. http://dle.rae.es/?id=DgIqVCc.

Diccionario marítimo español.1831. Ed. Martín Fernández de Navarrete. Madrid: Imprenta Real. http://archive.org/details/diccionariomart00Navagoog.

Encyclopedia of Latin American History and Culture. 1996. Edited by Barbara A. Tenenbaum. 5 vols. New York: Charles Scribner's Sons.

Encyclopedia Virginia. http://www.encyclopediavirginia.org.

Instituto de Historia y Cultura Naval. http://www.armada.mde.es/html/historiaarmada/tomo03/tomo_03_23.pdf.

The Original Catholic Encyclopedia. http://oce.catholic.com/index.

General Bibliography

Acosta, José de. 1979 [1590]. *Historia natural y moral de las Indias*. Edited by Edmundo O'Gorman. Mexico City: Fondo de Cultura Económica.

———. 1984 [1588]. *De procuranda Indorum salute. Pacificación y Colonización*. Edited by L. Pereña, V. Abril, C. Baciero, A. García, D. Ramos, J. Barrientos, and F. Maseda. Madrid: Consejo Superior de Investigaciones Científicas. [Complete title: *De Natura Novi Orbis libri duo, et de promulgatione Evangelii, apud barbaros, sive de procuranda Indorum salute libri sex.*]

———. 1998 [1590]. *Historia natural y moral de las Indias*. Study and facsimile edition by Antonio Quilis. Madrid: Ediciones de Cultura Hispánica.

Adorno, Rolena. 2000 [1986]. *Guaman Poma: Writing and Resistance in Colonial Peru*. Austin: University of Texas Press.

Ahern, Maureen. 1999. "Visual and Verbal Sites: The Construction of Jesuit Martyrdom in Northwest New Spain in Andrés Pérez de Ribas' *Historia de los Triumphos de nuestra Santa Fee* (1645)." *Colonial Latin American Review* 8 (1): 7–33.

Allen, Benjamin Mark. 2009. *Naked and Alone in a Strange New World: Early Modern Captivity and Its Mythos*. Newcastle upon Tyne: Cambridge Scholars Publishing.

Álvarez, Juan Pablo. *Avilés. Familia del Adelantado Pedro Menéndez de Avilés*. Edited by Francisco Mellén. www.euskalnet.net/laviana/gen_astures/aviles.htm.

Álvarez Maldonado, Juan. 1899. *Relación de la jornada y descubrimiento del Río Manu (hoy Madre de Dios) por Juan Álvarez Maldonado en 1567*. Edited by Luis Ulloa. Seville: Imp. y Lit. de C. Salas. http://pds.lib.harvard.edu/pds/view/4504374?n=27& print Thumbnails=true. Accessed 27 February 2013.

Antonio, Nicolás. 1783–1788. *Bibliotheca hispana nova, sive hispanorum scriptorum qui ab anno MD ad MDCLXXXIV floruere notitia*. Facsimile edition. Biblioteca Virtual Miguel de Cervantes. http://www.lluisvives.com/servlet/SirveObras/12705072225612 617543435/ima0925.htm. Accessed 10 August 2012.

Aquinas, St. Thomas. *The Summa Theologica*. "Question 23. Charity, considered in itself." New Advent. http://www.newadvent.org/summa/3023.htm.

Arias, David. *Spanish Cross in Georgia*. 1994. Washington, DC: University Press of America.

Arrom, José Juan. 1980. *Estudios de lexicología antillana*. Havana: Casa de las Américas.

Bandelier, A. F. "Luis Cáncer de Barbastro." *The Original Catholic Encyclopedia.* http://oce.catholic.com/index. Accessed 1 August 2015.

Benítez Sánchez-Blanco, Rafael, and Eugenio Císcar Pallarés. 1979. "La Iglesia ante la conversión y expulsión de los moriscos." In *Historia de la Iglesia en España.* Edited by Ricardo García-Villosalada, 4:255–307. Madrid: Editorial Católica (Biblioteca de Autores Cristianos).

Beyersdorff, Margot. 1993. "Rito y verbo en la poesía de fray Luis Jerónimo de Oré." In *Mito y simbolismo en los Andes: la figura y la palabra.* Edited by Henrique Urbano, 215–37. Cuzco: Centro de Estudios Regionales Andinos "Bartolomé de las Casas."

——. 2008. "Luis Jerónimo de Oré." In *Guide to Documentary Sources for Andean Studies 1530–1900.* Edited by Joanne Pillsbury, 3:472–75. Norman: University of Oklahoma Press.

Bible, the Latin Vulgate Old Testament. http://vulgate.org/ot/job_14.htm.

Bireley, Robert. 1999. *The Refashioning of Catholicism, 1450–1700: A Reassessment of the Counter Reformation.* Washington, DC: Catholic University Press.

Boyd, Mark F., Hale G. Smith, and John W. Griffin. 1999 [1951]. *Here They Once Stood: The Tragic End of the Apalachee Mission.* Gainesville: University Press of Florida.

Brickhouse, Anna. 2015. *The Unsettlement of America: Translation, Interpretation, and the Story of Don Luis de Velasco, 1560–1945.* New York: Oxford University Press.

Brown, Peter. 1981. *The Cult of the Saints: Its Rise and Function in Latin Christianity.* Chicago: University of Chicago Press.

Burgaleta, Claudio M., SJ. 1999. *José de Acosta, S. J. (1540–1600), His Life and Thought.* Chicago: Loyola University Press.

Burke, Peter. 1984. "How to Be a Counter-Reformation Saint." In *Religion and Society in Early Modern Europe.* Edited by Kaspar von Greyerz, 45–55. London: The German Historical Institute, George Allen and Unwin.

Burkholder, Mark A.1996. "Adelantado." *Encyclopedia of Latin American History and Culture.* Edited by Barbara A. Tenenbaum, 1:12. New York: Charles Scribner's Sons.

Bushnell, Amy Turner. 1978. "The Menéndez Marqués Cattle Barony at La Chua and the Determinants of Economic Expansion in Seventeenth-Century Florida." *Florida Historical Quarterly* 56: 407–31.

——. 1981. *The King's Coffer. Proprietors of the Spanish Florida Treasury, 1565–1702.* Gainesville: University Press of Florida.

——. 1990. "The Sacramental Imperative: Catholic Ritual and Indian Sedentism in the Provinces of Florida." In *Columbian Consequences. Vol. 2. Archaeology and History of the Spanish Borderlands East.* Edited by David Hurst Thomas, 475–90. Washington, DC: Smithsonian Institution Press.

——. 1994. *Situado and Sabana. Spain's Support System for the Presidio and Mission Provinces of Florida.* Anthropological Papers No. 74. New York: Museum of Natural History.

——, ed. 1995. *Establishing Exceptionalism: Historiography and the Colonial Americas.* Aldershot, UK, and Brookfield, VT: Ashgate/Variorum.

——. 2001. "Spain's Conquest by Contract: Pacification and the Mission System in Eastern North America." In *The World Turned Upside Down: The State of*

Eighteenth-Century American Studies at the Beginning of the Twenty-First Century. Edited by Michael V. Kennedy and William G. Shade, 289–320. Bethlehem, PA: Lehigh University Press.

———. 2004. "'None of These Wandering Nations Has Ever Been Reduced to the Faith': Missions and Mobility on the Spanish-American Frontier." In *The Spiritual Conversion of the Americas.* Edited by James Muldoon, 142–68. Gainesville: University Press of Florida.

———. 2006a [1989]. "Ruling 'The Republic of Indians' in Seventeenth-Century Florida." In *Powhatan's Mantle: Indians in the Colonial Southeast.* Edited by Gregory A. Waselkov, Peter H. Wood, and Tom Hatley, 195–213. Lincoln: University of Nebraska Press.

———. 2006b. "A Requiem for Lesser Conquerors. Honor and Oblivion on a Maritime Periphery." In *Beyond Books and Borders: Garcilaso de la Vega and "La Florida del Inca."* Edited by Raquel Chang-Rodríguez, 66–72. Lewisburg, PA: Bucknell University Press.

———. 2014. "A Land Renowned for War: Florida as a Maritime Marchland." In *La Florida: Five Hundred Years of Hispanic Presence.* Edited by Viviana Díaz Balsera and Rachel A. May, 103–16. Gainesville: University Press of Florida.

Bushnell, David I., Jr. 1919. *Native Villages and Village Sites East of the Mississippi.* Washington, DC: Government Printing Office.

Busto, José Antonio del. 1987. *Diccionario histórico biográfico de los conquistadores del Perú.* Vol. 2. Lima: Studium.

Cabeza de Vaca, Álvar Núñez. 2003. *The Narrative of Cabeza de Vaca.* Translated by Rolena Adorno and Patrick Charles Pautz. Lincoln: University of Nebraska Press.

Campos y Fernández de Sevilla, Javier. 2011. "Fiestas a la Inmaculada Concepción organizadas por la Universidad de Lima en 1619." *Revista Peruana de Historia de la Iglesia* 13: 205–52.

Cervantes, Fernando. 1994. *The Devil in the New World. The Impact of Diabolism in New Spain.* New Haven, CT: Yale University Press.

Chang-Rodríguez, Raquel, ed. 2006a. *Beyond Books and Borders: Garcilaso de la Vega and "La Florida del Inca."* Lewisburg, PA: Bucknell University Press.

———, ed. 2006b. *Franqueando fronteras: Garcilaso de la Vega y "La Florida del Inca."* Lima: Fondo Editorial. Pontificia Universidad Católica del Perú.

———. 2008. "La Florida y el suroeste: letras de la frontera norte." In *Enciclopedia del español en los Estados Unidos.* Edited by Humberto López Morales, 56–74. Madrid: Santillana.

———. 2014. "On the Trail of Texts from Early Spanish Florida: Garcilaso's *La Florida del Inca* and Oré's *Relación de los mártires.*" In *La Florida: Five Hundred Years of Hispanic Presence.* Edited by Viviana Díaz Balsera and Rachel A. May, 83–102. Gainesville: University Press of Florida.

———. 2016. "Felipe Huaman Poma de Ayala y Luis Jerónimo de Oré, dos ingenios andinos." *Libros & Artes* (Revista de Cultura de la Biblioteca Nacional del Perú) Año 13, 78–79: 11–14.

Chaplin, Joyce E. 2007. "Roanoke 'Counterfeited According to the Truth.'" In *A New World. England's First View of America.* Edited by Kim Sloan, with contributions from Christian F. Feest and Ute Kuhlemann, 51–63. London: The British Museum Press.

Cobo Betancourt, Juan Fernando. 2014. "Colonialism in the Periphery: Spanish Linguistic Policy in New Granada, c. 1574–1625." *Colonial Latin American Review* 23 (2): 118–42.

Codignola, Luca. 1995. "The Holy See and the Conversion of the Indians in French and British North America, 1486–1760." In *America in European Consciousness, 1493–1750.* Edited by Karen Ordahl Kupperman, 195–242. Chapel Hill: University of North Carolina Press/Institute of Early American History.

Coello de la Rosa, Alexandre. 2014. "Los *Memoriales* de don Juan Ortiz de Cervantes y la cuestión de la perpetuidad de las encomiendas en el Perú (siglo XVII)." *Colonial Latin American Review* 23 (3): 360–83.

Columbus, Christopher. 1982. *Textos y documentos completos. Relaciones de viajes, cartas y memoriales.* Edited by Consuelo Varela. Madrid: Alianza.

Cook, Noble David. 1992a. "Beyond the Martyrs of Florida: The Versatile Career of Luis Gerónimo de Oré." *Florida Historical Quarterly* 71 (2): 169–87.

———. 1992b. "Luis Jerónimo de Oré: una aproximación." In *Symbolo Catholico Indiano.* Edited by Antonine Tibesar, 35–63. Lima: Australis.

———. 1998. "Introducción." *Relación de la vida y milagros de San Francisco Solano.* Edition, prologue, and notes by Noble David Cook, ix–xxix. Lima: Fondo Editorial, Pontificia Universidad Católica del Perú.

———. 2008. "Viviendo en las márgenes del imperio: Luis Jerónimo de Oré y la exploración del otro." *Histórica* 32 (1): 11–38. http://www.scribd.com/doc/61753838/Viviendo-en-las-margenesdel-imperio-Luis-Jeronimo-de-Ore-y-la-exploracion-del-Otro-Por-Noble-David-Cook.

Cooper, Kate. 2014. Review of Candida Moss, *The Myth of Persecution: How Early Christianity Invented a Story of Martyrdom.* In *Times Literary Supplement.* 10 January.

Córdoba Salinas, Diego de. 1957 [1651]. *Crónica franciscana de las provincias del Perú.* Edited by Lino G. Canedo. Washington, DC: Academy of American Franciscan History y Jus.

Corse, Herbert M. 1942. "Names of the St. Johns River." *The Florida Historical Quarterly* 21 (2): 127–34. http://www.jstor.org/discover/10.2307/30138452?uid=3738800&uid=2129&uid=2&uid=70&uid=4&sid=56120100943.

Covington, James W., ed. 1963. *Pirates, Indians and Spaniards. Father Escobedo's "La Florida."* Translated by A. F. Falcones. St. Petersburg, FL: Great Outdoors Publishing.

Cruz, Fray Laureano de la, 1999. *Descripción de la América Austral o reinos del Perú con particular noticia de lo hecho por los franciscanos en la evangelización de aquel país.* Lima: Fondo Editorial, Pontificia Universidad Católica del Perú.

Cunningham, Lawrence S. 2005. *A Brief History of Saints.* Malden, MA: Blackwell Publishing.

Curtius, Ernst Robert. 1955. *Literatura europea y edad media latina.* Edited and translated by Margit Frenk and Antonio Alatorre. 2 vols. Mexico City: Fondo de Cultura Económica.

Cushner, Nicholas P. 1996. "Francisco Solano." In *Encyclopedia of Latin American History and Culture.* Edited by Barbara A. Tenenbaum, 5:140. New York: Scribner's.

——. 2006. *Why Have You Come Here? The Jesuits and the First Evangelization of Native America.* Oxford, UK: Oxford University Press.

Dandelet, Thomas James. 2001. *Spanish Rome.* New Haven, CT: Yale University Press.

Daniel, E. Randolph. 1975. *The Franciscan Concept of Mission in the High Middle Ages.* Lexington: University Press of Kentucky.

Daniels, Christine, and Michael V. Kennedy, eds. 2002. *Negotiated Empires. Centers and Peripheries in the Americas, 1500–1820.* New York: Routledge.

Domínguez Ortiz, Antonio. 1979. "Aspectos sociales de la vida eclesiástica en los siglos XVII y XVIII." In *Historia de la Iglesia en España.* Edited by Ricardo García-Villoslada, 4:5–72. Madrid: La Editorial Católica (Biblioteca de Autores Cristianos).

Elliott, John H. *Spain and its World, 1500–1700.* 1989. New Haven, CT: Yale University Press.

Emery, Theo. 2015 "Lost, and Found? Archaeological Finds Hint at the Fate of Colonists Who Disappeared in the 1500s." *The New York Times.* Science Section, 11 August: D1, D6.

Ennis, Arthur, OSA. 1977. "The Conflict between the Regular and Secular Clergy." In *The Roman Catholic Church in Latin America.* Edited and introduced by Richard E. Greenleaf, 63–72. Tempe: Arizona State University.

Escobedo, Alonso Gregorio de, OFM. 2015. *La Florida.* Annotated edition by Alexandra Sununu. Washington, DC: Academia Norteamericana de la Lengua Española.

Espinoza Soria, Miguel Ángel. 2012. *La catequesis en fray Luis Jerónimo de Oré OFM. Un aporte a la nueva evangelización.* Lima: Provincia Misionera de San Francisco Solano del Perú.

Estenssoro Fuchs, Juan Carlos. 2003. *Del paganismo a la santidad: la incorporación de los indios del Perú al catolicismo, 1532–1750.* Lima: Fondo Editorial, Pontificia Universidad Católica del Perú-IFEA, Instituto Francés de Estudios Andinos.

Feest, Christian F. 1995. "The Collecting of American Indian Artifacts in Europe, 1493–1750." In *America in European Consciousness, 1493–1750.* Edited by Karen Ordahl Kupperman, 324–60. Chapel Hill: University of North Carolina Press.

Figueroa del Campo, Cristóbal. 1994. *Franciscan Missions in Florida.* Madrid: ARS Magna.

Francis, J. Michael, and Kathleen M. Kole. 2011. *Murder and Martyrdom in Spanish Florida: Don Juan and the Guale Uprising of 1597.* Anthropological Papers No. 95. New York: American Museum of Natural History.

Galgano, Robert C. 2005. *Feast of Souls: Indians and Spaniards in the Seventeenth-Century Missions of Florida and New Mexico.* Albuquerque: University of New Mexico Press.

Galloway, Patricia. 2006. "*La Florida*'s Route through Maps: From Soto to the Present." In *Beyond Books and Borders: Garcilaso de la Vega and "La Florida del Inca."* Edited by Raquel Chang-Rodríguez, 75–90. Lewisburg, PA: Bucknell University Press.

Gannon, Michael V. 1992. *The Cross in the Sand: The Early Catholic Church in Florida, 1513–1870.* Gainesville: University Press of Florida.

García Ahumada, Enrique. 1990. "La catequesis renovadora de Fray Luis Jerónimo de Oré (1554–1630)." In *Evangelización y teología en América (siglo XVI): X Simposio Internacional de Teología de la Universidad de Navarra*. Edited by Josep-Ignasi Saranyana et al., 2:925–45. Pamplona: Ediciones Universidad de Navarra.

Garcilaso de la Vega, Inca. 1956 [1605]. *La Florida del Inca*. Edition and notes by Emma Susana Speratti Piñero; prologue by Aurelio Miró Quesada; bibliographical essay by José Durand. Mexico City: Fondo de Cultura Económica.

———. 1943 [1609]. *Comentarios reales*. Edited by Ángel Rosenblat. 2 vols. Buenos Aires: Emecé.

———. 1944 [1617]. *Historia general del Perú*. Edited by Ángel Rosenblat with an introduction by José de la Riva Agüero. 3 vols. Buenos Aires: Emecé.

Geiger, Maynard, trans. 1936. *The Martyrs of Florida (1513–1616)* by Luis Jerónimo de Oré. New York: Joseph F. Wagner, Franciscan Studies.

———. 1937. *The Franciscan Conquest of Florida (1573–1618)*. Washington, DC: The Catholic University of America.

———. 1940. *Biographical Dictionary of the Franciscans in Spanish Florida and Cuba (1528–1841)*. Franciscan Studies 21. Paterson, NJ: St. Anthony Guild Press.

Gilby, T. 1967. "Martyrdom (Theology of)." *New Catholic Encyclopedia*, 9:314–15. New York: McGraw Hill.

González de Barcia, Andrés. 1723. *Ensayo cronológico para la historia general de La Florida*. Madrid: Oficina real y a costa de N. R. Franco.

González Sánchez, Carlos Alberto. 2014. "El comercio de libros entre Europa y América en la Sevilla del siglo XVI: Impresores, libreros y mercaderes." *Colonial Latin American Review* 23 (3): 439–65.

Greene, A. E. 1967. "Canonization of Saints (Theological Aspect)." *New Catholic Encyclopedia*, 3:59–61. New York: McGraw Hill.

Guaman Poma de Ayala, Felipe. 1980 [1615]. *El primer nueva corónica y buen gobierno*. Edited by John V. Murra and Rolena Adorno. Translations from Quechua by Jorge L. Urioste. Mexico City: Siglo XXI.

Guevara-Gil, Armando, and Frank Salomon. 1994. "A 'Personal Visit': Colonial Political Ritual and the Making of Indians in the Andes." *Colonial Latin American Review* 3 (1–2): 3–36.

Guibert, Joseph de. 1986. *The Jesuits and their Spiritual Doctrine and Practice. A Historical Study*. Translated by William J. Young. St. Louis: The Institute of Jesuit Sources.

Habig, Marion A., OFM. 1947. *Heroes of the Cross. An American Martyrology*. Paterson, NJ: St. Anthony Guild Press.

Hann, John H. 1987. *Apalachee: The Land between the Rivers*. Gainesville: University Press of Florida/Florida Museum of Natural History.

Heawood, Edward. 1969. *Watermarks, Mainly of the 17th and 18th Centuries*. Hilversum, Holland: Paper Publications Society.

Henríquez Ureña, Pedro. 1936. *La cultura y las letras coloniales en Santo Domingo*. Buenos Aires: Imprenta de la Universidad.

Heras, Julián. 1966. "Bio-bibliografía de fray Luis Jerónimo de Oré, 1554–1630." *Revista Histórica* 29: 173–92.

———. 1983. *Los franciscanos y las misiones populares en el Perú.* Madrid: Cisneros.

Hitchcock, James. 2012. *History of the Catholic Church from the Apostolic Age to the Third Millennium.* San Francisco: Ignatius Press.

Hoffman, Paul E. 1984. "The Chicora Legend and Franco-Spanish Rivalry in La Florida." *Florida Historical Quarterly* 62: 419–38.

———. 2001. *Florida's Frontiers.* Bloomington: Indiana University Press.

———. 2004. *A New Andalucia and a Way to the Orient: The American Southeast during the Sixteenth Century.* Baton Rouge: Louisiana State University Press.

Honour, Hugh. 1975. *The European Vision of America.* Cleveland: The Cleveland Museum of Art.

Hsia, Florence C. 2009. *Sojourners in a Strange Land. Jesuits and their Scientific Missions in Late Imperial China.* Chicago: University of Chicago Press.

Hulton, Paul. 1977. *The Work of Jacques Le Moyne de Morgues: A French Huguenot Artist in France, Florida, and England.* 2 vols. London: British Museum Publications.

Jennings, Francis. 1975. *The Invasion of America. Indians, Colonialism, and the Cant of Conquest.* New York: W. W. Norton for the Institute of America History and Culture.

Kamen, Henry. 1997. *The Spanish Inquisition A Historical Revision.* London: Weidenfeld and Nicholson.

Klaiber, Jeffrey, SJ. 2001. "Review of *Relación de la vida y milagros de San Francisco Solano.*" *The Americas* 58 (2): 318–19.

Kupperman, Karen Ordahl, ed. 1995. *America in European Consciousness (1493–1750).* Chapel Hill: University of North Carolina Press/Institute of Early American History and Culture.

Lamana, Gonzalo. 2014. "Conocimiento de Dios, razón natural e historia local y universal en la *Nueva Corónica y Buen Gobierno* de Guaman Poma de Ayala," *Revista de Crítica Literaria Latinoamericana* 40: 103–16.

Lea, Henry Charles. 1955. *A History of the Inquisition of the Middle Ages.* 3 vols. New York: Russell & Russell.

Lewis, Clifford M., and Albert J. Loomis. 1953. *The Spanish Jesuit Missions in Virginia, 1570–72.* Chapel Hill: University of North Carolina Press.

Lisi, Francesco Leonardo, ed. 1990. *El tercer concilio limense y la aculturación de los indígenas sudamericanos: Estudio crítico con edición, traducción y comentario de las actas del concilio provincial celebrado en Lima entre 1582 y 1583.* Acta Salmanticensia. Estudios Filológicos 233. Salamanca: Ediciones Universidad de Salamanca.

Lockhart, James. 1986 [1972]. *Los de Cajamarca: Un estudio social y biográfico de los primeros conquistadores del Perú.* Translated by Mariana Mould de Pease. 2 vols. Lima: Milla Batres.

Lopetegui, León, and Félix Zubillaga. 1965. *Historia de la Iglesia en la América española.* Madrid: Editorial Católica (Biblioteca de Autores Cristianos).

López, Atanasio. 1931. "Prólogo." In *Relación histórica de La Florida escrita en el siglo XVII,* 5–54. Madrid: Imprenta de Ramona Velasco, viuda de P. Pérez.

López Baralt, Mercedes 1988. *Ícono y conquista: Guamán Poma de Ayala.* Madrid: Hiperión.

Lynch, John. 2012. *New Worlds. A Religious History of Latin America*. New Haven, CT: Yale University Press.

Lyon, Eugene. 1976. *The Enterprise of Florida: Pedro Menéndez de Avilés and the Spanish Conquest of 1565–1568*. Gainesville: University Press of Florida.

———. 1984. "Santa Elena: A Brief History of the Colony, 1566–1587." http://scholar commons.sc.edu/cgi/viewcontent.cgi?article=1184&context=archanth_books.

———, ed. 1995. *Pedro Menéndez de Avilés: Spanish Borderlands Sourcebooks*. New York: Garland Publishing.

MacCormack, Sabine. 1991. *Religion in the Andes: Vision and Imagination in Early Colonial Peru*. Princeton, NJ: Princeton University Press.

———. 2007. *On the Wings of Time: Rome, the Incas, Spain, and Peru*. Princeton, NJ: Princeton University Press.

Marotti, Frank. 1995. "Juan Baptista de Segura and the Failure of the Florida Jesuit Mission, 1566–1572." In *Pedro Menéndez de Avilés: Spanish Borderlands Sourcebooks*. Edited by Eugene Lyon, 413–25. New York: Garland Publishing.

Martín, Luis. 1968. *The Intellectual Conquest of Peru: The Jesuit College of San Pablo 1568–1767*. New York: Fordham University Press.

Martínez, Jaime [Bartolomé]. 1940. "Martirio de los padres y hermanos de la Compañía de Jesús." In *Los mártires de La Florida 1566–1572*. Edited by Rubén Vargas Ugarte, 79–99. Lima: Lumen.

Matienzo, Juan de. 1967. *Gobierno del Perú*. Edited by Guillermo Lohmann Villena. Vol. 11. Paris: Ministère des Affaires Étrangères, L'Institut Français d'Études Andines.

Matter, Robert Allen. 1990. *Pre-Seminole Florida: Spanish Soldiers, Friars, and Indian Missions, 1513–1763*. New York: Garland Publishing.

McEwan, Bonnie G. 1993. "Hispanic Life in the Seventeenth Century Florida Frontier." In *The Spanish Missions of La Florida*. Edited by Bonnie G. McEwan, 206–321. Gainesville: University Press of Florida.

Medina, José Toribio. 1987. *Biblioteca hispano-chilena (1523–1817)*. Santiago de Chile: José Toribio Medina.

Meier, Johannes. 1992. "The Organization of the Church," 55–68; "The Religious Orders in Latin America: A Historical Survey," 375–90. In *The Church in Latin America, 1492–1992*. Edited by Enrique Dussel. Maryknoll, NY: CEHILA, Burns and Oates, Orbis Books.

Melvin, Karen. 2012. *Building Colonial Cities of God: Mendicant Orders and Urban Culture in New Spain*. Stanford: Stanford University Press.

Mendoza y Enríquez de Cabrera, Ana de. http://www.cyclopaedia.es/wiki/Ana-de-Mendoza-y-Enriquez-de-Cabrera.

Menéndez de Avilés, Pedro. 2002. *Cartas sobre la Florida (1555–1574)*. Edited by Juan Carlos Mercado. Frankfurt am Mein/Madrid: Vervuert/Iberoamericana.

Mercado, Juan Carlos, ed. 2006. *Menéndez de Avilés y La Florida. Crónicas de sus expediciones*. New York: Edwin Mellen.

Michelson, Emily. 2013. *The Pulpit and the Press in Reformation Italy*. Cambridge, MA: Harvard University Press.

Milanich, Jerald T. 2006. *Laboring in the Fields of the Lord: Spanish Missions and Southeastern Indians.* Gainesville: University Press of Florida.

Milanich, Jerald T., and Susan Milbrath, eds. 1989. *First Encounters. Spanish Explorations in the Caribbean and the United States, 1492–1570.* Gainesville: University Press of Florida/Florida Museum of Natural History.

Miller, Lee. 2012. *Roanoke. Solving the Mystery of the Lost Colony.* New York: MJF Books.

Millones Santa Gadea, Luis, ed. 1990. *El retorno de las huacas. Estudios y documentos sobre el Taqui Onqoy.* Lima: Instituto de Estudios Peruanos/Sociedad Peruana de Psicoanálisis.

Miranda Larco, Giuliana. 2008. "Misiones y catequesis en el Perú del XVI: Fray Luis Jerónimo de Oré (1554–1630), el *Symbolo catholico indiano* y el *Rituale seu manuale peruanum.*" *Allpanchis* 69: 14–82.

Molinari, P. 1967. "Canonization of Saints (History and Procedure)." *New Catholic Encyclopedia,* 3:55–59. New York: McGraw Hill.

Morales, Francisco, ed. 1993. *Franciscanos en América: quinientos años de presencia evangelizadora.* Mexico City: Conferencia Franciscana de Santa María de Guadalupe.

Moss, Candida. 2013. *The Myth of Persecution: How Early Christianity Invented a Story of Martyrdom.* New York: HarperOne.

Muldoon, James. 1979. *Popes, Lawyers, and Infidels: The Church and the Non-Christian World, 1250–1500.* Philadelphia: University of Pennsylvania Press.

———. 1994. *The Americas in the Spanish World Order: The Justification for Conquest in the Seventeenth Century.* Philadelphia: University of Pennsylvania Press.

———, ed. 2004. *The Spiritual Conversion of the Americas.* Gainesville: University Press of Florida.

Mumford, Jeremy Ravi. 2012. *Vertical Empire. The General Resettlement of Indians in the Colonial Andes.* Durham: Duke University Press.

Nadal Iniesta, Javier. 2008. "Fray Antonio de Trejo: el primer príncipe contrarreformista de la diócesis de Cartagena." *Congreso internacional de imagen y apariencia,* 2008. http://congresos.um.es/ imagenyapariencia/imagenyapariencia2008/paper/viewFile/2571/2521.

Ocaña, Diego de. 2013 [c. 1608]. *Memoria viva de una tierra de olvido: Relación del viaje al Nuevo Mundo de 1599 a 1607.* Introduction and edition by Beatriz Carolina Peña. Barcelona: CECAL/Paso de Barca.

O'Connor, Sister Mary Catharine. 1942. *The Art of Dying Well. The Development of the Ars moriendi.* New York: Columbia University Press.

O'Malley, John W. 2013. *Trent: What Happened at the Council.* Cambridge, MA: Harvard University Press.

Pagden, Anthony. 1995. *Lords of All the World: Ideologies of Empire in Spain, Britain and France c. 1500–c. 1800.* New Haven, CT: Yale University Press.

Palau y Dulcet, Antonio. 1948–1977. *Manual del librero hispanoamericano; bibliografía general española e hispano-americana desde la invención de la imprenta hasta nuestros tiempos, con el valor comercial de los impresos descritos.* Edited by Agustín Palau Claveras. 2nd ed. 28 vols. Barcelona: Antonio Palau Dulcet.

Palma, Ricardo. 1957. *Tradiciones peruanas completas.* 3rd ed. Madrid: Aguilar.

Parkman, Francis.1996 [1865]. *Pioneers of France in the New World.* Edited by Colin G. Calloway. Lincoln: University of Nebraska Press.

Pello, Xavier. 2000. "Los últimos días de Luis Jerónimo de Oré (1554–1630): un nuevo documento biográfico." *Bulletin de l'Institut Français d'Études Andines* 29 (2): 161–71.

Peña, Beatriz Carolina. 2011. *Imágenes contra el olvido. El Perú colonial en las imágenes de fray Diego de Ocaña.* Lima: Fondo Editorial, Pontificia Universidad Católica del Perú.

Perry, Mary Elizabeth. 2005. *The Handless Maiden: Moriscos and the Politics of Religion in Early Modern Spain.* Princeton, NJ: Princeton University Press.

Phelan, John Leddy.1970. *The Millennial Kingdom of the Franciscans in the New World.* 2nd rev. ed. Berkeley: University of California Press.

Polo, José Toribio. 1907. "Luis Jerónimo de Oré." *Revista Histórica* 2: 75–91.

Porras Barrenechea, Raúl. 1952. Prólogo. In Diego González de Holguín. *Vocabulario de la lengua general de todo el Perú llamada lengua qquichua o del Inca (1608).* v–xliv. Lima: Instituto de Historia, Universidad Nacional Mayor de San Marcos.

Puente Luna, José Carlos de la. 2014. "The Many Tongues of the King: Indigenous Language Interpreters and the Making of the Spanish Empire." *Colonial Latin American Review* 23 (2): 143–70.

Quinn, David B. 1990. *Explorers and Colonies: America, 1500–1625.* London: The Hambledon Press.

Quinn, David B., et al., eds. 1979. *Major Spanish Searches in Eastern North America: Franco-Spanish Clash in Florida: The Beginnings of Spanish Florida.* vol. 2. *New American World: A Documentary History of North America to 1612.* New York: Arno Press.

Ramos Soriano, José Abel. 2011. *Los delincuentes de papel. Inquisición y libros en la Nueva España (1591–1820).* Mexico City: Instituto Nacional de Antropología e Historia, Fondo de Cultura Económica.

Reilly, Stephen Edward. 1995. "A Marriage of Expedience: The Calusa Indians and Their Relations with Pedro Menéndez de Avilés in Southwest Florida, 1566–1569." In *Pedro Menéndez de Avilés: Spanish Borderlands Sourcebooks.* Edited by Eugene Lyon, 383–409. New York: Garland Publishing.

Reyes Ramírez, Rocío de los. 1989. "Fray Jerónimo de Oré, Obispo de Concepción en Chile." In *Actas del III Congreso Internacional sobre los franciscanos en el Nuevo Mundo (siglo XVII). La Rábida, 18–23 de septiembre de 1989.* 1099–114. Madrid: Deimos.

Ricart, Robert. 1966 [1947]. *The Spiritual Conquest of Mexico: An Essay on the Apostolate and the Evangelizing Methods of the Mendicant Orders in New Spain, 1523–1572.* Translated by Lesley Byrd Simpson. Berkeley: University of California Press.

Richter, Federico. 1986. "Primera parte: Fray Luis Jerónimo de Oré (biografía) 1554–1630. Segunda parte: Información de oficio en la Real Audiencia de La Plata del Perú, de los méritos del biografiado (tres piezas)." In *Anales de la Provincia Franciscana de los Doce Apóstoles de Lima.* 1–41. Huamanga: Imprenta de la Universidad de San Cristóbal de Huamanga.

———. 1990. *Fray Luis Jerónimo de Oré, OFM, Obispo de Concepción.* Santiago de Chile: Archivo Franciscano.

Rivera de Tuesta, María Luisa. 1970. *José de Acosta, un humanista reformista*. Lima: Universo.

Sáinz Sastre, María Antonia. 1992. *La Florida, siglo XVI: Descubrimiento y conquista*. Madrid: Mapfre.

———. 2012. *La Florida en el siglo XVI: Exploración y colonización*. 2nd rev. ed. Madrid: Mapfre.

Saranyana, José Ignacio, and Carmen José Alejos-Grau. 1993. *La teología trinitaria de Fray Jerónimo Oré, OFM (1554–1630) en su "Symbolo catholico indiano."* Valencia: [s.n.].

Shields, William E., SJ. 1961. *King and Church: The Rise and Fall of the Patronato Real*. Chicago: University of Chicago Press.

Sloan, Kim, ed. 2007. *A New World: England's First View of America*. With contributions by Joyce E. Chaplin, Christian F. Feest, and Ute Kuhlemann. London: British Museum.

Solís de Merás, Gonzalo.1990. *Pedro Menéndez de Avilés y la conquista de la Florida (1565)*. Oviedo: Grupo Editorial Asturiano.

Stewart, George. 1945. *Names on the Land: An Historical Account of Place-Naming in the United States*. New York: Random House.

Sununu, Alexandra. 1992. "Escobedo y su poema, *La Florida*." *Boletín de la Academia Norteamericana de la Lengua Española* 8: 37–49.

Tauro del Pino, Alberto. 2001. *Enciclopedia ilustrada del Perú*. 3rd ed. 17 vols. Lima: Peisa.

Thigpen, Paul. "The Georgia Martyrs: Heroic Witnesses to the Sanctity of Marriage." http://www.catholicculture.org/culture/library/view.cfm?recnum=7662.

Tibesar, Antonine, OFM. 1953. *Franciscan Beginnings in Colonial Peru*. Washington, DC: Academy of American Franciscan History.

———. 1955. "The *Alternativa*: A Study in Spanish-Creole Relations in Seventeenth-Century Peru." *The Americas: A Quarterly Review of Inter-American Cultural History* 11: 229–83.

Tineo, Primitivo. 1990. *Los Concilios Limenses en la evangelización latinoamericana: Labor organizativa y pastoral del Tercer Concilio Limense*. Pamplona: Ediciones Universidad de Navarra.

Tord, Luis Enrique. 1992. "Luis Jerónimo de Oré y el *Symbolo Catholico Indiano*." In Luis Jerónimo de Oré, *Symbolo Catholico Indiano* [1598], 15–34. Lima: Australis.

Trent, Council of. 1941. *Canons and Decrees of the Council of Trent*. Translated and introduced by Rev. H. J. Schroeder, OP. Rockford, IL: Tan Books.

University of West Florida. *Spanish Florida Resources*. http://uwf.edu/jworth/index.htm.

Utrera, Fray Cipriano. 1978. *Noticias históricas de Santo Domingo*. Edited by Emilio Rodríguez Demorizi. 6 vols. Santo Domingo: Taller.

Vargas Ugarte, Rubén, SJ. 1935. "The First Jesuit Mission in Florida." *Historical Records and Studies* 25: 71–72.

———. 1938. *Manuscritos peruanos del Archivo de Indias*. Lima Talleres Tipográficos La Prensa.

———. 1940. *Los mártires de La Florida 1566–1572*. Lima: Lumen.

———. 1945. *Manuscritos peruanos en las bibliotecas de América*. 4 vols. Buenos Aires: A. Baiocco y Cía.

———. 1949. *Historia del Perú*. Vol. 1. Buenos Aires: A. Baiocco y Cía.

———. 1951–1954. *Concilios Limenses (1551–1772)*. 3 vols. Lima: Talleres Gráficos de la Tipografía Peruana.

———. 1953–1961. *Historia de la Iglesia en el Perú*. 2 vols. Lima: Burgos.

———. 1978. *Historia general del Perú*. Vol. 3. Lima: Milla Batres.

Vázquez, Isaac. 1979. "Las controversias doctrinales postridentinas hasta finales del siglo XVII." In *Historia de la Iglesia en España*. Edited by Ricardo García-Villosalada, 419–74. Madrid: Editorial Católica (Biblioteca de Autores Cristianos).

Villarroel, Gaspar de. 1943 [1656]. *Gobierno eclesiástico pacífico*. Prólogo y selección de Gonzalo Zaldumbide. Quito: Imprenta del Ministerio de Gobierno.

Vitoria, Francisco de. 1991. *Political Writings*. Edited by Anthony Pagden and Jeremy Lawrence. Cambridge: Cambridge University Press.

Voigt, Lisa. 2009. *Writing Captivity in the Early Modern Atlantic: Circulations of Knowledge and Authority in the Iberian and English Imperial Worlds*. Chapel Hill: Omohundro Institute and University of North Carolina Press.

Weber, David J. 1992. *The Spanish Frontier in North America*. New Haven, CT: Yale University Press.

———. 2005. *Bárbaros: Spaniards and Their Savages in the Age of Enlightenment*. New Haven, CT: Yale University Press.

Wolfe, B. 2014. "Don Luis de Velasco/Paquiquineo (fl. 1561–1571) (2014, September 17)." In *Encyclopedia Virginia*. http://www.EncyclopediaVirginia.org/Don_LuA. Accessed 23 July 2015.

Worth, John E. 1998. *The Timucuan Chiefdoms of Spanish Florida*. Vol. 1, *Assimilation*. Gainesville: University Press of Florida.

———. 2007. *The Struggle for the Georgia Coast*. Tuscaloosa: University of Alabama Press.

Zavala, Silvio A. 1988. *Las instituciones jurídicas en la conquista de América*. 3rd ed. Mexico City: Porrúa.

Zubillaga, Félix. 1941. *La Florida, la misión jesuítica (1566–1572) y la colonización española*. Rome: Institutum Historicum S. J.

———, ed. 1946. *Monumenta Antiquae Floridae (1566–1572)*. Rome: Monumenta Historica Soc. Iesu.

———. 1983. "P. Pedro Martínez (1533–1536): La primera sangre jesuítica en las misiones norteamericanas." *Archivum Historicum Societatis Iesu* 7: 30–53.

Index

Page numbers in italic text indicate illustrations.